Date Due

JUN 0 6 1989	OCT 1 0 2001
MAY 2 5 RECD	
DEC 1 6 1991	MAR 0 7 2005
DEC 1 7 1991	MAR 2 9 2005
MAY 2 6 1993	NOV 2 5 2008
MAY 2 5 RECD	
MAY 2 3 1994	NOV 1 1 2008
MAY 2 0 1994	
NOV 0 1 1999	
NOV 0 2 1999	
OCT 1 1 2001	

Mann, Ralph.
    After the Gold Rush : society in
Grass Valley and Nevada City,
California, 1849-1870 / Ralph Mann. --
Stanford, Calif. : Stanford University
Press, 1982.
    xv, 302 p. : map ; 23 cm.
    Bibliography: p. [287]-295.
    Includes index.
    0804711364 : $25.00
    ISBN 0-8047-1136-4

    1. Grass Valley (Calif.)--History.
2. Nevada City (Calif.)--History.
3. California--Gold discoveries.
I. Title

After the Gold Rush

SOCIETY IN GRASS VALLEY AND
NEVADA CITY, CALIFORNIA,
1849–1870

RALPH MANN

After the Gold Rush

SOCIETY IN GRASS VALLEY AND
NEVADA CITY, CALIFORNIA
1849-1870,

Stanford University Press, Stanford, California   *1982*

Published with the assistance of the E. M. Kahn Fund

Stanford University Press, Stanford, California
© 1982 by the Board of Trustees of the Leland Stanford Junior University
Printed in the United States of America
ISBN 0–8047–1136–4
LC 81–52825

This Is Nancy's Book

·❧ ❧·

Preface

This book is a study of the two largest California gold mining towns, Grass Valley and Nevada City, from first settlement in 1849 to civic maturity in 1870. I undertook an analysis of mining towns because I believe that western American history is largely an urban history, and the aftermath of the Gold Rush of 1849 offers a nearly unique opportunity to investigate the rapid development of town society. I chose these two towns because they are only four miles apart, they were both important mine centers, their mining economies came to differ substantially by 1870, and abundant historical materials relating to them survive. By 1851, Nevada City had the second newspaper to appear in the mines, and there is at least one newspaper file extant for all the following years under study; for most of the period there are two or more. Town directories published in 1856, 1861, 1865, and 1867 provide details on the populations and contemporary histories of both towns. Because many gold rushers were self-consciously engaged in making history, and the towns, especially Nevada City, were famous placer camps, many diaries and memoirs describing their first years survive, although as the romance faded from mining, personal records became scarcer. In addition, Alonzo Delano—humorist, moralist, and one of the best-known contemporary commentators on Gold Rush society—resided in Grass Valley for most of the 1850's and 1860's.

The heart of the study's data was drawn from the manuscript census records of the two towns for 1850, 1860, and 1870, which supplied information on occupations, ethnicity, household size and composition, and real and personal property holding. These data were correlated by a computer program, the Statistical Package for the Social Sciences (SPSS), developed by Norman Nie, Dale H. Bent, and C. Hadlai Hull in 1968 and subsequently updated several times. The cross-tabulation of the census materials, by establishing the ethnic, occupational, and property structures of the towns, provided a base from which to analyze the social values and behavior of the townspeople.

The reader, then, will find three different types of historical writing here, based on different types of sources. First, there is a narrative of events drawn largely from newspapers, town directory histories, and contemporary accounts of the mining industry. Second, this narrative pauses for analyses of social structure as it appeared in the years of the federal censuses. Third, I have attempted to examine the social values, living conditions, and dominant concerns of town residents in each period on the basis of diaries, sermons, travel descriptions, and, especially after the 1850's, newspaper editorials. My presentation is chronological because I believe that economic growth, social structure, and civic issues are interdependent, and because they interacted to create environments that changed radically during the towns' early histories.

Certain terms need to be clarified at the start. Much of this book revolves around comparisons between the "American-born" and the "foreign-born" as to occupation, family composition, and property holding. I use the terms literally to mean those who were born in the United States and those who were not. The 21-year span of the study, the youth of the townspeople, and their tendency toward direct migration reduce the statistical importance of the American-born children of immigrants within the two communities. However, some counted here as natives may well have identified themselves, and been identified by others, with the immigrant cultures in which they grew up. I often refer to the town leaders—professionals, businessmen, and mining entrepreneurs and their families—as "middle class." By national standards most of these people would hardly have qualified financially for the term, but they regarded themselves as natural civic leaders and consciously undertook the civic roles and behavior of Eastern professional and merchant groups. A group of wealthier mine owners existed briefly in both towns, but it was small, largely invisible in town life, and, when visible, firmly allied to the middle class. Finally, I refer constantly to "traditional" or "orthodox" American values. I mean, first, what townspeople themselves explicitly called "American" and, second, what historians agree to have been the definitions, beliefs, and frames of reference that most Americans took for granted during the mid-nineteenth century.

In the course of research and writing I ran up many scholarly and personal debts, and I would like to acknowledge the courtesy and cooperation of a wide variety of friends, librarians, and historians. First of all, the staffs of the Stanford University Library, the Bancroft Library of the University of California, Berkeley, and the California Historical Society Library, San Francisco, gave me material aid throughout my research. Thanks are also due to the staffs of the California State Library, Sacramento, the Wells Fargo History Room, San Francisco, the Searls Memorial Library, Nevada City, and especially the Nevada City Public Library. The illustrations on pp. 47 and 158 are reproduced by kind permission of the California State Library, Sacramento. Mr. Jepson Garland of Menlo Park, California, made a special effort to obtain valuable family papers for my use. Money for travel and photoduplication was provided by the University of Colorado's Council on Research and Creative Work, most importantly through a Summer Research Initiation Faculty Fellowship, and by the Penrose Fund of the American Philosophical Society. Grants from the Stanford Computation Center and the University of Colorado Computing Center allowed access to the computer. A grant from the Committee on University Scholarly Publishing, University of Colorado, helped defray the costs of the final preparation of the manuscript. Boyd Paulson, Jr. and Mike Johnson demonstrated the utility of the computer and SPSS program to me; Scott Allman of the University of Colorado Computing Center advised and instructed me throughout the process of data tabulation and correlation. Earlier versions of parts of this book have appeared in the *Pacific Historical Review* (November, 1972) and in *American Workingclass Culture*, edited by Milton Cantor (Greenwood Press, 1979). I thank the *Pacific Historical Review* and Greenwood Press for permission to reuse this material.

Grass Valley and Nevada City residents Hjalmer Berg, Doris

Foley, and the late Lyle White were generous with their time and knowledge of the towns. Paul Seaver introduced me to the range of methods and questions possible in social history, and the teaching of Earl Pomeroy exerted great influence on the research design and on the writing of this book. Carl Degler's superb eye for coherence immeasurably improved the first draft. As the work progressed, I received valuable criticisms, suggestions, and support from Bill Carver, Norris Hundley, Milton Cantor, Bill Taylor, Robert R. Dykstra, and Rodman Paul. My greatest scholarly debt, however, is to Don Fehrenbacher, who makes every effort to help his students and ex-students meet the dauntingly high historical standards he sets for them. Finally, without Nancy, my wife, I could not have written this—or any other—book.

R.M.

Contents

·✦ ✦·

Tables

After the Gold Rush

SOCIETY IN GRASS VALLEY AND NEVADA CITY, CALIFORNIA, 1849–1870

Introduction

Grass Valley and Nevada City, four miles apart in the lower foothills of the Sierra Nevada, were the two richest and largest gold
towns in California. Both began as placer camps, where individuals
and small collectives washed the gold from stream gravels, but they
soon diverged economically: Nevada City's growth was founded on
hydraulic and quartz mining, supplemented by commerce and
county government, while Grass Valley thrived on its hard-rock
quartz operations. They survived their more notorious contemporaries because their gold deposits could support the development,
by the late 1860's, of large-scale industrial mining economies. The
growth of mining, then, is the underlying story of these towns in
the two decades under study, starting with the small, loosely organized gravel-washing companies of the Gold Rush and finishing
with the highly capitalized and technological wage-labor mining
of the industrial era. This book's chief concern, however, is not this
economic development but the social changes that accompanied it
and their relation to the larger American society.

The California Gold Rush was not an aberration in nineteenth-
century American history, nor were the forty-niners alienated
from the values of their time. The Gold Rush granted young men
access to opportunities and experiences approved by their society—even identified by it as uniquely American—but seldom
found in the established towns of the East and Midwest. It offered
adventure in a land drenched in literary romance; participation in
the nation's God-given imperial destiny; incredible wealth, appar-

ently free to any man unafraid of physical labor or hardship; and a legitimate, temporary escape from elders and from feminized respectability. To middle-class youths it offered an extension of their customary period of experimentation; the stampede to California let them prove themselves, improve themselves, and seek the capital for their chosen careers.

Once in California, the adventurers intended to live and work as Americans. When gold discoveries made permanence possible, those who stayed converted their camps to towns that would further the oldest, most basic dream of American frontiersmen—to rise with a new region. The forty-niners and the town builders, then, are linked by a continuous commitment (on the part of the native-born majority) to contemporary national mores. Since townsmen aimed to recreate what they had left behind, the approach of the social historian, with its emphasis on social structure, and its data drawn from sources that allow comparisons to other American societies, is especially appropriate to the study of the Gold Rush camps and the towns that superseded them.

In 1850, Grass Valley and Nevada City served as the trading centers for a mercurial aggregate of young, single miners, centers populated largely by small merchants almost indistinguishable in age and attitude from their customers. During the 1850's and 1860's the two camps progressed confidently toward the commonplaces of American town life, and quickly reproduced many of them: churches, schools, occupational stratification, and governmental institutions. But so long as Grass Valley and Nevada City remained the focal points of California's richest mine districts, they could only progress toward urban norms, never reach them. Their populations would remain much too male, too transient, and later, too foreign for the two towns ever to reach their founders' expectations. Grass Valley, in particular, became more and more alien, an industrial mining town shaped by its Cornish population, in contrast to the Americanized Nevada City.[1] Besides the social changes that came with the permanent mining economy, this book focuses on the ways cultural and social groups coped with each other, with the failure of their expectations, and with the need to protect their own cultural practices.

The history of Grass Valley and Nevada City between 1849 and 1870 falls into three distinct periods: 1849 through 1856, a time when town survival and the establishment of American middle-

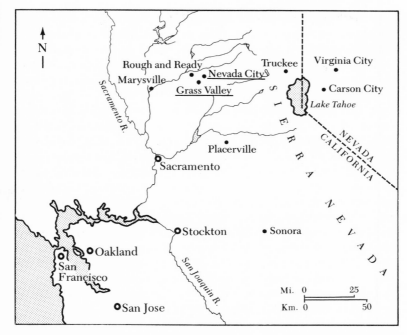

Modern map of northern California showing the principal Gold Rush communities.

class mores were the central concerns; 1856 through 1863, a time of economic depression and political reorganization, but also of relative ethnic and class tranquility; and 1863 through 1870, a boom time in industrial mining when clashes of interest between miners and owners, and between the foreign- and native-born, were the major civic issues. The manuscript census returns provide a benchmark for each period. By tabulating their information on social patterns, I can go on to chart the development of occupational and ethnic stratification, describe the creation of a family-oriented society, illustrate the changing roles of women, and examine the impact of industrial mining on occupations, property holdings, and household membership. Lastly, I can link changes in the social structure with contemporary perceptions of public social issues (the needs for moral reform, for permanent populations, for mine unions, and so forth) and place both within the context of the towns' erratic economic careers and relevant national events.

Transience, mine failures, an ethnically diverse population, and the rapid imposition of industrial order all, at times, threatened town cohesion. But society in the gold towns was held together by two complementary principles: continuity and innovation. First, in the midst of the seeming chaos of the Gold Rush, there existed from the beginning the values, and most of the necessary institutions, that would shape the development of Grass Valley and Nevada City. Commercial and financial systems arrived intact from the East, as did political parties and fraternal organizations, all important sources of status and self-identification. These entities, furthermore, kept their links with social privilege and deference; different types of people had different places in politics and business. Storekeepers, predictably, dominated local affairs. When clergymen arrived to call congregations, their public responsibility was clearly understood. So too with sex roles; the "cult of true womanhood" was pervasive enough that early town leaders expected the advent of families virtually to eliminate disorder. Families, of course, would strengthen complementary institutions such as churches and schools, which would extend the private morality of the home into the public realm.[2]

Settlers also transplanted racial and ethnic stereotypes intact. Occupational categories were popularly defined by ethnicity: Yankee lawyers, black menials, Jewish dry-goods merchants, and, early on, Cornish miners and Irish laborers. Fear of aliens and a tendency by the native-born to trace all threats to the foreign-born—to amoral Chinese or bloodthirsty Mexicans—remained a constant over the two decades studied here. The sense that American civilization had to overcome rival cultures carried with it, as we shall see, the seeds of moral coercion, Know-Nothingism, and at times mob action. The foreign-born were no more inclined than the natives to abandon their own cultures, and their defensiveness compounded the dangers inherent in the American-born's defensiveness.[3] Long-established rivalries and prejudices among the foreign-born also contributed to the potential for social strife. Battles between Cornish and Irish miners were common. And all whites joined in enforcing the segregation of blacks and Chinese.

The continuity of values and institutions, then, provided a base for the new communities, but it also threatened their peace. A second characteristic was necessary for these two towns to function well: the ability to innovate, to adapt. The changes that had to be made were not minor; no platitude of family life or morality went untested. Mining did not pay well, and for many households the family, though ideally inviolate, had to be opened to lodgers so that the mother might augment family income.[4] Cornish miners had to cooperate with Irish miners to maintain a union. And any group that felt threatened had to content itself with establishing boundaries within which it could thrive unchallenged. Native-born reformers could only segregate, not eliminate the haunts of the miners. Mine owners had to accept the fact that Grass Valley's industrial mining depended on Cornish expertise, and the Cornish had to accept an absentee owner class.

As long as the towns' diverse elements had reasonable hope for jobs and felt their cultural identities secure, peace prevailed. When the peace in the mining towns broke down, the reasons went far beyond the economic uncertainty, ethnic prejudice, and population turnover that were endemic there. Each crisis was rooted in a particular group's perception of a threat to its traditions. And before any crisis became major, such agitation had to be reinforced by some outside agency—a nativist reform crusade, a Sinophobic political campaign—with values and solutions that seemed relevant to the needs of the community.[5]

Grass Valley and Nevada City always shared the problems, prejudices, and intellectual currents of American society; therefore, although the Gold Rush and the later mining industry precluded any close resemblance to more settled cities, legitimate comparisons can be made between the two towns and their civic peers, especially other frontier and mill towns. The questions asked here parallel some of the questions asked in other town studies that use census data and similar analytical techniques. Selective comparisons with relevant studies can cast light on the social impact of mining, demonstrate patterns within the settlement process, and suggest commonalities in the experience of industrialization. They can also further attempts to bring the history of the frontier, especially the Far Western frontier, into the mainstream of American social history and its general re-evaluation of the American past.

PART I

FOUNDING
PERMANENT TOWNS

1849-1856

⟡ 1 ⟡

Merchants and Miners

GOLD RUSH SOCIETY

Nevada City and Grass Valley thrived during the first half of the 1850's as did no other California gold towns, primarily because their gold-bearing gravels and veins were rich enough to pay despite speculative greed, ignorance of mining techniques, and the vagaries of weather and water supply. During these years there took shape in the two towns a society—all male, uncommitted to either occupation or residence—that seemed alien to orthodox American mores. This society was shaped by three basic facts. First, continual technological innovation made mines more predominantly consolidated, highly capitalized enterprises, and miners more likely to be simply employees. Second, the entities called Nevada City and Grass Valley differentiated into two parts, the mining areas and the towns proper, and two populations, miners and merchants, mutually dependent but distinct in location, in function, and in styles of living. Third, for miners and storekeepers alike, their former homes in the East remained paramount in determining identity and personal prejudices, and also in determining with whom a man would live and work and for whom he would vote. After extensive gold discoveries held out a promise of reasonable permanence for the towns, editors and town boosters, although they tacitly accepted functional distinctions between the diggings and the business districts, began to argue that the fluid, formless society of the Gold Rush threatened orderly business and mine production. By 1856, changes in mining had made the dreams accompanying the Gold Rush seem obsolete and the characteristics and attitudes of Gold Rush society seem destructive.

Gold-Town Societies

Late in the first season of California's gold excitement, in the autumn of 1848, a few men entered the lower Sierras to prospect along Wolf Creek, a tributary of the Bear River lying roughly 75 miles north-northeast of Sutter's Mill. Others a short distance farther to the northeast panned in Deer Creek, a branch of the Yuba. Both parties found traces of gold, but not enough to risk a winter isolated in the mountains, and they moved on, leaving no physical evidence of their brief stay. The next summer, in a small valley watered by Wolf Creek, forty-niners impatiently recruiting their animals for the trek down to the Sacramento filled the wait by searching the stream bed and the dry gullies opening from it. Overlanders already knew this site, called Grass Valley for its waist-deep grasses, as a regular resting place off the Truckee Route; gold did not figure in its reputation. But now digging uncovered paying placers—gold-bearing gravel deposits laid down by streams—and two groups of men decided to remain and continue mining over the winter. In September one company pitched permanent camp on Wolf Creek one-half mile below the grassy valley, in a ravine they named Boston after their home. In December a Frenchman, Jules Rosiere, opened a rudimentary trading post there to provision miners taking advantage of the seasonal rains to scour the surrounding creeks and rivulets. Most of that first winter's gold seekers gravitated to the collection of log huts and canvas shanties that grew up in Boston Ravine.[1]

Four miles to the northeast, parties of prospectors working up Deer Creek in the fall of 1849 struck very rich placers on two of its branches, Little Deer Creek and Gold Run. Word spread that these were "pound diggings," where a man could get twelve (troy) ounces of gold per day, and miners flocked in to excavate the streams and dry washes tributary to Deer Creek. Storekeeper A. B. Caldwell followed his customers upstream and in September threw up a square canvas tent on the hill overlooking Little Deer Creek. Here he vended salt pork, moldy biscuit, and four-bits-a-shot whiskey and gave the area its first mailing address, Caldwell's Upper Store. The locality's alternative name, Deer Creek Dry Diggings, indicated that most of the gold lay in the seasonally dry ravines rather than the creek bottoms. Gold-bearing dirt had to be packed out on mules, in carts, or on miners' backs to be washed in Deer Creek. Perhaps a thousand men mined through the very severe winter of 1849–50, braving snowstorms and icy mud, for winter was the only time when water ran in the gullies and claims could be worked on site. Snow and rain closed the newly cut trails to Marysville and Sacramento for weeks at a time, and foodstuffs became scarce and expensive. While bad weather halted supply wagons and pack trains, the diggings' rich reputation continued to persuade would-be nabobs to risk their health and go into debt for uncertain transportation there. All winter long new arrivals fought their way up the almost obliterated tracks to the tent and brush-hut city that sprawled over the hills above Deer Creek.[2]

In the spring of 1850, as the washes dried out, miners dug ditches to water sources, rapidly extending them in pursuit of the constantly retreating streams. A growing water shortage worsened as a new influx of miners, far greater than the first, came with the spring into diggings where the original discovery sites had already been blanketed by claims. The newcomers, variously estimated to number between 6,000 and 16,000, perforce took up new ground, widening dramatically the area being worked, with continued good results. Merchants also took advantage of opened trails to ship wagonload after wagonload into the area, at once lowering prices and improving the miners' meager diet. Difficult terrain, composed of pine- and oak-covered ridges cut deeply by ravines converging at Deer Creek, surrounded the paying claims. So the newly arrived entrepreneurs seized on the only level spot near the mines, a little flat that lay across Deer Creek from Caldwell's Store, and ignoring its swampiness marked out a sketchy thoroughfare. Insubstantial emporiums interspersed with supply wagons lined the street, perhaps prematurely known as Main, while a gambling saloon in a round tent, surmounted by a flag and complete with a band, commanded the scene.

The short, marshy street with its flimsy structures supplied a focal point for the previously formless collection of tents and cabins; diggings began to turn into a mining camp. In March, several robberies and a murder persuaded the population along Deer Creek of the necessity of some form of government to keep order. Accordingly, at an election held on the flat, the merchants and miners chose an *alcalde,* an official taken over from Californio practice who combined administrative and law-enforcement duties. Storekeeper O. P. Blackman, acting as judge for this election, proposed, and the voters ratified, "Nevada" as the camp's permanent name.[3]

That spring and summer the mines paid well; a fortunate few left for their old homes with thousands of dollars to show for their season's labor. The hordes of miners, however, soon worked out the placers in the stream system around Nevada. The diggings and the stores alike would have faced abandonment, except that in May men attempting to trace dwindling gold deposits to their sources discovered in a ravine north of the camp a lead that widened as they followed it into the bank. When surface pits could no longer reach the gold, they sank a shaft to bedrock that proved rich enough to inspire other miners to burrow into neighboring hills. The imagined resemblance of the resulting pits to coyote holes gave this type of mining its name, "coyoteing."

By 1850 mining operations had already left gold pans and one-man rockers behind; sluices and long toms (a kind of large rocker), worked by organized companies of miners, dominated the diggings. Coyoteing demanded even more planning and cooperative effort, and new knowledge and technology. Miners had to learn to map the courses of the ancient underground stream beds where the deposits lay, to sink shafts that would not cave in, and to get workers, tools, and fresh air to the bottom of them. Miners also had to raise capital for the expensive work of digging and equipping shafts before any returns were possible. The coyote lead saved Nevada, but irreversibly changed the nature of mining opportunity in the camp. Men arriving at the coyote mines alone and with little cash had to go to work for those with enough of a stake to pay wages. Experience in underground mining was at a premium and unskilled labor at a discount; Charles Ferguson of Ohio could join a mine crew only by claiming to have worked in the lead pits of Galena, Illinois, while John Steele commanded $16 a day, despite his inexperience at practical mining, on the strength of his Wisconsin origins and lead miner's costume. Coyoteing forced organization, but few of the informal joint stock companies held enough funds to withstand much delay before producing gold; most missed the main coyote lead and quickly dissolved after their first failures. Nevertheless, a new tent city, Coyoteville, mushroomed on a hill

Grass Valley and Nevada City conspicuously lacked the traditional sources of social stability. The populations of the two camps seemed just as transitory and unstable as their canvas-walled buildings. In 1850 almost all of the inhabitants of both the diggings and the commercial centers were male (Table 1)* and most were young; mining entailed hard physical labor and rough living conditions. Men between 20 and 30 years of age made up over 60 percent of the towns' working populations; men between 20 and 40 made up 90 percent (Table 2). Few families graced either town, and neither contained many men long experienced in commerce, the professions, or community leadership.

Home life in the mines almost parodied American orthodoxy. Most men shared cabins with two to five other men. These households, like the farm families many of the miners had grown up in, commonly composed an economic unit. In some, the men together staffed a mine, trading post, or saloon. Other cabins might house diverse but cooperative endeavors, each man earning what he could at whatever job he could find and contributing to a common treasury. Domestic duties were parceled out; traditionally defined sex roles were impossible in the camps. Since only three men in a hundred had wives and children with them, since collective effort was necessary for productive mining, and since the camps' lack of social organization nursed fears of robbery or unattended sickness, cooperative households were the most practical, almost the only logical way to live.

Living arrangements reflected the homes men hoped to return to, not new associations or new homes they might make for themselves in Grass Valley or Nevada. Miners sought out men from the same state or region as themselves or, in some cases, lived with fellow members of the overland associations formed in their home towns for the trip west. Of a sample of 50 houses in the Grass Valley area, 16 contained men identifiably related, usually brothers, and 35 had two or more inhabitants born in the same state (Table 3). Half the cabins included men born in adjoining states, especially states along the routes of westward migration; very possibly some of these men had lived as adults in the same localities. A similar pattern prevailed in Nevada: a representative cabin might

---

* The tables are grouped for convenient reference in the Appendix, pp. 223–66.

contain two brothers, one born in Tennessee, the other in Missouri, and three unrelated men from Missouri, Tennessee, and Kentucky. Only about one dwelling in six contained a man born in a different section of the United States or a different country from the majority of the inhabitants.

When Edwin Morse arrived at Wolf Creek in 1850, the first man he met directed him to Boston Ravine and the New England company living there, because Morse said he came from Boston. After establishing the geographical tie, men evidently found it easy to accept complete strangers not only as cabin mates but as business or mining partners. Iowan Jasper Hill wrote comfortingly to his mother that he had found a good group of Iowa boys to move in with. In Grass Valley a gang of toughs called by themselves the Baltimore Boys, by others the Baltimore Hounds, banded together ostensibly for mutual protection—some thought from justice. The names of claims and town business concerns commonly advertised the home loyalties of their owners and founders; merchants expected to attract a clientele in part on the strength of mutual backgrounds. And by 1851, Nevada had a New England society that celebrated the anniversary of the landing at Plymouth Rock and dedicated itself to preserving the values of Puritan ancestors.[10]

Camp residents were disposed not only to trust and to associate intimately with men from their own sections of the country, but also to distrust and segregate themselves from natives of other sections. The plurality of the population in both camps came from east of the Mississippi and north of the Mason-Dixon line, but Southerners and men from the old frontier beyond the river, especially Missouri, taken together, slightly outnumbered the Northerners (Table 4). No group dominated enough to stamp the towns with its own characteristics, despite early New England prominence in merchandising and Southern strength in politics. The camps clearly shared the intense sectional tensions of the early 1850's; propinquity did not lessen suspicions. When New Yorker Benjamin P. Avery came to the Deer Creek diggings in 1850, he found the ground monopolized by clannish "long-haired Missourians" who in turn eyed him warily because of his Northern dress and accent. Ohioan Alonzo Delano described an acquaintance, "Old Mississippi," as a "typical" Southern frontiersman, good-humored but drunken, uncouth, and untrustworthy. Sectional rivalries were always at least potentially violent, but surfaced mostly in slighting references to "the Chivs" (of the "chivalric" South) or to "damned mackerel catchers" (of New England), or in outright refusals to live and work, or even to worship, with men from other geographical sections.[11]

Northerners or Southerners, miners heavily outnumbered men in all other occupations. In Nevada in 1850, eight out of ten men dug for gold, and in Grass Valley, seven of ten. Still, men did not permanently adopt one occupation, nor did they hold any one job for long. Sometimes too broke from the journey to buy equipment or too inexperienced to prospect with any chance of success, newcomers after a brief experiment with mining alone typically became employees of others, doing the manual labor of coyoteing or ditch construction or perhaps shoveling dirt into a long tom. Some men took up their hometown trades, while others attempted occupations for which only willingness to try and the shortage of skilled labor qualified them. A man who listed himself as a miner in the census of 1850 might have been on that day a mining employee or an entrepreneur, and on the next a teamster or a merchant. Gold drew men to the camps but did not necessarily support them, although most at least tried mining. Garrett Low and his companions, for example, went searching for placers immediately after reaching Nevada. Finding none, they split up, each member of the party turning his hand to whatever he could find to do. Low, a skilled craftsman, passed the summer alternately earning good money as a carpenter or millwright and wasting it in vain prospecting. Daniel Fletcher found employment with a Boston Ravine mining company, then left it to go mining on his own, only to return to work for others by the week or month when his independent efforts did not pay. When bad weather or bad luck halted operations, he turned to cutting cordwood or splitting shingles until work resumed. Fletcher's constant goal was to buy into a mining company so that he would hold shares in the claims he worked.

The high wages created by a shortage of skilled artisans and of men willing to do menial labor meant that a man could probably consistently earn more as an employee than in taking up claims. High prices cut deeply into earnings, of course, reducing the attractiveness of working for hire; living expenses almost dictated that a man dig for gold if he were to have any chance of going home with the large stake he sought in California. In addition, prospecting fascinated men because it offered both the certainty of independent labor and the chance of riches; Englishman J. D. Borthwick implied that the only men who worked for wages were "cold-blooded philosophers," those immune to the excitement of the Gold Rush, or "men not energetic enough to direct their own labor." When mining paid, most men of all backgrounds searched for gold. The slightly larger proportion of non-miners in Grass Valley than in Nevada in 1850 (Table 5) simply indicates that Grass Valley's claims were less productive and that men there had turned to other pursuits.[12]

A large number of men engaged in merchandising; around Nevada, for every nine men working the placers, one sold provisions. At Grass Valley the ratio was about four to one (Table 5). Most of these men did not claim to be merchants, but rather used the term "trader," which denoted an individual with small stocks and a small income. Like other callings in the camps, trading could be a temporary activity; a man who had won a small stake in mining might invest it in canned goods or whiskey, and bad luck in choosing merchandise or overextension of credit might quickly return him to the pick and shovel. Some men changed occupations seasonally, speculating in hogs or mixing drinks or peddling boots while waiting until the rainy season to resume mining. Trading, therefore, did not distinguish a man from the bulk of the camps' populations. Traders dressed like miners and lived with miners, and according to Alonzo Delano, who had been both, the close ties between vendor and customer undermined hard-headed business practices and helped ensure that many budding entrepreneurs would return to the ranks, bankrupted by their generosity with credit.[13] The large proportion of traders in Grass Valley in 1850—too large to be economically viable—like the small proportion of actual miners, proclaims that the camp was living on hope for the future. For the present, the mines had not produced well in Grass Valley, but the quartz discovery promised a coming prosperity when some traders might find new customers and others might return to mining.

The small occupational elite of the two camps resided and worked in the commercial cores; the town centers, especially in Nevada, were set off from the surrounding mining districts physically, functionally, and by the status of many of their inhabitants. In the diggings lived the mass of miners and small traders, but along the few streets of the embryo towns lodged businessmen and professionals with clear occupational identities. An attorney or a druggist or a dry-goods merchant usually remained in that role. At a lower level of prestige, artisans likewise tended to live in the town centers, unless their skills related directly to mining operations, and the blacksmiths, millwrights, or carpenters normally stuck to those trades. Men whose occupations called for special skills, schooling, or experience tended to stay with their crafts more than men with less formally defined jobs. Upward movement could be rapid; Hamlet Davis, a shrewd and fortunate grocer, within a year after arriving in Nevada outgrew his canvas shed and became the proprietor of a large provision store, an investor in ditch property and town lots, and, like many merchants, a holder of mining paper. So could downward movement, for an unsuccessful speculation could easily break a man who habitually had all his capital at stake in commodities or claims.

Professionals—doctors, attorneys, and dentists actively engaged in their callings—composed about 3 percent of each camp's population (Table 5). A society of single young men, engaging in dangerous, sometimes legally ambiguous work and living under makeshift conditions, created opportunities for gifted lawyers and doctors, but also for frauds. A few men like Sherman Fletcher and William Stewart, who observed that professionals resuming their old vocations got more gold than those digging it from the ground, apprenticed themselves to leading doctors or lawyers; others simply assumed the titles and status. Town merchants and town professionals alike lived in a symbiotic relationship with the mines, winning a competence by selling goods and services, and nurturing the gold-based economy through investments, organizing abilities, and the establishment of precedents in mining law. But the way of life in the trading centers illuminated the social distances already established by 1850. Nevada storekeeper Peter Decker, bunking in the back of his Broad Street store, warmed by a large "sheet iron stove," taking his meals at a boarding house, spending his evenings in the society of the few families in town, lived a much more comfortable, regular life than most of his mining contemporaries.[14]

The formation of local governing bodies and political participation in the camps' first years further demonstrate that town and mines were separate but interdependent. Newspapers and town directories preserve only the names of the winners of the first elections in Grass Valley and Nevada; of those whose occupations can be discovered, professionals and merchants composed the great majority. The victors lived in the business centers or else at the sites of such vital enterprises as sawmills or water ditches. From 1850 through 1853, in areas overwhelmingly populated by men calling themselves miners, the candidates represented the commercial centers; the central political concern remained the governance of the towns, not the diggings, and townsmen, not miners, ran the elections and filled the offices. In the first elections merchants and lawyers did not impose their rule on miners; rather they undertook to organize the separate business districts. The miners voted, if not in great numbers, for the same town professionals and storekeepers who supplied them with goods and services, and came to the camps for law and justice just as they did for credit and provisions.

Governing themselves as nearly according to American norms as they could manage, especially after the formation of Nevada County in early 1851, the men of the two towns reproduced partisan caucuses, conventions, and rhetoric. Party politics exacerbated tensions between Northerners and Southerners just as they did in the nation at large; residents segregated themselves by geographic origin politically as well as physically. Partisan elections were passionate affairs; Southern Democrats, seizing control of the party structure, used a man's position on slavery as a test for party support, excluding several Northern Democrats from running for office. The bitterness evoked caused several near-duels, which further highlighted cultural differences: a Southerner in the heat of a campaign might challenge a Northern opponent to a duel and discover to his baffled rage and contempt that his adversary looked on the Code as evidence of Southern barbarity. The occasional challenges were spectacular exceptions to the general rule of barely suppressed hostility; still, ancient loyalties fueled local party politics, raising issues that had little to do with the mines.[15]

Mining Innovation and Town Survival

High hopes and rapid growth characterized both camps in 1851. Nevada City, its name augmented to distinguish it from the new county, strengthened its economic base by expanding trade and express connections with the Sacramento Valley. The legal business generated by the county offices attracted attorneys, and the whole business and professional community profited, for men who came to town as petitioners often became customers. The gravel leads had already made Nevada City and Coyoteville, taken as a unit, the most important gold district in the state, and the works continued to produce at a high rate. Gold, the county government, and a growing commerce gave Nevada City a much stronger economic base than most California mining camps.

Reflecting this prosperity, during 1851 Nevada City began to acquire the appearance of a permanent town. Its entrepreneurs laid out new commercial streets lined with impressive-looking buildings, some two-storied, some false-fronted. It possessed several standard town institutions: two churches, two theaters, a post office, several hotels, boarding houses, and restaurants, and a newspaper, the *Nevada Journal*. In March, an arsonist almost leveled the original town site by setting a fire that destroyed 125 buildings—at least as local boosters defined buildings. Flimsy construction promoted the rapid spread of the blaze, but the equally flimsy, hasty reconstruction that followed meant that the fire only interrupted growth. This first conflagration did, however, force a rapid turnover among businessmen—a process that would be repeated in later fires; individual merchants who had turned all their profits back into inventory were ruined and disappeared from the camps, only to be quickly replaced by others attracted by the camps' widely publicized potential. A business directory published in the newspaper in September listed ten attorneys, six physicians, ten grocers, fifteen general stores, thirteen hotels, six clothing stores, and eight saloons.

Early in 1851, Nevada City's population felt sanguine enough about the town's future to establish a full-fledged municipal government. Ignoring the protests of a few who felt the new order unnecessary, enthusiasts for a "real" town structure chose a mayor, ten aldermen, a recorder, a constable, a postmaster, and various minor officials. Although the election of Eastern-style officials might have seemed to signal the town's coming of age, residency requirements demanded only that a candidate have lived in town three months, a voter 30 days. Details of the campaign were not reported in the newspaper, but later commentators hinted that the election had pitted two factions of local businessmen against each other; the winning mayoral candidate, Moses Hoit, represented a group of gravel and ditch investors. The new government quickly proved overambitious: embarking without sufficient funds on a civic building program, Hoit soon had to admit a deficit of nearly $6,500.[16]

Proportionately, Grass Valley grew much faster than its neighbor in 1851, while remaining smaller in population and in volume of trade. At the beginning of 1851 only a handful of stores and boarding hotels occupied the little valley, but in the first months of that year merchants responding to the quartz news rapidly filled up Grass Valley with ramshackle structures. Mining in Grass Valley skipped some of the usual stages of development; it jumped from rather small-scale placer operations to the expensive experimental mills of the quartz interests, without a middle phase such as Nevada City's coyote works. Although the raw shake cabins and canvas sheds of Grass Valley's living area resembled those of most camps, boosters claimed that the rude buildings sheltered a uniquely peaceable population. Grass Valley managed to enforce its laws with the aid of only one justice of the peace; its people felt no need for a system like Nevada City's. Both towns, however, despite Grass Valley's assertions of sobriety and stability, lived in expectation of a quartz boom.[17]

Ignorance of the most crucial process of quartz mining, separating the gold from its quartz matrix, did not prevent merchants and mine owners in both towns from organizing joint-stock mining companies that tied up large percentages of the camps' capital resources. Meanwhile, newspaper propaganda and fulsome prospectuses of individual mines circulated in the East had spawned New York and Boston companies, which sent managers as incompetent and inexperienced as the locals to direct operations at leads often bought without investigation. By autumn of 1851, more than twenty mills in the two towns haltingly attempted to break up quartz ore. That winter, however, while gravel mining boomed, the *Journal* frequently contained notices of auction sales of quartz stock, as the holders let it revert to the companies rather than meet assessments to support more fruitless experimentation.[18]

While seasonal water supplies continued to govern the ebb and flow of men into the diggings, and therefore the economy, individual miners found other conditions changed from the days of the forty-niners. Jasper Hill wrote his brother several times in 1851 warning him against coming to California, because all the easily available ravine and surface claims had been worked over and over until they were worthless. By that year combines of investors had managed to control entire placer mining districts by consolidating many claims. An independent miner had little hope of developing coyote or gravel claims, which required investment capital and organized work forces; at best he might locate a promising claim, then sell out to a combine. And although coyoteing and other types of placer mining expanded in scope and became more sophisticated in method, most of the public excitement in Grass Valley and Nevada City revolved around quartz. Quartz mining required capital to support not only operations but experiments in technology; the more emphasis on quartz, the less possibility of successful independent mining. Men who located obviously rich veins usually could not exploit them, so even more than in coyoteing the hope was to sell claims, not to work them. The men lauded by Warren B. Ewer of the *Journal* for attempting to develop quartz mining were local businessmen who invested heavily in mining companies, but even they probably could not command the necessary financial power. The newspaper, in 1851, already looked to San Francisco to secure the future of quartz mining.[19]

The quartz excitement came to a head early in 1852 at a Nevada City mine known as the Bunker Hill. Many of Nevada City's leading citizens, including several city officials, deeply involved themselves in the highly publicized operation. Newspaper accounts marveled at the mill's massive waterwheel and smokestack, and at the risk capital it represented. Unfortunately, the theory behind the mill emanated from the imagination of a charlatan, a spurious doctor named Rogers. He supervised the construction of a huge blast furnace on the hypothesis that melting the quartz would free the gold, held like honey in a honeycomb, from its matrix and it would then sink to the bottom of the firebox to be readily removed. The fact that the town heavily backed this scheme sums up both the speculative nature of the local economy and the state of the science of quartz reduction. The whole town, in carnival, turned out for the initial test of the scheme. The results, after several trials, toppled many overly credulous merchants and the town government, several of whose members joined Rogers in the flight from financial reckoning. A businessman's government had proved only as good as the business sense of the mine investors who ran it. In the aftermath, the state legislature answered the petition of the citizens of Nevada City and dissolved the remnants of the administration.

Other attempts to separate gold from quartz by crushing the ore were more practical than Rogers's, but lack of capital, ineffective crushing equipment, imperfect methods of saving gold, and poor financial direction together doomed all operations except at the very richest mines. At one point in 1852, only one quartz mine at Nevada City and two near Grass Valley continued in production. Aaron A. Sargent of the *Journal*, reluctantly admitting the existence of a business depression in Nevada City following the quartz debacle, confidently predicted that spring production from the gravel hills would end hard times. But the late winter of 1852 brought floods all over the mining regions, and for once, an excess of water halted all placer work. Then a flash flood washed away several buildings, and soon afterwards, a fire set by incendiaries destroyed part of Nevada City's commercial district. Arson with intent to loot was only the crest of a crime wave rooted in the dearth of work and lack of law enforcement. As theft and robbery grew to epidemic proportions, beleaguered businessmen posted watches and formed vigilance committees to fill the vacuum in peacekeeping caused by the sudden dissolution of the Hoit regime. At the same time they sought credit from San Francisco and Sacramento. One vigilante group signaled its serious intent by assessing each member 25 cents to buy a rope. No hangings followed, but a suspected thief was whipped out of town. In 1852 Nevada City concentrated on survival.[20]

Grass Valley's quartz had not boomed as wildly as Nevada City's, and, because of the richness of the Gold Hill leads, did not bust as completely. A few mines, paying in spite of inefficient management and milling processes, attracted and held enough Eastern and English backing to maintain continuous production. By the start of 1852, Grass Valleyans claimed that the Gold Hill mines had yielded $4 million in gold. Placer mining, though plagued by water problems, supplemented quartz operations. A few ex-miners turned to stock raising and gardening and prospered, since milk sold for more than twice as much as whiskey and only the seller's conscience held down the price of fresh vegetables.

Again in the winter of 1852–53 severe storms disrupted business by cutting off communications with Sacramento and Marysville, the two most important transshipment points for the northern mines. Shortages of foodstuffs followed, as did hoarding and profiteering. But after the weather broke and commerce resumed, promoter Alonzo Delano, as always extracting the best he could from the business situation, assured the towns that the worst was over; fires and quartz failures had merely tested their metal, burning off the dross. The men left behind would be better for the experience.[21]

Signs of economic recovery and portents of future economic stability multiplied throughout 1853. "Fireproof" brick buildings started to appear as merchants attempted to protect investments with iron shutters, composite roofs, and locally manufactured masonry; by the mid-1850's "bricks" dominated both downtowns. Telegraph service linked both towns to Sacramento. A Nevada City company built a reservoir and by means of wooden pipes supplied much of the town with mountain spring water. And in June a reincorporated town government replaced Nevada City's impromptu citizens' groups. Composed of a salaried sheriff, an unpaid board of trustees, and a handful of administrative officials, the new order clearly reflected the dampening effects of the quartz crash. Its ordinances concentrated on fire protection, street repair, and public safety.

The launching in 1853 of a second newspaper in Nevada City, the *Young America*, later the *Democrat*, indicated returning confidence, as well as partisan fervor. While exchanging rancorous personal and political charges with the Whig *Journal*, the newcomer joined its rival in promoting nonspeculative growth. Grass Valley's new paper, the *Telegraph*, undertook to remain nonpartisan and spent its energies extolling the quartz interests, usually at the expense of the mines of Nevada City. Despite editor J. W. Oliver's assurances that Grass Valley would soon eclipse its industrially backward neighbor and would need more government, the citizens of the quartz town still did not find it necessary to incorporate. Perhaps the best evidence of returning prosperity in the two camps comes from court cases in Nevada City, where in late 1853 lots on the outskirts of town became the objects of litigation. Six months earlier they had been worthless.[22]

For Grass Valley, "the daily din of the quartz mills" signaled solvency, as "cool, cautious businessmen with hard earned experience" took control of the industry from speculators and dreamers. Six successful mills were in operation by mid-1853 and even the somewhat envious Sargent of the Nevada City *Journal* had to admit that quartz mining had become both stable and lucrative. The belief that enormous wealth would reward those who solved the technical problem of separating gold from quartz attracted skilled mechanics and draftsmen to Grass Valley; John A. Collins's mill plans won a medal for design at the 1853 fair of the Mechanics Institute in New York City. Unfortunately, nothing could guarantee a mining bonanza, so while the industry stabilized and production mounted, individual concerns continually failed. The basic combination necessary for a successful quartz mine remained constant: a rich claim, skilled management, a high-quality mill, capital adequate to overcome unforeseen accidents and delays, and good luck. The company that first opened a promising quartz lead rarely participated in its ultimate development, and often the original locator did not even realize the price of his claim, as companies frequently could not meet their debts. Jonas Winchester, who operated Grass Valley's most ambitious mining and milling undertaking in 1853, had both executive experience and powerful financial contacts in New York. In addition, his company ran a sawmill that helped defray local expenses. But bad weather and bad roads delayed the delivery of vital equipment, and as debts mounted his Eastern financial support dried up, because the long suspension of production had reinforced suspicions that California quartz was a bad investment. Creditors forced a foreclosure before Winchester could really get started.[23]

While quartz mining languished, then rallied, placer production had steadily improved in both efficiency and volume, so that even in the depths of the quartz depression, as long as the weather permitted, the two towns enjoyed a constant mining income. The gravel-mining industry sustained two tendencies established early: use of water, and the accompanying concentration of paying claims and solvent companies into fewer and fewer hands. Ditch companies pushed their flumes and conduits farther into the mountains in the attempt to maintain year-round water supplies. Legal battles for the control of creeks and rights-of-way accompanied the expansion, sometimes ending only with the merger of competing ditch concerns.

The water companies became doubly vital to the placer economy as gravel technology turned more and more to the intensive use
of water both for mining and to separate gold from ore. Ground
sluicing, that is, packing gold-bearing dirt in rock-lined trenches
and then diverting a creek through them, permitted washing on a
very large if wasteful scale, especially after canvas hoses replaced
rerouted streams as the water source. Early in 1853, miners discovered that placing brass nozzles on the hoses produced a controllable
high-pressure spray that rapidly removed the dirt. Further experiment proved that this current could also be directed against the
banks and hillsides of the placer sites themselves to wash down the
gold-bearing gravel. Called hydraulic mining, this method rapidly
replaced other techniques at important diggings and enhanced the
pivotal role of the ditch companies. Threatened boycotts and work
stoppages by individual miners and small companies might temporarily reduce prices charged for water but could not reverse the
ditch companies' continual gain in economic power. Hydraulicking also accelerated the ravaging of the countryside; the destructive force of the water and the public acceptance that mining
rights took precedence over all others resulted in the undermining
of roads, bridges, even working farms. At Coyoteville, all paying
claims were gradually concentrated into the hands of one hydraulic company, the commercial area was abandoned, and finally the
site of Nevada City's onetime rival was literally washed away. Of
course, hydraulicking also perpetuated the part weather played in
prosperity; between 1852 and 1857, only in 1856 did adequate
rainfall allow hydraulic methods to reach maximum efficiency.[24]

The way the miners lived and worked directly reflected the
changes in the industry. For many men the fortunes of mining
became the fortunes of the company that employed them; by now
most new arrivals actively sought wage work, and more than one
recorded that he made better money when he worked for someone
else. For all the uncertainties of quartz and hydraulic mining—the
work stoppages caused by weather, the pay reductions and layoffs
as firms ran out of capital or paying ore—wage earning held out
more security than prospecting. Miners began to move into town,
some for the common labor or construction work available there,
others for the boarding houses and restaurants. Most miners continued to live in cabins outside towns, but hotels, families that took in
boarders, and eating places that offered weekly or monthly rates

all found customers happy to abandon domestic duties. A few mining companies provided food and a place to live at low cost for their employees; Jonas Winchester transformed a family servant into a boarding-house cook and, using half of the "best house in the county" and a chickencoop, boarded several of his miners for his own profit and their convenience. By 1853, passable cooks, laundries, baths, barbers, seasonal farm produce, and improved transportation and shipping facilities all contributed to the physical comforts of the two camps; a miner on a spree could enjoy at any season anything that could be bottled or tinned. If the miner was solvent, roughing it, in the sense of cooking short rations over open fires and dwelling in makeshift huts, was a thing of the past.[25]

The Problem of Impermanence

Brick buildings and mechanically sophisticated mills could give an illusion of physical permanence and solidity, but nothing could make the towns' populations appear settled. Rushes to new gold strikes were only the most noticeable of many forces pulling at the miners. Individual movements in response to personal events—the failure of a claim or the opening of a business opportunity elsewhere—went on continuously. And of course, any extended work stoppage or recession would be accompanied by departures of miners and merchants alike. While newspapers dismissed the major exoduses as involving only the worthless portions of the working population, the flow of departures revealed not only the fluctuations of a mining economy, but also the persistence into the mid-1850's of the Gold Rush credo: get rich and get out. In the newspapers, condemnations of infatuated miners pursuing will-o'-the-wisps shared editorial space with compliments to members of the business community returning home to invest their profits; no occupational group seemed to have a lasting commitment to the camps. Mining investor Henry Crandall played active roles in Nevada City's politics and commerce, but once his mining company had struck a good lead and was producing consistently, he left for Massachusetts to marry and establish a home. Almost no one who had enjoyed the flush days, when some Nevada miners found a pound of gold a day or when Grass Valley prospectors sold quartz leads to enthusiastic and wealthy mining speculators, remained to see the mining industry dominated by technology and large combines.[26]

Of the men enumerated in the 1850 census, only about 7 in 100 appeared in the Nevada City directory of 1856 (Table 6). Neither of these documents is completely trustworthy, but their unreliability alone could hardly account for these outmigration figures. Only about 3 percent of the miners of 1850 worked in the town, in any occupation, in 1856. Professionals and proprietors were much more likely to stay than miners but in no way constituted a stable population. By late 1850, when the census was taken, Nevada already supported a well-established business community; only one member in five was still there six years later. Nevada City's small group of artisans, whose services and products commanded a constant market, was the most stable occupational group; one in three remained in 1856. No equivalent directory exists for Grass Valley, and the Nevada City directory listed Grass Valley's businessmen but none of its other citizens, so no comparison between miners and merchants within that town is possible. In 1850 there had been neither a major gold strike nor a business community in Grass Valley; very few of the traders and professionals listed for 1850 remained to be counted in 1856.

Outwardly the towns seemed prosperous and stable for the most part; newspapers offered in evidence Nevada City's brick buildings or Grass Valley's quartz mills. Indeed, compared to other mining camps, the two were prodigies, the largest in the state in both population and gold production. Nevada City ranked fifth among California towns in number of inhabitants, Grass Valley sixth. Only the largest commercial centers could claim more merchandisers than Nevada City's 98; no town had more mills—lumber, flour, and quartz—than Grass Valley. But there could be no real economic security in either town as long as bad weather, a major fire, or a mine failure could disrupt commerce or gold production, and these common dislocations, with the resulting population turnover, shaped the character of the towns. The towns were potentially as transient as their people.

Impermanence showed itself in shoddy workmanship. Town boosters congratulated themselves on the new "bricks," but in 1854 several in Nevada City collapsed under the weight of a spring snow, and in 1856 rains damaged many new structures because of the inferior materials in them. Outside of massive mining collapse, the single greatest threat to the towns and to individual businessmen in them was fire. But despite fund-raising bazaars by the ladies, and despite the membership of "the best young men" in the fire companies, neither town maintained an effective fire-fighting organization through the mid-1850's. In September 1855, a Grass Valley fire that burned uncontrolled all night destroyed 300 buildings at a loss of $400,000, and in July 1856, Nevada City was almost blotted out. During the Nevada City fire, faith in "fireproof bricks" cost ten lives when men took up stations inside to defend them. And even the volunteer fire companies formed in the aftermath of the conflagrations soon lapsed from lack of members.[27]

In the face of citizen apathy and mobile populations, the responsibility to promote town stability fell to the local governments, which, however, proved unable to maintain even their own continuity. In 1855, Grass Valley followed the example of Nevada City and incorporated under a system of trustees, who passed ordinances, and a marshal, who enforced them. But in 1856 attorney William Stewart, seeking to overturn a client's conviction on a misdemeanor charge, successfully challenged the constitutionality of the towns' incorporation before the state supreme court, and the state ordered both town governments to dissolve. Nevada City, after a brief outbreak of rowdiness as law enforcement stood in abeyance, reincorporated under the same system as before through a special act of the legislature, but Grass Valley did not find it necessary to reorganize until 1861. Despite their inability to enforce fire ordinances, their chronic financial weakness, and even their uncertain legal position, the town governments continued to be recognized as the most direct guardians of the town, at least by editors who insisted that interests which profited from disorder— saloon keepers, peddlers, and criminals—lay behind the refusal of Grass Valley's voters to reincorporate. There were no alternatives to town governments; the two towns' experience with fire companies could have satisfied no one as to the citizens' ability to protect their own property.[28]

While nonpartisan businessmen's town governments struggled simultaneously to survive and to promote order, the violently partisan conflict over the highly visible county and state offices contributed to further disorder. Party politics provided colorful amusements, a sense of belonging for activists, and an avenue of success for ambitious young men; population turnover meant that a man with the right social and ideological credentials could move directly into important roles almost immediately after arriving in the towns. But party politics undermined local loyalties. In 1855, as in 1850, parties fought over national issues and frequently enlisted voters according to sectional biases against blacks or immigrants. Party politics also shared some of the social characteristics of the towns themselves: constantly changing personnel, an emphasis on immediate individual opportunity, and emotional commitments centered elsewhere.[29]

By the mid-1850's the business communities, the most vocal proponents of the town corporations and order, openly acknowledged that the towns were dangerously out of control. The fault lay mostly with themselves; they dominated both town governments and partisan politics, they built the shoddy bricks and failed to maintain the fire companies. Their fears were for the commercial cores more than for the diggings: fluid social conditions might lead to the collapse of the towns despite the productivity of the mines.

The merchant's ideal town was stable, orderly, and, of course, prosperous—terms that may seem obvious but which in fact were employed in specific senses, limited in certain important ways. "Prosperity" meant lasting commercial success, as opposed to mining booms. Although money was made in the chaos of the Gold Rush, merchants much preferred quiet business conditions and the pursuit of long-term profits. Prosperity required stability enough that owners and investors could make reasonably accurate predictions and projections. And these businessmen assumed unquestioningly that a stable community must be composed of settled, nonmigratory individuals committed to the future of their towns.

In promotional writings, in resolutions passed at public meetings, and above all in editorials, businessmen and their journalist allies consistently homed in on "the great canker to the prosperity of California": the speculative, sojourner's attitude that most town inhabitants assumed toward their temporary homes. Some editors even dared to condemn those who had achieved the most common ambition of townsmen, to leave after "making their pile." In 1856 W. F. Anderson of the *Democrat* charged such men with having "sucked the life blood out of our state." To businessmen who aspired to build towns modeled on American orthodoxy, the perpetuation of Gold Rush attitudes and conditions was unthinkable.[30]

Against the Gold Rush

DISORDER, REFORM, AND SEGREGATION

The people of Grass Valley and Nevada City were as responsive to the intellectual currents of the 1850's as they were to the political ones. In particular, influential men among the native-born shared in the rise of nativism and moral reform movements and like many other Americans tended to link the two together, equating immorality and alien birth. Stereotyped images of foreign groups and their faults served as a background to social relations in the two towns, to be brought into play when needed. "Irish drunkenness" became an issue at elections, "Chinese servility" during hard economic times. These minor crises between the American- and foreign-born, often artificially inspired by outsiders, had only temporary impact on the towns. But in the mid-1850's a congruence of external example, shared prejudices, and, among Nevada City leaders, fear of moral disorder fueled a reform movement that briefly degenerated into violence against the Chinese. The underlying issue was the lingering effects of the Gold Rush—a toleration of gambling, prostitution, and crime believed by merchants and editors in both towns to be rooted in a lack of commitment to the towns themselves. The constant expectation of moving on endangered morality as well as prosperity, and ministers and town promoters offered the same solutions. The towns needed families, churches, and schools to establish orthodox mores and to attach population to place, and responsible merchants and professional men to serve as models of orderly living. In short, the reform movement aimed at ending the effects of the Gold Rush on town businesses and residents—the diggings were not involved. Reform would continue, and the foreign-born would remain its potential targets, until "American" institutions were securely established.

The Persistence of the Gold Rush

"All are here for money" is how Nevada City storekeeper Peter Decker flatly summed up his neighbors. His 1850 contemporary Charles Ferguson recalled that "a strong desire for adventure" beyond the bounds of civilized society reinforced "visions of gold" as inspiration for his overland journey. Observers disagreed whether the pursuit of wealth or an anticipated freedom from restraint was paramount in shaping Gold Rush society; either—and certainly both together—could and did produce what many saw as social chaos. The camps had no cohesion, Decker argued, because "the sociable man is lost in the money making." Miner Garrett Low agreed: "Money is one's only friend."

Expecting excitement, and with nothing hindering, miners could keep the camps of 1849 and 1850 in a continual uproar; late at night someone might fire at a wolf or an enemy, or just at random, and others would answer with shots until "for a mile around, it would seem like a regular battle." As gold mining proved devoid of romance, the simple need for diversion perpetuated the practices of the camps' first years. Grass Valley miner Edwin Morse, defending his fellows against sensationalist charges of debauchery, answered that "drinking and gambling were indulged in to a great extent in the dearth of other amusements." Greed, boredom, and anticipated license all helped give rise to a society outside accepted mores. The men in the tent cities along Gold Run, Little Deer Creek, and Boston Ravine that first winter gambled and drank far into the night. When the Deer Creek mines gave birth to the trading center that became Nevada City, a gambling saloon dominated the first collection of wagons and provision sheds on the site. Gamblers and prostitutes were just as mobile as miners and envisioned the same moral unconstraint, though in a more professional light. A tent, a deck of cards, and a barrel of anything alcoholic could complete the equipment of a Gold Rush resort. By 1851 and early 1852, as the two camps began to look like real towns, they acquired all the amusements peculiar to California's flush times. Theaters presented everything from Shakespearean tragedy staged

by famous professionals to vulgar farces performed by mounte-
banks before large and sometimes blindly enthusiastic audiences.
Circuses, minstrel shows, spiritualists, and phrenologists passed
through, as they did in small towns across the country. And in the
early days Nevada City possessed a crudely built bullfighting are-
na, where "Spanish" matadors used spears to dispatch somewhat
suspect fighting stock, and where upon occasion bulls and bears
were set on each other.[1]

While touring players, bullfighters, and mediums made brief
appearances and then moved on to divert or defraud the next
camp, the gambling halls remained, the largest, best furnished, and
most amply provisioned places of resort in the towns. A contemporary observer reported that these saloons had made the first attempts at ornamentation in the camps; gilt mirrors, nudes in oils,
stained-glass panels, crimson draperies, and mahogany bars contrasted sharply with the canvas walls and dirt floors of the miners'
cabins. The calculatedly luxurious, licentious, and frenetic gaming
ambience could give the miner at least the illusion of wealth and
adventure. In a Nevada City rebuilding after the fire of 1851, two
gambling saloons, the Empire and Barker's Exchange, were the
most impressive structures; in Grass Valley, the Alta enjoyed a
similar prominence. Men like Peter Decker and Garrett Low were
shocked to find that the "gaming palaces," like those of any booming mining camp, were most crowded on Sunday. Businesses, legitimate and questionable alike, claimed to do four times their
usual trade on the Sabbath.

Complaints about rowdy amusements and miners' Sabbaths expressed more than anger at disrupted rest or reckless use of fire-
arms or the like; diarists and journalists early recognized that string
bands and affable gamblers could supply cover for a criminal
underworld. In Grass Valley, disputes between "tinhorns" and
miners resulted in at least one homicide and one near-lynching.
The extreme preponderance of males generated sexual tensions
and jealousies easily aggravated in the atmosphere of the back-
room bordellos, and newspaper accounts of drunken brawls over or
between whores became common in 1851 and 1852. Twice in those
years homicide trials involved prostitutes, once as victim and once
as the bait in a robbery-and-murder plot. Worse, John Steele asserted, in Nevada City "the gambling houses had developed and shel-

tered a vicious class . . . so emboldened by the lack of organized government that they greatly hindered legitimate business."[2]

Despite moralists' rumblings of outrage and fading miners' dreams of unbridled adventure, mining society stayed fundamentally the same throughout the first half of the 1850's. The populations of both camps remained overwhelmingly young, single, and male, and both amusements and respectable women remained scarce. The quartz collapse of 1852 ruined some speculators and daunted others, and only the most deluded miners still dreamed of instant wealth after that date, but boredom and biology still urged the men toward the recreations of the flush times. A drifter for a coyote company labored just as hard as anyone had working on his own claim; he was equally starved for breaks in his routine, and perhaps even more hungry for the semblance of luxury and daring the gambling halls and brothels could supply. In 1853, a Grass Valley correspondent extolling town prosperity reported that "business is lively here on Sunday and the hotels and public places thronged with people." Nevada City's most famous, if not its most elaborate, gambling establishment opened in 1854, presided over by Eleanore Dumont, later known as Madame Moustache. Brothels such as the Recreo Flor de Maria figured prominently in disturbance-of-the-peace cases in the mid-1850's; neither the availability of prostitutes nor their power to provoke violence had diminished. Brawling, drunkenness, and petty crime remained newspaper staples.[3]

Two conflicting interpretations of mining society appear in the memoirs and journals from these years. The more favorable (and less common) version stressed the honesty, generosity, and sometimes even the piety of the Gold Rush miners and emphasized mutual trust, cooperation, and fair and sure popular justice. The devout Luther Melanchthon Schaeffer described a hymn-singing, contented, and good-humored Grass Valley in 1851, where "everyone seemed anxious to have our little village distinguished for its morality," though he had to admit that gambling and drinking thrived. In the same vein, Luzena Wilson recounted how she kept her boarders' gold in her bedroom, in a house with no locks, never imagining the possibility of theft. But the dominant analysis of camp society emphasized its moral dangers to individuals. "California turns men profane, drunken [and] lawless," J. W. Oliver of the *Grass Valley Telegraph* bluntly stated; through "criminal indulgences," some men had "lost the finer feelings of the soul." Men seemed to feel that their actions did not matter: "We are in California, without associations . . . in a short time we will return to the states where somebody lives, and then we will reform." Without the checks of traditional social institutions, the gambling saloon and bordello shaped society in their image, so that, as newspapers reported, morality had "little importance in the mountains," its practitioners sneeringly called "Christians" by all "lovers of fun and California liberty."

The camp moralists who promulgated this ominous analysis of mining life, either in newspaper editorials, like Aaron Sargent of the *Journal* and Warren Ewer of the *Journal* and the *Telegraph*, or in magazine sketches, like Alonzo Delano, almost invariably contrasted the two camps with an idealized East of Sunday schools, scrubbed children, and respectful laborers. Isolation caused part of this felt inferiority; newspapers reported that a returned Californian felt out of his element in proper society and uncomfortable in intelligent conversation simply because he had fallen behind in general information. But much more importantly, the moralists always lamented the absence, or even more frightening, the fragility of the traditional bulwarks of society: homes, churches, schools, and respect for the "better classes." And these were absent, or frail, because it seemed that few cared enough about the towns to attempt to maintain them.[4]

Neither sinners nor the godly would remain in the towns to reap what they had sown. Here the analysis of the moralists coincided exactly with that of the business community, who saw lack of commitment as the bane of town prosperity. Such unanimity is hardly surprising, though, as the most influential voices for business stability and for moral reform were those of the same men speaking to the same audience. Sargent, as a lay religious leader and as editor, mining investor, and politician, was publicly committed to the New England example. Banker and mine developer Delano, in his humorous sketches, combined local boosterism with nostalgia for village American piety. Ewer, mining expert and temperance man, emphasized the importance of peace and quiet to attract investment. Delano came to Grass Valley in 1850, Ewer and Sargent to Nevada City in 1851, and each plunged immediately into promoting morality and his town, consciously addressing the region's literate middle class. The three writers were representative of their audience, men they expected to share their values. They were educated "natural leaders"—the kind of men automatically chosen in early elections. They were men of business, but also active in social clubs and churches. Most importantly, they had unusually strong roots in the two towns. They and others like them counseled that together moral order, business order, and governmental order might create healthy communities, while separately none of these would prove obtainable.[5]

Throughout the lives of Nevada City and Grass Valley, editors and orators had proclaimed that they would become as permanent as Eastern towns. These boasts stemmed from an almost instinctive boosterism on the part of frontier businessmen and reflected the conviction that California would become "American," that all aspects of American society would be reproduced there. In the first days, then, most locally published discussions of the future and moral failings focused rather broadly on California, not on the camps themselves. But after the discovery of the deep gravel deposits and the quartz leads, the successful capitalization of several mining companies in 1851 and 1852, and the reestablishment of commerce in 1853 presaged possible long-term prosperity, spokesmen began to concentrate on local concerns. They clearly tied future economic success to morality: gamblers, prostitutes, and thieves no longer endangered primarily individuals, but the commercial interests in general. Disorder could obviously damage trade; less directly, the same lack of commitment that allowed gambling to flourish permitted fire protection to lapse. By 1855 the local editors, essayists, ministers, and merchants speaking in citizens' meetings had suggested the outlines of their model society, one that combined piety and profits in the form of accepted American practice. The means of "Americanizing" the camps were to be threefold: stabilizing and diversifying their economic base, restoring class distinctions that had been blurred during the Gold Rush, and importing women and children to guarantee the future.

From the first newspaper predictions on the future of the camps, the debaters had acknowledged that the mines alone, no matter how rich or seemingly inexhaustible, could not guarantee long life. Any extractive industry would eventually work itself out. Moreover, placer mining had created the social conditions that plagued the camps, and hydraulic and quartz mining seemed to perpetuate them. Finally, mining as the economic base for a whole community was simply foreign to the experience of those in the business community. Editors and publicists proposed farming—the most traditional economic base possible—along with ranching and lumbering as supplements to gold mining and as eventual substitutes for it. Warren Ewer felt that California and the two camps needed artisans, small farmers, and mechanics, to supply the daily wants of an established society, far more than they needed more miners.

All of the business community spokesmen agreed, furthermore, that even a diversified economy by itself could assure neither prosperity nor permanency: economic stability also required an end to the rampant "gambling" attitude of early mining investors and the merchants themselves. Where at first almost any speculator had received respectful attention in the newspapers and often backing from the towns' merchants, by 1852, especially after Nevada City was almost ruined by a town government tied to Rogers's quartz-reduction scheme, "speculator" became a term of contempt. The attitudes of mine developers toward the towns and toward their own roles in the community would have to be radically altered if the promise of the gold resources were to be fulfilled. Men aiming to get rich quickly must be replaced by men interested in moderate returns over the long haul. The towns also needed investment capital and funds to support further technological experimentation; one representative of a New York bank was worth dozens of mining boomers. Developing the leads already discovered and building a mining industry far outweighed prospecting for new strikes, just as rooted farmers were more important to the towns than new swarms of transient miners.[6]

Proponents of stability expected that a sophisticated mining industry, with its heavy capitalization and a definite managerial structure, would produce other benefits besides unprecedented wealth for the two towns. The first descriptions of quartz mills in Grass Valley often pointed out that they gave the camp the semblance of a New England factory town and implied that they had also brought Lowell-style paternalism and social control. Editors referred to Grass Valley as a "village," in sharp contradistinction to a "camp," because of these associations with mill villages, and local boosters argued that Grass Valley was superior to Nevada City and other mining camps because its quartz industry created stable employment and therefore a stable society. The development of large-scale mining not only would undercut the economic basis—the dreams of quick wealth—of Gold Rush attitudes, it would impose order and discipline on the laboring populations and create a permanent management class.[7]

One of the most vaunted social consequences of the Gold Rush had been the supposed democratization of society. The process of acclimatizing to gold-camp life—turning from a greenhorn to a "bully honest miner"—involved hiding one's earlier identity behind a beard, a red flannel shirt, dirt, and an aggressively hail-fellow manner, or so most early narrators agreed. No American society had achieved the appearance of democracy so well as the gold camps; Grass Valley visitor Mallie Stafford reported that "all honest citizens, merchants, officials, mechanics and miners, adopted the recognized uniform of the mines, . . . so that a man's background or present status could not be determined by his exterior." In the *Nevada Journal*, "practical miner" meant respectable citizen, and Luther Schaeffer, a jack-of-all-trades sojourning in Grass Valley, boasted that "no false distinctions of society" existed and that "no mushroom aristocratic notions were tolerated." Supposedly, neither family background nor mining luck created accepted class distinctions.

But democracy manifested itself more in outward show than in real changes in values. Moralists and businessmen openly called on men exceptional in ability and position to shape the towns into traditional forms. The celebrants of camp equality typically hastened on to point out that men superior to the herd in training and attainments hid behind long hair and patches. Alonzo Delano attributed more scientific and literary accomplishments to "these . . . uncouth looking miners than I have ever seen among the same number of men at home." Moreover, according to optimistic reporters like Stafford and Schaeffer, this disguised elite controlled camp mores: "The influence of a few moral and intellectual gentlemen kept in check the turbulent spirit that needed only a spark to ignite it into flame." The majority, less sanguine, argued that the chaotic social conditions they saw hindering camp commerce and endangering individuals resulted precisely from the failure of the natural middle-class leadership to fulfill its responsibility and take control. Whether one believed that the camps had been saved or needed to be saved, social equality was not conducive to order.[8]

The roles of successful industrial mining and of educated middle-class men in bringing order were invariably linked by post–Gold Rush writers with another, more fundamental source of order, the family. Grass Valley's quartz mining would promote peace in the town by making it practical for the mining employees to bring in their families. And when either town's editors made their repeated (and premature) claims of new prosperity and tranquility, they always cited the increase in the number of women and children and "neat cottage homes" as well as the business acumen of the enterprising merchants and the thriving mine operations. When editors noted their town's shortcomings, the brothels, brawls, and floating populations, the corrective always in some way depended on established families. "We must have families here and make this land a home"; the towns must become "scenes of happy associations and personal interests." With his wife and children present, the husband would develop a "centralization of feelings" there, and concern himself with laws, education, and religion in order to protect his family. Women and children would be the catalysts—not necessarily active agents—of social change. The mere presence of women would, through the automatic respect and deference men owed them, alter the behavior of the male population. Women in their most traditional role, as the focus of the home, the bearers of religion, and the stewards of a natural conservatism, would control men; editors specifically called for "womanly women" for the towns, rejecting bluestocking feminists who would meddle in male affairs. The women the moralists wanted, inherently pious, would support churches; the concerns of parents would promote schools; and both institutions, through preaching and teaching, would further advance customary American beliefs. Moreover, by creating order the family would also generate wealth; "the healthy and softening influence of women and morality" would "form the basis of a lasting prosperity."[9]

Industry to provide steady work and steady discipline, middle-class men to supply moral and political leadership, and women to keep their men in the towns and out of the saloons and brothels together would tame the gold towns, it was claimed. Unfortunately, far from being eliminated, the vices and irresponsible attitudes of the flush times seemed in practice to infect the very individuals and institutions expected to tame the two towns.

Industrial mining did not promote the type of stability business-men had expected from it. The owners of the major mines were interested in profits, not paternalism; they made no attempts to control their employees' demands for the same sort of releases—gambling and prostitution—the forty-niners had demanded. And the mine owners' failure mirrored that of middle-class society in general to separate itself from questionable activities. In the first years there had been no unambiguous distinctions between legiti-mate, lawful society, the demimonde, and the violent criminal class. The owner of a prominent gambling saloon enjoyed enough respectability to be elected alderman in Nevada City's overinflated government of 1851; the Grass Valley vigilance committee of that year elected E. B. Lundy its captain while he was standing trial for killing his opponent in the diggings' most notorious duel, settled at fifteen paces with Colt revolvers. Nevada City's most spectacular shootout erupted when the defeated Democratic candidate for state assemblyman in 1853 opened fire on the man he blamed for his loss; both survived, slightly wounded, after a battle waged in the middle of Broad Street. That year J. W. Oliver of the *Telegraph* charged, with obvious accuracy, that leading citizens coun-tenanced rowdyism, shirking their responsibility to be models for the rest of society. Some of them, in fact, had questionable origins. Henry Crandall, in a letter to his fiancée, bluntly stated that "Ne-vada is starting to have its Aristocracy and they require [for mem-bership] rather too much in a pecuniary way . . . and too little as to character of morals. Sporting gentlemen and Profligate Women are by no means excluded if only they come well supplied with the Oro."

The democratic disguise, hiding differences in individual social position, might itself be dangerous. Alonzo Delano feared this; he professed relief to discover in himself "a small portion of the soul" and "an innate sense of decency" despite his dirty matted hair and beard. His works, especially his play, "A Live Woman in the Mines," focused on characters who had been professionals in the East but in the mines had become déclassé, now ignorant of the usages of polite society and helpless to restore themselves. By embracing Gold Rush mores, a man could lose his self as well as his money and social status.[10]

Even pious women refused to accept the stereotyped passive part assigned them in saving the towns and townsmen. As Charles Ferguson shrewdly noted concerning the first respectable women in Nevada City, "they were anxious to make money by honest industry[,] also to improve society"; making money took precedence. Luzena Wilson, thinking how to aid her husband who had gone into debt transporting the family to Nevada, decided, "as always occurs to the mind of a woman," to provide for boarders. Starting from an outdoor table constructed from two doors, the Wilsons "made money fast" and in six months had $10,000 invested in a hotel and store. Similarly, Madame Penn, after mining at her husband's side, started a boarding house, and Mrs. Philips's dried-apple pies attracted throngs of miners willing to pay a dollar each.[11]

In 1850, thirteen women lived in what was to become Grass Valley. Eight were housewives, one was a servant, and four took in boarders. Five husbands listed "trader" as their occupation, so their wives probably assisted in keeping store, but only in the case of the boarding houses were the women certainly using domestic skills to help support their families. Nevada in 1850, with a clearly defined business center, gave women opportunity for a more obvious economic role. Twenty-three adult white women lived in the midst of a male population of over 2,600 (Table 1). Twelve of them either accepted boarders or ran hotels with their husbands, two were servants, and three more worked in family-run taverns that supplied bed and board to single males. Six women lived in nuclear families, and three of them, married to prominent merchants, kept male servants. These three households with Irish, Mexican, and black servants may have been the embryo of a middle-class society, but almost three-fourths of the respectable women listed—and the census taker enumerated only respectable women—worked essentially at domestic tasks gone public, in the business area that became Nevada City.

In both towns, but especially in Nevada in 1850, a disproportionate number of men with wives and families operated small businesses of some kind. Some could afford the luxury of transporting non-working wives to the mines, but in most cases wives and children worked alongside husbands and fathers. Standards of female respectability had to be modified. Just as saloon keepers could be leading citizens in the camps, women could make beds and work in taverns without becoming social pariahs. Accepted Eastern roles for middle-class women—and the merchants and tavern keepers were certainly middle-class by camp standards—did not seem to be completely relevant in the two camps, and the first respectable women did not act as passive inspirers of social control.[12]

In 1851, Charles Ferguson and his companions, weary of cooking for themselves, began to board at the Grass Valley establishment of Mrs. Coates. Mr. Coates, who mined while his wife cooked, soon acquired a reputation for desperate jealousy. Mr. Coates's response was rational, if extreme. The scarcity of women that made their "sweet seductive voices" devastating lures to both gaming tables and church-bazaar baked goods tables, that led men "to come forty miles over the mountains" to look at the obviously married and admittedly unhandsome Luzena Wilson, induced other men to try to break up marriages. William Stewart, on Nevada City jury duty, discovered divorce cases to be commonplace, as prosperous young miners persuaded wives that they had married beneath themselves and helped engineer their freedom by serving as witnesses at their trials. Stewart had to admit that mining-camp conditions could corrupt women as well as men. Alonzo Delano, an ardent advocate of female-inspired reform, ruefully agreed; his "former ideas of the purity and stern morality of the opposite sex," he wrote, "had been somewhat lowered" because women often "adopt the code of morals of the country and instead of endeavoring to stem the current, float along with it." The Grass Valley and Nevada City of the flush times were not safe for the middle-class women and families expected to save them and more than one man refused to allow his wife to join him.[13]

After 1852, as the towns began to seem more permanent, more and more merchants and investors began to visit their old homes to collect families or choose wives. The number of women and children increased rapidly, but two conditions remained constant: the Gold Rush practice of wives contributing to family survival continued, and merchant society was still tainted by contact with those less respectable. The wife of a leading Nevada City hotel keeper made dresses; a politician's wife operated a "fancy goods" shop.

Professional and business families quickly banded together and followed a self-conscious round of recreations, notably sit-down dinners and dances, conducted as formally as possible and duly chronicled in the newspapers. Since the only buildings large enough to host a large party or ball were saloons or hotels, the evenings of the elite became perforce subscription entertainments, staged for profit by restaurant, tavern, or hotel keepers. For example, participants in a "fashionable cotillion" in Grass Valley danced until midnight and then marched in to supper at the Alta, the town's most lavish gambling saloon. Even though "the guests both male and female were of the best class in the community," at this and similar affairs society's parties remained public, commercial, frequently located in resorts of ambiguous repute, and liable to disruption by disreputables.[14]

Churches and schools, the institutions commonly identified with the middle class in bringing civilization to the towns, shared the insecurities of that group. Organized religion had recognized California as a fertile missionary field from the beginning of the gold excitement, and the first formal churches in Nevada City and Grass Valley were founded by ministers dispatched and supported by national denominational bodies. These men faced camp life straightforwardly, condemning excesses and naming names without fear, and preaching, if need be, in front of or in saloons. Congregationalist James Warren held services in the Dramatic Hall on Sunday morning; in the evenings the usual performances took place. The camps, although courteous to the ministers, largely ignored them. From the first, declaimed Warren in his farewell sermon, "I have been almost a professional beggar," making the rounds of the diggings, largely in vain, trying to raise an edifice and then maintain it. Early accounts of camp religion stress the believers' sense of being few against many, the small band of churchgoers opposed to the crowds of celebrants in the saloons. When the first Methodist chapel in Nevada City was planned, the members decided to locate it on a hill outside town, out of earshot of the Sunday street revels the churches were unable to control. Nevertheless, churches and congregations attempted to fulfill their expected parts. Ministers tried to act as moral arbiters, and churches supplied bases of operations for reform by sheltering temperance clubs and Sabbatarian meetings. And middle-class

Grass Valley (top) and Nevada City (bottom) in 1856. (Lithographs in the
California State Library.)

women constituted the foundation of church support; their sub-scription campaigns, suppers, auctions, and fairs became common features of camp life.[15]

The other archetypical family institution also had failed to estab-lish itself firmly in the two camps. Neither town made an effort to support public schools at first as the number of school-age children did not warrant large investments in education. Both towns did have short-lived private primary schools conducted by women for a few scholars. Grass Valley's first public school opened in 1853, and Nevada City followed suit the next year; the towns, however, did not offer adequate financial support for the schools. Nevada City's school exhausted its allotment after one term and closed. A benefit given by a touring circus allowed it to reopen. Most of the time subscription campaigns, public dinners, and school exhibi-tions in which children sang and recited lessons before doting, ticket-buying parents and friends kept the systems barely afloat.[16]

By 1853, none of the agents expected to bring order and with it prosperity had proved successful; instead, all had themselves been marred or hampered by camp conditions. Vice daily intruded on virtue; when a drunken miner mistook a minister's wife for "Fanny the Whore" and burst into the parsonage, Aaron Sargent fulminat-ed in the *Journal* against town attitudes that allowed Fanny to locate her "neat cottage" among the homes of the middle class. Orthodox values and institutions had not taken hold.[17]

Alien Peoples and Perceptions of Disorder

In the first issue of the *Nevada Journal*, Warren Ewer gave a prominent place to an editorial on the glories of the Anglo-Saxon race; racial self-consciousness was one of the essential values Amer-icans carried with them to the mines. And when the middle class failed to extinguish the influence of the Gold Rush, racial stereo-types provided a ready explanation: members of "alien races" did not share the moral virtues of Americans. The native-born associat-ed the towns' underworlds with the foreign-born; moreover, nativ-ists claimed, the vices of inferior peoples could undermine the towns' Americanness, since men led astray by the lures of the demimonde became somehow less than American.

In the beginning, the two towns' foreign-born were accepted as part of the exotic Gold Rush experience. This dispassionate good humor was not universal and was soon sorely tested as the number of the foreign-born rapidly increased. And, as Nevada lawyer Lorenzo Sawyer noted in 1850, "we see people here from all parts of the world and have the opportunity of observing their habits and customs . . . for they still retain their distinguishing characteristics"—that is, the foreign-born were not assimilating. The census takers, working in the fall of 1850, did not record the range of nationalities suggested by Sawyer. Instead, they found that the 5 percent in both camps who were foreign-born came mostly from Great Britain, Ireland, and Germany, with small numbers from Canada, Latin America, and France (Table 8). Almost certainly undercounting men from the different Spanish-speaking nations, the enumerators may also have ignored Chinese miners who were present in the camps by late 1850. Still, in 1850 the towns had been overwhelmingly American-born, and many contemporary observers drew an easy connection between the large numbers of immigrants arriving in 1851 and 1852 and the problems of order during those years.[18]

Two national groups bore the blame for nearly all the crime associated with the first years of the towns. Englishmen who arrived in California via Australia were assumed to be veterans of the penal colony there and were automatically suspected of any unsolved robbery or assault. Edwin Morse reported that some of the "Sidney Ducks" lived decent lives, but more frequented certain "lewd dens" in Grass Valley, looking for criminal opportunities. If the Sidney Ducks had the reputation of being "very hardened" characters, the "Spanish" were believed worse, men who would "dabble their hands in human gore as a pastime" and kill "with fiendish delight." Chileans, Sonorans, and Californios, indiscriminately called "Spanish," were more directly identified with the perceived foreign threat to the Americanness of the camps than any other group. In November 1851, vigilance committees in both camps, believing that the crimes they had organized to end were perpetrated by Sonorans, prepared for pitched battles with them. Aaron Sargent cheered on the vigilantes: "the extermination of such Ishmaelites is the only safeguard of society." Mexican brigands failed to appear, so no bloodshed issued from the hasty mobilization for war, but the beliefs that had triggered lynchings in other camps clearly had alarmed Grass Valley and Nevada City.

According to the American-born, vice as well as violence was the near-exclusive province of the "Spanish." When Edwin Morse reported that upon his arrival only one English-speaking woman lived in Grass Valley, he meant only one respectable woman; "Spanish woman" or "senorita" almost invariably denoted a prostitute, and "Spanish house," regardless of the nationality of owner or inmates, referred to the lowest dives or dance halls. Almost all Spanish-surnamed women who appeared in the public record were being tried for prostitution. Most Hispanic men mined or teamed, but in the popular image they pimped and rolled drunks in the bordellos. Newspaper and ministerial moralists emphasized that the most alien and bloody gold-camp amusement, the bullfight, was "Spanish," and since undeniably American men packed the rings, they condemned the Mexican performers for reducing civilized men to savagery. To some, the Americanization of California meant above all the elimination of Hispanic cultural influences.[19]

Most of the European-born rarely experienced enmity from the American-born, and only the presence of common national stereotypes—pugnacious Irishmen, stolid Germans, mercurial Frenchmen—hinted at tensions. Anti-Semitism rarely became public. The small community of Jews, mostly German-born, concentrated their efforts in merchandising, and maintained good relations with Christian customers and competitors. In 1851, some "ladies of Nevada City" convinced George Dornin that he "would do well" to start a store there because "an American establishment would be met with general patronage." Dornin soon discovered that his Jewish rivals, more experienced than himself, consistently undersold him and also enjoyed "the trade of the ladies who had protested loudest against Jewish merchants." Dornin sold out.

The two largest European groups, the Irish and the Cornish, did not arrive in number until the development of large-scale mining was well under way. Unfortunately for the Irish, this process coincided with an upsurge of political nativism. Anti-Irish sentiment was almost always tied to Whig or Know-Nothing partisanship, and had little to do with the Irishmen's local activities, beyond their loyalty to the Democratic Party. The Cornish, of all the large foreign groups the most similar in appearance, values, and religion to the American-born (they even shared antipathies toward the Irish), the most accustomed to the emerging industrial mining life, and, because of their skills in hard-rock mining, the most vital to economic development, entered easily into town society.[20]

Stereotyped images of attributes and behavior were especially important in determining attitudes toward the two native-born non-white groups in the camps, the Nisenan (the local California tribe) and blacks. The diarists and letter writers of 1850 and 1851, anticipating romanticized Plains warriors, described the simple material culture and retiring personalities of the Nisenan with contempt. For example, Peter Decker dismissed them as "mere animals although mostly of good physical development." Physical conflict between whites and the Nisenan occurred only in 1850; in May a tribal party attacked two sawmills near Grass Valley and killed a man. Whites later agreed that the raid was revenge, either for miners' incursions in pursuit of allegedly stolen cattle, or for one miller's practice of "insulting"—molesting—Indian women. At the time, however, whites overreacted, frantically calling for aid from neighboring camps and military officials, and staging a series of punitive attacks on Nisenan villages before imposing a peace settlement late in the year. For most whites, after the scare had ended, the Indian camps became curiosities, places where men paid a dollar admission to watch dances and remark on the nudity of the performers. Other whites held, paternalistically, that the Nisenan had to be protected against white vices and should be on reservations, despite their obvious reluctance to give up their semi-nomadic ways and the protests of sympathetic whites that they were harmless. By 1855 one-quarter of the Nisenan were on the Nome Lackee reservation; the rest remained under the control of an Indian agent named Bovyer. In five years the Nisenan had gone from objects of fear to objects of pity.[21]

Few blacks lived in the camps (Table 9), but they also elicited a response based on common expectations about their behavior, complicated by the difference in regional attitudes toward slavery in the 1850's. In 1850 six black males lived in Grass Valley, six males and one young girl in Nevada. All were quartered with whites; there were no black families. Proximity did not mean equality, however, for despite California's Free Soil constitution, most of the blacks were held as slaves or at best as quasi-free servants in white households. Only two men, listed as mulattos, born in Ohio, and working as cook and waiter in a tavern, clearly controlled their own lives. They stayed in the hostelry with the other waiters, who were white. At the other extreme, two Grass Valley black males, three Nevada men, and the girl had no surnames and served Southerners. The status of the others was more ambiguous. A mulatto boy, born in the Cherokee Nation and living with a white trader's family, probably enjoyed no freedom; three Nevada blacks, listed as baker, washer, and miner and residing in the store of a Virginia-born grocer, may have been technically free, although they probably contributed labor to the grocer's enterprise. Occupations ranged from cook and baker, the most skilled, through those who mined beside their probable owners, to those simply listed as servants, commonly with white families who took in boarders.

The numbers of blacks in the two camps increased steadily but slowly during the early 1850's, always remaining only a small proportion of the total residents. The illegal practice of slavery quietly died out; in 1852 Grass Valley's population was augmented by the breakup of a nearby mining operation worked by slaves. Slavery in that mine was ended by the death of its Georgia-born owner, not by the pressure of public opinion. Most of the time, the few blacks were ignored, and the few newspaper and diary references to them depicted blacks working at menial tasks and laughingly recounted their battles and love affairs, incidentally reiterating imputations of loose morals and unbridled behavior. In March 1852, Grass Valley whites held a citizens' meeting to protest what they called a "negro riot." Perhaps called in response to the influx of blacks from the defunct slave mine, the assembly's actual discussion emphasized the disturbance to white families created by blacks living nearby. The citizens resolved to protect white neighborhoods by force, and convinced the owner of one house rented by blacks to evict his tenants. Grass Valley had established housing segregation. Excitement flared in 1854 in Nevada City when a mulatto girl enrolled in school and the next year in Grass Valley when children "suspected of being tainted with Indian or Negro blood" attempted also to attend school. In both cases the children were expelled. A brief, sharp, public debate followed on the propriety of taxing blacks to support schools their children could not attend, even though the state law requiring school attendance did not specifically exclude students by race. The editorial consensus called for separate schools, but nothing resulted beyond continued rejection of children even suspected of being non-white, and the acceptance of segregation in the newly established schools in both camps, to match the already existing segregation in neighborhoods. Paternalism coexisted with discrimination; while he endorsed seg-regated schools, Warren Ewer lauded Grass Valley blacks for pur-chasing their freedom and then acquiring property and congratu-lated "respectable" blacks for founding a church. Good blacks, in sum, worked hard and went to church; bad blacks intruded them-selves into white society.[22]

The Chinese were the largest non-white presence in the two towns; 2,000 lived in Nevada County by 1852. Again, racial and social stereotypes of the Chinese helped make them curiosities in white eyes, very much like the other exotic, racially different group in the diggings, the Nisenan. Lorenzo Sawyer found the Chinese "the most sober, honest and industrious people in this country"; others, especially merchants, expected them, as cheap labor and profitable customers, to benefit white businesses. On the other hand, some whites characterized all Chinese as liars and thieves, and argued that their clannishness and obtuseness made it impossible for them to learn American ways. In the main, the newspapers displayed more interest than enmity as long as the Chinese did not compete directly with whites in the search for gold, although references to heathen ways, slavery, and teeming millions of potential immigrants were common.[23]

Although the numbers of Chinese declined in both camps after the Foreign Miner's Tax of 1852, definable Chinese districts began to develop in both Grass Valley and Nevada City. The Chinese leased buildings in the cheapest and roughest downtown blocks, and there, surrounded by white men's saloons and prostitutes' flim-sy cribs, they established their own stores, restaurants, and gam-bling dens. White ethnic groups did not form homogeneous neigh-borhoods because they lacked both the necessary numbers and the outside pressures that operated on the Chinese; like the blacks, the Chinese lived apart. Wherever Chinese migrated away from their home villages, they established discrete communities for mutual support, but in the two camps, this separation also reflected white racial antipathies, backed by force. "I pity the poor devils," hedged

Grass Valley mining entrepreneur Jonas Winchester, who refused to give shelter in his woodshed to some flooded-out Chinese, "yet could not have a houseful of them quite so near me."

Since Nevada City was more oriented toward placer mining than Grass Valley, where white miners excluded the Chinese from quartz work, it had a larger Chinese community. The Chinatown of Nevada City, already a distinct enclave by late 1853, offered a wider range of services to Chinese miners, having more merchants and more skilled and semiskilled craftsmen. Grass Valley's smaller Chinatown began on the town's outskirts and did not permanently establish itself downtown until late in the 1850's. Both Chinese districts reflected in their populations the facts of Chinese migration. Except for a handful of well-to-do merchants and doctors, the Chinese came to America as single men, dependent on regional companies organized by entrepreneurs from their home prefects for passage, jobs, protection in the mines, and consumer goods. A Chinese did not perceive himself as part of the environment he inhabited; he lived with his kind, earning for his family in China as rapidly as possible so he could return home as soon as possible.[24]

In many ways, then, the life and aspirations of a young Chinese miner resembled those of his American-born counterpart or a miner from any ethnic group. Originally attracted by hopes of quick wealth and a quick return home, he gave up that dream in exchange for steady work, often wage labor, in the mines. For the duration of his short stay, he would tolerate otherwise unacceptable privations and unsettled social conditions; he left his family behind, and he had little identification with the camp as a possible home. The Chinatowns served the same purposes as the towns' commercial cores; men resorted there for supplies, contacts with home, and gambling and women to ease the monotony of mining. Whites, however, saw the Chinese as the most racially and culturally alien of all the groups in the mines, and as the least affected by the forces gradually changing mining society—industrial mining, the ideal of permanent settlement, and the establishment of traditional American institutions.

In 1852, Sinophobic and nativist undercurrents briefly surfaced as both Grass Valley and Nevada City, along with several other camps, reacted violently to calls for a Foreign Miner's Tax intended in part to slow immigration. That year, sporadic clashes between American-born and foreign-born erupted in both camps, and American citizens' meetings called for exclusion. Newspapers and diary references to nativist political agitation, and to violence directed against foreigners, were concentrated in early and mid-May 1852, immediately after and in some cases in direct response to Governor John Bigler's "Special Message" warning of the dangers of massive foreign migration. The fact that men like the usually levelheaded Ohioan John Banks shared the general perception of the foreign-born, especially Chinese, as "arriving in the thousands and offering to work very low, some for board," demonstrates how the fear of competition for jobs in the economically troubled Grass Valley and Nevada City of 1852 could help Bigler's partisans to exploit the foreign question. But other factors conditioned the response besides economics; Grass Valley, with a larger immigrant population and seasoned anti-foreign activists, experienced more excitement than Nevada City, even though it had suffered less from the quartz failure earlier that year.

A Grass Valley public meeting, called to protest foreign miners' taking up claims, resolved against "foreigners coming to America to extract wealth without rendering the duties and benefits expected of citizens," and concluded to petition the California legislature that no "foreigner be allowed to locate and hold mining claims in this township," because "they pay no taxes." The resolutions—echoing Bigler—struck harder at the Chinese than at European miners; men desiring to become American citizens could take up claims, but the "Chinese and other colored races" of course could not be naturalized. Although Bigler's message focused on the Chinese, all foreigners suffered. A week after the meeting, John Banks reported that some native-born counseled cruel treatment to drive the foreigners from the mines, and then, a week later, that a party of twenty citizens had stoned a small group of Englishmen. The anti-foreign movement in Grass Valley climaxed at the end of May in a riot over the election of a district recorder of mining claims. The foreign-born and the American-born held separate elections, and when non-citizens attempted to participate in the natives' election, a fight broke out that ended with one man dead and another badly hurt. The citizen party's choice for recorder took office; the native-born had affirmed their control of town politics. The statewide campaign culminated in the passage of a tax technically applicable to all foreign miners, although often collected only from the Chinese and Mexicans. After its enactment, overt nativist action declined in the two camps, although the foreign-born continued to arrive in numbers; no important local concerns had ever really been at stake.

Governor Bigler's supporters had drawn on prejudice and the visibly increasing foreign presence, but their rhetoric had also stressed unfair competition for specifically American riches. This mixture of Manifest Destiny and greed maintained that only citizens deserved the wealth of California. Economic arguments lost prominence in the years immediately after 1852, giving place to charges that the foreign-born refused to accept American customs and laws. A Grass Valley correspondent of the *Nevada Journal* in 1853 identified the town's only problem as a portion of the population, mostly foreigners, who resisted and thwarted the *ad hoc* mining laws. "Americus," as the writer signed himself, hinted at a common counter to such menaces to the peace: vigilante justice. Anti-foreign prejudices, self-serving beliefs in exclusively American rights, economic fears, and the tendency to make the foreign-born scapegoats for breakdowns in order—all remained current, if subdued, into the mid-1850's, ready to emerge in any social crisis.[25]

Reform Movements and Segregation

In response to the failure of industrial mining and traditional agencies to bring the two towns toward Eastern social norms, the sporadic, disjointed efforts at reform coalesced into a thoroughgoing moral crusade. Led by the same men—Delano, Sargent, Ewer, Warren—who had earlier exhorted the townspeople to change, still drawing sustenance primarily from the churches, and reinforced by continued arrivals of families and middle-class women from the East where similar evangelical campaigns flourished, the reformers brought every aspect of town society under scrutiny. The movement, already under way in 1853, came to a climax in 1855, as did crusades against vice all over the state. In reform, as in politics, the two towns were current with a national wave of temperance agitation and a rather unstructured California campaign to limit gambling (and, by inference, prostitution) and to require Sunday closing. Probably the editors and evangelical ministers and their female allies took involvement in moral reform for granted, as an activity natural to their social roles, but certainly the towns presented them with direct, personal challenges. The influence of national movements and Eastern values was augmented locally by the felt threat of social disorder to inspire a concerted effort toward social change.

The local situation determined both the scope and the focus of moral reform. The ultimate purpose was to make the towns—not the mines—safe for women, children, churches, and schools, so that they in turn could promote prosperity by making the towns safe for long-term commitment and investment. Reform was directed primarily inward, at the middle class itself, and aimed to cleanse it of Gold Rush survivals. Reformers concerned themselves with the mining areas only because miners coming to town largely supported the saloons and gambling halls, but at the same time miners' pay was essential to legitimate business. In consequence, reform-minded townsmen did not undertake (except in the temperance election of 1855) to impose their moral views on the miners. Their solution to the problem of catering to the miners yet fostering virtue was to segregate the brothels and saloons of the miners' society from the homes and churches of the middle class.

The most formally organized local reform group was the Sons of Temperance, with an elaborate system of officers and rituals and strong ties to evangelical congregations. The Sons firmly grounded themselves in both towns by 1853, then turned all the standard reform techniques against drink: resolutions, parades, public debates, and a children's branch organization operating in conjunction with the Sabbath Schools, the Cadets of Temperance. While drawing strength from being part of a national club involved in a national anti-alcohol campaign, at the same time the Sons expressed perfectly the perceived moral needs specific to the towns. Drinking, argued J. W. Oliver in the *Telegraph,* had been excusable only "when there were hardly any women here," but now behavior had to be altered, in deference to women and in order to increase their influence on society. "Even more important than the Sons, 'the Cadets' would train up your children in a course of virtue," thus assuring their and the towns' future prosperity. At first content to use moral suasion, then to pass resolutions calling on the political parties to nominate temperate men for office, the Sons declined suggestions that they nominate separate candidates, evidently because of informal leadership ties with the Whig Party. In 1855, with the local Whig organization moribund, the Sons reversed themselves and accepted the decision of state leaders to campaign independently for a Maine Liquor Law for California. In the resulting preferential vote, Nevada County expressed a desire for a liquor law, but the state as a whole rejected it. Shortly after the election defeat, the state organization in disarray, the towns' chapters collapsed.[26]

A second moral reform movement, Sabbatarianism, operated entirely under the aegis of the evangelical churches and initially emphasized closing all businesses on Sunday. This program pitted the religious reformers directly against one of the most distinctive practices of the Gold Rush, the transaction of most retail business on Sunday, and could not hope to succeed until the working habits of the placer miners had ceased to determine commercial patterns in the camps. Attempts in Nevada City in 1851 and in both towns in 1853 and 1854 to shutter businesses on Sunday came to nothing. The evangelicals had to acknowledge the economic importance of Sunday commerce and its convenience for miners working a six-day week. Drawing closer to other local reformers, the Sabbatarians began to concentrate their fire "on the avaricious and ungodly," that is, on the gamblers.[27]

Sabbatarianism and local attempts to suppress gambling and prostitution shared both activists and goals, as Sunday disturbances centered in the gambling dens and brothels. Editors' and ministers' arguments against gambling emphasized a man's duty to his parents and family back home and like the sermons of the Sabbatarians set the hells and dives in direct competition with the churches. By the mid-1850's gamblers no longer had an aura of romance; accounts of them stressed dishonesty, lechery, and penury. One newspaper story described two "blacklegs" sneaking away to avoid paying for a restaurant meal. The saloons themselves figured in the press mainly as disturbers of the peace. But direct action did not prove effective against the hells and their denizens, for local ordinances and the state law of 1855 banning open gambling were only erratically enforced.[28]

The parallel movement against prostitution was unique among the reform efforts in that it depended heavily on pressure from law-enforcement officials. Ideally, constables arrested madams and raided brothels for disturbing the peace. To reformers, a brothel was at best a disorderly "pest to the neighborhood"; at worst it exposed women and children to the "open, undisguised abodes of vice." Niles Searls of the *Democrat* condemned the number of prostitute's cribs scattered around the town, urging that they be at least confined to one locality. A law went on the books to "drive such scenes from sight"—and remained unenforced. Other local laws against breaking the peace and state laws against keeping disorderly houses proved ineffective; defendants won acquittal or had convictions overturned because of the difficulty of proving participation in disturbances and the vagueness of the state laws. In general, the town governments found controlling prostitution too difficult, and given the sexual imbalance of the camps, many inhabitants thought prostitution a necessary evil.[29]

The various moral crusades had explicitly used reform as a means toward stability and prosperity. "Friends of good order" were expected to vote for prohibition and to be gratified by the decline in the number of gambling houses. Prostitution and Sabbath-breaking directly menaced the family and the church, the institutions charged with shaping camp behavior "as becomes an enlightened and civilized community." The reform movement provided a way for professionals and merchants of the two towns to assume moral leadership, and moralists deplored their lack of courage when they failed to do so. Businessmen who stayed open on Sunday had not only failed to recognize their true economic interest, they had shirked their duty as natural leaders. Inseparable from the demands of a middle-class moral economy was the need to replicate in Grass Valley and Nevada City the idealized image of the Anglo-American childhood homes of the reformers. But with the ever-increasing foreign-born population, the relevance of that tradition suddenly came into question for the first time; it might prove impossible to establish orthodox Eastern values. A thread of nativism inescapably ran through the reform efforts. Two statewide anti-foreign movements flourished alongside the temperance and "blue law" campaigns and reinforced the tendency of the moralists to explain their failures with racist or nativist arguments. The first, directed against the Chinese, aimed at exclusion through raising the tax on foreign miners to prohibitive levels. The second, climaxing in the San Francisco Vigilance Committee of 1856 but also active in several other towns, combined attempts to control crime with anti-Catholic and anti-Irish attitudes. Neither movement became very active in Nevada City or Grass Valley although both received appreciable local publicity.[30]

Some of the prominent reform leaders, especially Sargent and Delano, manifested this nativism by leaving the dying Whig Party to become Know-Nothings at the height of the reform drive. Reformist ideas were certainly not the exclusive property of the local Whigs; Democratic politicians and editors also contended that stability and prosperity depended on morality and families, and no well-known politico openly opposed the forces of righteousness. But the Whigs and the openly nativist American Party (Know-Nothings) claimed and used reform as their own; charges that Irish Democrat ruffians prevented the respectable from voting augmented accusations of Irish drunkenness and claim-jumping. Except for the economically irreplaceable Cornish, who had a reputation for hymn-singing and nonpartisanship, all major ethnic and racial groups found themselves tainted in nativist eyes with suggestions of immorality. Stereotypes shifted slightly in response to the needs of the moral crusades. A new complaint against the Nisenan surfaced in the mid-1850's: their nudity shocked women and children. As the Spanish-speaking miners departed after 1851, and fears of Mexican ferocity declined, the word "Spanish" appeared almost exclusively in reference to prostitution. Sabbatarian debaters accused Jewish merchants of refusing to respect the Christian Sabbath. Journalists still depicted blacks, despite their Grass Valley church, as sexually loose and potentially violent. But the Chinese bore the brunt of the moral agitation, especially its xenophobic, sometimes violent ramifications.[31]

The ambiguous, contradictory set of attitudes Americans held toward the Chinese made them available scapegoats in times of social crisis. The Chinese had suffered more than other foreign groups during the agitation of 1852; they had been singled out in Governor Bigler's "Special Message" and in the Grass Valley resolutions, and then by tax collectors and the thugs who put politics into brutal practice. At that time images of the Chinese as men who passively accepted both employers' orders and incredibly low standards of living made them vulnerable to charges of unfair competition for jobs. But after that excitement died down, newspaper references to the Chinese once again became neutral or favorable, usually stressing their ignorance of American ways and their willingness to work hard. Then in the mid-1850's another part of the stereotype—that they were incurably amoral—began to take the most prominent place in descriptions of the Chinese.

As the most distant in behavior from the reformers' Protestant family ideal, they were natural targets. Only a handful of the Sidney Ducks and "Spanish" remained in the towns, while the Chinese, after the abrupt decline caused by the Foreign Miners' Tax, increased in number and because of their growing concentration in the Chinatowns became more conspicuous. During the mid-1850's references to "China Street" and the "Celestial District" became commonplace in Nevada City newspapers. While white community leaders, disregarding the actual transience of the white population, talked of promoting permanence and investing in the camps' futures, the Chinese openly remained sojourners intending to return their profits to their homes. While the white gamblers and fallen women responded to the reformers and became more circumspect, Chinese merchants kept open their gaming dens and houses of prostitution; the Chinese districts seemed to flaunt vice in the face of the reformers. In the eyes of the American-born all Chinese became identified with these institutions.

The Chinese seemed the antithesis of what the reformers and businessmen hoped to establish in the towns and the exemplars of what they feared most in white society. No longer just amusingly naive, the Chinese now appeared to live by choice in the midst of their "abodes of vice." If American women represented everything conducive to order, Chinese women, all assumed to be prostitutes, represented the opposite. A telling warning against Chinese influence in the camps stressed the cruelty of Chinese men toward females; Chinese women were slaves, not saviors. By the middle of the decade, newspaper accounts of brawls and robberies in Chinese cribs, involving whites as well as Chinese, had begun to replace similar reports from "Spanish houses." White association with Chinese women evoked especially bitter denunciations that alluded to the need for public pressure to keep these men from debasing the entire white community.[32]

In 1854 and 1855, at the height of the moral campaigns, moral vigilantes descended on the growing Chinese section of Nevada

City on three occasions, dispersing the denizens of the "Chinese houses of ill-fame." The raids failed, for as the *Journal* expressed it, despite the "summary cleansing . . . the vermin have crawled back to their nests and hold out as aforetime." Chinese women were rounded up along with "Spanish" and American-born prostitutes in the legal drives to control vice; the difference lay in the indiscriminate use of duress against the Chinese, and the unofficial status of the perpetrators. Violence against the Chinese could now be defended before the white community in the name of morality. The newspapers pointed out that some disreputables, "natives of Port Sidney," had used moral indignation as a cover for looting Chinese dwellings, but in general the attacks were condoned, even when the violence spread from brothels to Chinese miners' homes. Humor marked the usual journalistic response; "the boys" were having fun, and if the means were slightly reprehensible, the ends were widely accepted. The imagined link between the Chinese and disorder permitted the vigilantism of 1851–52 to return, with its conviction that the foreign-born could be blamed for all community troubles. And with the successful establishment of families and therefore of the towns themselves at stake, few whites would oppose even brutal anti-Chinese actions.[33]

In 1855, anti-Chinese agitation peaked all over the state. Alarmed at the increase in Chinese immigration during a depression, the state legislature passed a new Foreign Miners' Tax, directed at the Chinese and intended to be exclusionary, and coupled it with a prohibitive capitation tax to be paid by the ship's captain for every Chinese he brought into California. The basic argument for these bills charged that Chinese took work from whites. In other mining areas, especially Shasta County, whites drove out Chinese, again alleging unfair job competition. Grass Valley and Nevada City newspapers such as Aaron Sargent's *Journal* accepted the raids on Chinese brothels, but opposed the higher tax on the grounds that the Chinese could not pay it, and condemned it and efforts to expel the Chinese because these measures would deprive mining counties of needed tax revenue and infringe upon the legal rights of the Chinese. In the two towns, anti-Chinese actions were shaped by local social needs rather than by the economic issues that prevailed in most of the state in 1855; local whites could adopt pragmatic, even paternalistic attitudes toward the Chinese if the emotional issues of alien vice and town stability could be avoided. Nevada City residents attempted to close Chinese brothels in the towns by force, but did not try to drive the Chinese out of the mines. Mining in the camps was relatively prosperous in the mid-1850's; while the immediate economic future of Grass Valley and Nevada City was not thought to be in question, morality was.[34]

Local conditions also determined that Nevada City would be the center of excitement in 1854 and 1855, as Grass Valley had been in 1852. Grass Valley had never been as deeply or publicly committed to moral evangelism as Nevada City, perhaps because its people believed their own assertions of superiority in peace and order. Although Grass Valley had a greater proportion of foreign-born than Nevada City, its largest groups, the Irish and Cornish, were essential to technological mining as labor and as experts. Furthermore, they were northern Europeans, not very different from the native-born in cultural values, and the Irish, despite the adverse stereotypes, had enough political power to defuse anti-Catholic agitation. Nevada City, much more dependent on commerce, perhaps felt to a greater extent the need for public order to safeguard its trade. Nevada City was also home to most of the prominent and active Whig leaders; among the Whig moralists only Alonzo Delano lived in Grass Valley. Nevada City's foreign-born population—which included a greater proportion of Chinese—seemed both more unassimilable and more ambiguous economically than that of Grass Valley. As a commercial center and a wealthier town, Nevada City simply had more, and more elaborate, gambling saloons and bordellos than Grass Valley; the sources of wealth in Nevada City, trade and placer mining, seemed to exacerbate problems of morality and order, while Grass Valley's quartz mining seemed to ease them.

After 1855, reform campaigns in the towns became less strident, although certainly not silent. The national and state movements had lost energy as temperance advocates split over moral suasion versus prohibition statutes, and nativism briefly declined as Know-Nothingism foundered on the question of slavery. At the local level, events had partially solved the perceived social problems. Although the moralists failed to create Alonzo Delano's nostalgically remembered pious villages—they had not really attempted to do so—they had contributed to a basic change in town life. The insulation of middle-class families and institutions from evil had begun. The rougher amusements of a male society began to move out of the towns or to become concentrated in particular sections within them. In 1854 Hughes' Union Race Course opened, located on undeveloped land between Grass Valley and Nevada City and convenient to both. Although its owners designed it for horse racing, other sporting events took place at the Union Course, including boxing matches and bullfights. These spectacles at least occurred out of respectable hearing; meanwhile the bullring in Nevada City decayed.

More significantly, newspaper accounts of brawls in the dives began to show patterns of contiguous addresses. By 1853 in Nevada City, the most notorious offenders against the peace congregated on the upper end of Broad Street, one of the town's original thoroughfares, and in portions of adjacent streets and alleys. Likewise, a portion of Main Street in Grass Valley began to be associated with "disorderly houses." From the first, the movement against prostitution had aimed primarily at removing the evil from public view. By late 1855, Warren Ewer could boast that "vice and immorality" were mostly restricted to "lurking in the by places." Even segregating prostitution remained a constant struggle; there were common newspaper complaints of the "shameless boldness with which Cyprians take up their residences in the immediate vicinity of respectable families," but limits had been fairly clearly defined. While the number of prostitutes probably remained relatively steady, the number of gamblers declined. By the summer of 1854 only three gambling establishments remained in Nevada City, and in 1856, Aaron Sargent claimed that all the dens were either closed or no longer visible; gambling had retired to the back rooms of the red-light district. By the end of 1855, most stores remained shuttered on the Sabbath, and the boast "as quiet as Eastern towns" could be legitimately made.[35]

This outward peace and quiet resulted partly from state laws passed in 1855 against open gambling and "barbarous and noisy" amusements on the Sabbath, for example, but lack of enforcement limited their impact. The change depended more on industrial mining; while prostitution continued to flourish because of the nature of the work force, the establishment of fixed shift schedules lessened the need for Sunday business, and, as it was argued at the time, working for wages reduced miners' willingness to gamble. The reformers had also contributed to the pacification process, mostly by calling attention to potential problems.

The physical segregation of "moral lepers" could help promote the community of values advocated by reformers, but the rise of middle-class neighborhoods could do more. By the mid-1850's, a gradual increase in the numbers of families—overwhelmingly the wives and children of professionals and merchants—had resulted in the development of identifiably family-oriented neighborhoods. The districts were not large, since most men of the business class were still unmarried and boarding, or living in their places of business. Nor were they exclusive, as shops and single miners' cabins were interspersed with the dwellings of bankers' families. But, especially in Nevada City, family neighborhoods had early been recognized. In 1853, hills around Nevada City's commercial area had begun to be improved by an "array of pleasant cottages" that spoke, perhaps inevitably to editorial minds, of "growth and confidence in the future." One such area, Aristocracy Hill, received its name in derision of the pretensions of the bachelor mine developers who built "Bourbon Lodge" there, but the name came to have real meaning. By 1856, a cluster of professionals' and merchants' homes had assembled on these hills, on the upper reaches of two of the towns' main streets. Two streets just north of Grass Valley's main business district also began to have definite middle-class and family characteristics. That year, each town claimed approximately 150 families with children. The school-age population increased rapidly, Nevada City's growing by almost half between 1853 and 1856. As the sites of homes, schools, and churches, family neighborhoods promised social stability.[36]

Life in these neighborhoods suggested that traditional mores could coexist with gold mining. In a Nevada City where sewing circles, lyceums, Sunday-school picnics, and philharmonic clubs could flourish, and in a Grass Valley where Edwin Morse could court his future wife by walking her home from church, obvious strides had been made away from Gold Rush conditions. A middle-class woman's arrival in town remained something of an event; newcomers had to cope with stares and personal questions, but once having run the gantlet of the curious, they found a small society of lawyers' and merchants' wives, complete with social calls and teas. A coterie of the newly-well-to-do with boldly figured brocades and silks and showy gold ornaments, this society jolted ladies of more fastidious backgrounds when they heard their new peers complain about the shortage of good servants in a brogue or a frontier drawl. The elites of both towns retained their rough edges; although formal duels ceased, prominent men might still brawl in the streets. Emily Rolfe recalled one fight: "George Jacobs knocked my husband down. I screamed and ran toward them. I fell down and in getting up I picked up a rock. . . . I caught Mr. Jacobs by the hair he being on top of Mr. R and struck him on the head with the rock." Mr. Jacobs required three stitches to close the wound, and on the way back into the house, the Rolfes "picked up my petticoat that had fallen off when I fell down." Rolfe and Jacobs were leading mining and real-estate investors in Nevada City; they were fighting over a land deal gone sour.

Subscription cotillions and dinners at local saloons or restaurants continued to be patronized by the towns' prominent citizens, but newly built church halls and private homes gradually offered alternative sites for gatherings uncontaminated by evil associations. The hall of the Sons of Temperance became the locale of the social occasions of the respectable: benefit suppers for schools and churches, uplifting lectures, and debates on the issues of the day. Signs of Eastern gentility made their appearance in the form of short-lived dancing schools and fencing clubs, and ceremonious New Year's calls "in the New York manner." After 1853, May Day and the Fourth of July became accepted days for children's church outings. Local enthusiasm over them surpassed even the usual nineteenth-century sentimentalism about pious infants; journalists reacted to the sight of a Sunday-school picnic in tones previously reserved for gold strikes.[37]

The red-light districts, the relative invisibility of vice, and the family streets all served to ease the disquiet of the merchants and moralists and defuse the moral crusade. As long as the neighborhoods offered reassuring physical evidence of commitment and solvency, a bored and lonely miner could be permitted to find excitement and to buy companionship if he did not disturb the homes of the middle class. For by the necessity of a mining economy, the two societies had to coexist. Towns and mines, merchants and miners still were mutually dependent. So family concerts competed with saloon string bands, church teas with free-for-alls, Irish Democrats with Whig nativists. The Fourth of July of 1855 was celebrated with patriotic readings, a Sunday-school procession, a circus, and a bear-and-bull fight.[38]

PART II

PEACE WITHOUT PROSPERITY

1856-1863

·❧ 3 ❧·

The Towns Grow Apart

NEW ECONOMIES, NEW PEOPLE

During the late 1850's and early 1860's, stampedes to the Fraser River and Comstock strikes, coupled with cycles of flood and drought, once again brought the survival of Nevada City and Grass Valley into question. Miners decamped and civic institutions crumbled as if the days of the Gold Rush had returned. Smaller mines and businesses lacked the resources to weather the hard times, so that the processes of consolidation and large-scale capitalization accelerated. In response to mining depression, Nevada City turned even more to commerce. Grass Valley's quartz industry, hurt less than placer mining, hung on, in the end benefiting from the example of the Comstock Lode. Town economic bases, already dissimilar, became more strikingly so, and since different industries and jobs attracted different groups of people, the towns also grew less alike in racial and ethnic structure. But economic crises did not end in economic strife. A constant turnover in population generated a constant need for both manpower and skills. Accordingly, most immigrant groups had access to jobs and advancement even at a time when occupational classification and stratification was sharpening. Peace between classes usually prevailed within the towns, but between them diverging populations promoted conflict as ethnic party loyalties placed Grass Valley and Nevada City on opposite sides during the rabid partisanship of the Civil War era. Political identities and enmities were the clearest evidence of economic and ethnic differences.

Depression Years

Many Nevada City storekeepers entered 1857 in debt to San Francisco commercial houses for replacements for stock lost in the fire of 1856, only to be plunged deeper into depression by excessive winter rains that cut off stage and wagon connections to surrounding towns, effectively disrupting the trade needed to recoup losses. The storms also raised creeks enough to hinder mining operations. In January and February both main economic props of the town neared collapse. Then, in mid-February, a dam being constructed across Deer Creek six miles above Nevada City by Amos Laird, the region's leading hydraulic mining entrepreneur, broke under the additional volume of water. The resulting flood swept away two bridges, six houses, three stores, and half a hotel. Since Laird was not held legally responsible for damages, the already impoverished town government could not quickly repair the bridges, and trade was further retarded. Business remained slow for the rest of the year, and several major stores were boarded up after failing to work off the debts of 1856.[1]

Grass Valley entered 1857 far stronger economically than its neighbor because of the prosperity of the quartz mines. Employing larger work forces and less vulnerable to disruptions by the weather, quartz mining provided steadier returns than Nevada City's placer mines. San Franciscan, Eastern, and foreign capital remained available, and the new Nevada Foundry expedited repairs and improvements by manufacturing casings, fittings, and steam engines. But the mining base of Grass Valley rested narrowly on the production of at most seven major mines, augmented only slightly by smaller, even one-man, quartz and placer works. And capital and business experience could never ensure success. In 1856, the New York owners of the Rocky Bar Company sent out Michael Brennan to run their works on Massachusetts Hill. Heartened by initial success, Brennan erected a mill and sank a deep shaft, gambling that it would reach high-grade ore before his finances were exhausted. He failed, the property was lost to creditors, and in February 1858, Brennan poisoned himself and his entire family. Brennan's disaster was only the most horrific; the Eureka, the Osborne Hill, and the Lafayette Hill mines, all of which had been worked since 1852, closed down at various times.

Only the Empire, the Scadden, and the Allison Ranch mines enjoyed relatively uninterrupted profits in the late 1850's.[2]

Economic uncertainty made the area vulnerable to rival mining sites. When word of a new gold field on the Fraser River of British Columbia, advertised as a second Forty-nine, reached the two towns in 1858, the miners listened and many believed. T. H. Rolfe of the *Nevada Democrat* estimated that one-quarter of the town's voters had joined the exodus to the Fraser; Warren Ewer in the *Grass Valley Telegraph* reported that 400 men had departed. The Fraser River excitement was brief, as the Canadian mines soon proved to be highly overrated, and 1859 promised a return to prosperity. Nevada City merchants once again filled the streets with wagons destined to supply neighboring camps, and Grass Valley quartz mines and mills had full complements of workers. Cornishman John Coad, who directed a small mining outfit, had planned in 1858 to abandon Grass Valley as a place where a man with a family could not make a living. But the "quartz failure" ended in 1859; in May he was able to lend a friend $1,200, and in April 1860 his share of sold claims totaled $3,000. Then the news of a silver discovery in the far western part of Utah Territory—the Comstock Lode—burst upon local mine investors and miners. The initial rush was led by "enterprising quartz operators" in the summer of 1859, trailed by the "best working miners"; all were willing to abandon producing mines. Edwin Morse, a small mining entrepreneur, estimated that two-thirds of the men of Nevada City and Grass Valley attempted Comstock mining at one time or another, as the seasonal flow across the Sierra Nevada continued for the next three years.[3]

The effect of the Comstock rush was to paralyze local mining temporarily by drawing off capital, expertise, and manpower, but not in the long run to disrupt it completely. At the time, however, editors who had long assumed that a stable population was necessary to the two towns' prosperity could see only the immediate danger and waxed extremely bitter over the Comstock bonanza. In despair, they condemned their ex-townsmen as hopeless gamblers who would eagerly abandon steady pay for a chance at a jackpot and sneeringly reminded their readers, "more victims are daily added to the thousands long shivering on the bleak sidehills and among the sage brush of Virginia City." Meanwhile, the search for new economic supports for Grass Valley and Nevada City became nearly hysterical. In the spring of 1860, the reputed memory of rock similar to the Comstock "blue stuff" led to the staking of a silver claim seven miles above Nevada City on Deer Creek. As rumors spread, a brief but frantic rush resulted; men flooded the road out of town, and in one day claims were laid out for a distance of six miles along the creek. No one found silver—none had ever existed—but in the reeling towns of 1860 the flimsiest evidence had to be tested.[4]

Despite prophecies of doom in some quarters, the important local producers of gold continued to work, potentially important new leads were located in both townships, and the strongest Grass Valley mining concerns undertook important investments in 1858 and 1860 to deepen shafts and improve steam pumping and hoisting equipment. Then, starting in 1861, a cycle of drought and flood severely damaged mining operations. Drought struck the whole state of California in 1861, particularly damaging Nevada City's hydraulicking interests. In Grass Valley, fears that there would not be enough water to serve the town's inhabitants, fight fires, or water crops led to requests that the available water be contracted for town use, since there would obviously not be enough for effective mining that year. Winter broke the drought with a vengeance; January 1862 was a month of floods. Several of the best paying mines in Grass Valley were drowned, despite the use of steam pumps; several months passed before they could be worked again, and the combination of higher costs and interrupted production forced more mining entrepreneurs out of business. The stoppage in quartz depressed all types of business in Grass Valley, and the town's skilled miners flowed over the mountains. Nevada City was also badly damaged, for high water on the Yuba and Bear Rivers almost isolated both towns, again disrupting commerce and inflating food prices. The next two winters were dry, and depression continued in both towns. In January and February 1863, what business there was moved by credit as coin would remain unavailable until mining resumed. In Nevada City in 1863, note holders commonly attached mercantile stocks and raffled off the goods to meet their own obligations. With business at a standstill, the Comstock mines in Nevada Territory (formed in 1861 from Utah Territory) was ever-present in the public mind; more notices of men "rushing off in crazy haste to silverland" appeared in the newspapers in 1863 than in any previous year. The weather-induced migration hurt Grass Valley and Nevada City far more than the initial silver excitement.[5]

Even while climate and the Comstock rush paralyzed commerce, Nevada City and Grass Valley continued to mature in appearance. Both downtown centers were largely brick by the early 1860's, had planked streets, wooden sidewalks, and domestic water service, and were lighted by gas locally produced from pitch pine and coal. Nevada City got a daily newspaper, the *Transcript*, in 1860; that year the county commissioners, responding to state directives, opened a hospital near Nevada City to care for indigent patients and to house permanently disabled men. The towns seemed more tame after the isolation of the dives. Although violence remained a part of mining life (the worst outbreak, an 1858 battle over claim rights, ended with four dead and several badly wounded) and stage holdups offered spectacular proof of the persistence of a criminal class, the last attempt at lynch law, in response to a botched plot to fire Grass Valley, had taken place in 1855 and had quickly failed. The patient rolls of the new county hospital revealed the actual dangers of mining life; gunshot and stab wounds were very rare, while mining accidents, rheumatism, and venereal diseases accounted for many cases. In 1862, again in obedience to state law, the county sheriff constructed a temporary shelter behind the courthouse so that an execution for murder would not be public.[6]

Sidewalks, running water, and private hangings alike were enthusiastically greeted in the press as evidence of growing "civilization" and thus stability. At the same time, editors took it upon themselves to prod local officials to maintain these marks of permanence, pointing to the usual disrepair of roads and bridges and to the collapse of fire companies and citizens' groups. The editors' watchdog role was one of their legitimate functions, but often they seemed oblivious to the depression-related handicaps the town trustees labored under.

The town governments were the most important case of a civic institution buffeted by events and by popular attitudes. Local jurisdiction developed the rough framework of a lasting system during these years, in the face of citizen indifference and even hostility against local taxes and restrictive ordinances. In 1857 township lines, following creek patterns, formally defined both towns' mining districts and perpetuated by law the original relationships of camp and diggings. The incorporated towns of Nevada City and (after 1861) Grass Valley lay inside and separate from the townships of the same names, taking the form of business districts, and increasingly of residential districts, encompassed by mines, mills, and ranches.

The structure of local authority accentuated this division between town and township. Justices of the peace, county supervisors, and a sheriff handled crime and provided services outside corporate limits; within the towns they shared authority and sometimes financial responsibility for improvements with the town governments. The marshal had the pivotal role among town officials, enforcing the laws passed by the town trustees and fulfilling roughly the same functions for the towns as the sheriff did for the county. An elected official and thus the object of partisan criticism, the marshal drew a salary, held no other job, and had to possess a certain level of professional competence. He headed a small body of salaried men known at various times as constables, policemen, or deputy marshals. Like other western towns, Nevada City and Grass Valley risked sometimes ambiguous relationships between these small bands of semiprofessionals and the criminal subcultures they dealt with; more than one lawman proved criminal or at least suspect himself. More prosaically, the occasional incompetent marshal could, through inertia, bring the entire town government to a halt.[7]

The town trustees held legislative authority in both towns. Unsalaried and recruited as before from the businessmen, they continued to serve as the voice for commercial stability in local government. They, of all local officials, had to deal most directly with the problem of promoting institutional continuity in the midst of flux. The job, while necessary, meant a year of dealing with the minutiae of town affairs under conditions of near-bankruptcy; storms damaged not only roads and bridges but the towns' ability to pay for repairs. Chronically short of cash and needing state legislative approval to raise tax rates, the town trustees commonly found themselves in debt, ignored and overburdened with the details of their jobs. And after 1856, legal crusades against raucous saloons and brothels gave way to clearing sidewalks of storekeepers' boxes or barrels, or licensing the packs of dogs that roamed the streets, and trying to convince irate owners of cattle that their property's presence downtown was unbecoming in maturing towns. Frustrated by their inability to enforce even ordinances as essential as fire regulations, many trustees refused to serve a second term. At times it became difficult to fill vacancies on the boards, and by 1863 the office of trustee had, at least for election purposes, become the appendage of the office of marshal. Any competition for the job was usually between slates formed by rival aspirants for marshal to reinforce their candidacies. Minor functional offices such as those of recorder, clerk, or assessor supplied continuity in services to citizens, but the record of the trustee-and-marshal system was just as checkered as the economic history of Grass Valley and Nevada City during these years.[8]

Still, compared to private civic organizations, the town governments appeared remarkably successful. In 1858, "the leading business and professional men" of Nevada City, led by political attorney Henry Meredith, started a militia company, the Nevada Rifles. In 1860, when the men of the Rifles felt impelled to avenge the death of Meredith, who had joined the silver rush and fallen at the Pyramid Lake Indian fight, the outfit had to reconstitute itself completely and send to Sacramento for percussion caps before it could embark on a punitive campaign. In 1861, the company broke up, its remaining membership depleted by the distant war between the states.[9]

The fashionably officered and manned fire brigades led similarly brief, erratic lives, in spite of the more immediate danger to individuals and the towns from fire. In Nevada City, the volunteer fire brigade hastily created after the catastrophic conflagration of 1856 barely survived into 1857, and the property holders, nearly insolvent, did nothing to replace it, refusing even to grant exclusive rights to a local company to supply piped water. In late May of 1858 the business district burned again, with less destruction than in 1856 only because the fire spread more slowly and owners had more time to save merchandise. Instead of building a waterworks or maintaining a fire company, townspeople chose to blame the Chinese for the fire and passed an unconstitutional ordinance that temporarily drove them out of town. Grass Valley had a hook-and-ladder brigade; in 1860 an incendiary fire destroyed 30 buildings in spite of its efforts, and in 1862 the company lost its firehouse during a downtown fire.

By 1861 Nevada City appeared to have solved the problem of fire protection, with two volunteer companies and a town waterworks hailed as "the most valuable improvement ever projected for the town." Then in November 1863, after the cumulative effects of the drought and the Comstock rush, the town was again destroyed by fire. Men rallying to fight the flames found no pressure in the pipes, because no one had maintained the system during the water shortage. Many members of the fire brigades were missing, and the elaborate governing system designed to ensure cooperation between the two companies did not function because "the Chief Engineer was engaged in saving the duds of his strumpet." The loss, $500,000, was less than in 1856 because most residences were now built on the hills beyond downtown, but also because property values had declined. Coming on top of the depression, the fire seemed to sound the death knell for Nevada City. All major buildings were gone, and court business was transacted in the only remaining public edifice, the Baptist church. Some merchants abandoned the town as a hopeless cause, and although two joint-stock companies of local entrepreneurs organized to build hotels as new foci for town business, at the end of 1863 the survival of Nevada City was very uncertain.[10]

However, the source of survival was already at hand; the much vilified Comstock Lode proved the catalyst for economic development in both towns. Carson City and Virginia City could not feed themselves, while Grass Valley and Nevada City townships each contained over 30 thriving farms. Nevada City had long been a distribution point for goods destined for nearby camps. It had a flour mill, large hardware concerns, and a foundry; trade with Nevada Territory offered new life to business interests that according to John Hittell had already been responsible for maintaining its position as the "first town in the mountains." But that trade would not fall automatically to Nevada City; both Sacramento and Marysville had been impinging on its area of commercial dominance, and Placerville businessmen who had seen the saving value of commerce with the Comstock mines were promoting a route across the mountains designed to bypass Nevada City. When engineer Theodore P. Judah traversed the region, surveying possible railroad routes over the Sierra, he was given a hero's welcome in the local press. But although citizens of the two towns greatly desired a railroad, a wagon road was deemed more practicable. In Nevada City, the town's leading entrepreneurs called for a corporation to build a toll road, and work commenced almost immediately on a route through the Henness Pass. Eventually, two trans-Sierra toll roads serving Nevada City were granted much of the credit for restoring "her wonted busy and lively aspect."

The ranches in the two townships supplied farm produce, flour mills and breweries processed grains, and the foothills around the towns supported flocks of sheep. Nevada City's trustees had to revoke the ordinance against livestock loose in the street to accommodate the herds of cattle being driven through on the way over the mountains. In both towns, but especially in Grass Valley, sawmills produced lumber for the nearly treeless Comstock towns. These markets helped move Nevada City further away from its dependence on mining. At least while the roads stayed open, the town supported itself largely through trade, and the promise of trans-mountain commerce, not mining, convinced local investors to revitalize Nevada City by undertaking projects such as rebuilding downtown hotels. With mining at a halt for long periods in the early 1860's, the town was crippled but not dead.[11]

The Comstock country served as more than a ready market; it helped confirm Grass Valley in the production of quartz gold. Oscar Maltman and G. F. Deetken had made the first practical attempts to reduce gold sulfides with chlorine gas in Nevada City in 1858. Failing, they had gone to the Comstock mines, where they learned new metallurgical techniques. Returning to Nevada City in 1860, they had immediate success with a new process that improved the efficiency with which the hard-rock mines could be worked. By 1862 Grass Valley had its own reduction works. The deep-shaft Comstock mines gave many men experience in the methods needed to open quartz mines, while successful Comstockers accumulated capital to invest; by late 1863 expert mine engineers, superintendents, and investors were drifting back over the mountains to Grass Valley, and before the year was over three of the most important leads had been reopened. On Saturday night, reported the *National*, Mill and Main Streets were thronged with miners, the most in eighteen months.[12]

New Economies, New People

Too much gold underlay the two townships for the sites to be easily abandoned; fires and floods could only temporarily stop production. Several mines continued to be developed despite disruptions, most spectacularly the Allison Ranch mine, which proved not only that with competent management a mine could be expanded right through the worst of the depression but also that poor men might still find stupendous success. In 1854, a party of Irish prospectors who had spent two years working a placer site on Wolf Creek three miles below Grass Valley uncovered a quartz lead. Only after finding no buyer for the claim at $1,000 did they attempt to open the vein. The man they hired, fellow countryman Con Reilly, proved exceptionally able and the mine exceptionally rich; by 1860 the mine, popularly thought inoperable, was acknowledged to be the most valuable mining property in the state.

Still, the depression reshaped the mining industry in ways that made the luck of the Allison Ranch Irish even more unlikely than before. Only the strong survived; in quartz mining, Deetken's process and the other technological advances from the Comstock mines, especially in pumping and tunneling operations, tended to drive up the capital required to work mines and therefore were practical only for the richest leads. Grass Valley mining, accordingly, fell into the control of fewer and larger concerns during the early 1860's. In Nevada City, although promoters had finally shaken off the revulsion against quartz, hydraulic mining dominated the township. The ditch and water companies centered there exceeded in extent of works and value all others in California. Hydraulic operations, of course, were vulnerable to the cycle of flood and drought, and in the late 1850's small operators consolidated claims to pay debts or in an attempt to use water more efficiently. Even so, many claims fell into the hands of bankers. When the drought broke in 1864, the hydraulic companies of Nevada City were smaller in numbers and greater in size. The influx of capital and expertise after 1863 found sound and growing mining economies already in place in both towns, and already in fewer, richer hands.[13] The drought pushed ahead a process well begun by coyote-ing.

Developments in the technology of mining, the Fraser River and Comstock rushes, and Nevada City's turn toward commerce and Grass Valley's toward quartz together profoundly altered the population composition of the two towns. The census of 1860, taken after the first rush to the Comstock district and before the cycle of flood and drought, found the town of Nevada City (3,070) still larger than Grass Valley (1,265), while the township of Grass Valley, which included Boston Ravine and clusters of miners living around major mines, most importantly at Allison Ranch, counted greater numbers (3,840) than the township of Nevada City (3,679; Table 1). Some conditions remained similar to those of the early 1850's; societies in both towns were heavily male and still dominated numerically by men calling themselves miners (Table 5). Not surprisingly, Grass Valley township had a greater proportion of miners, more than seven men in ten, than Nevada City township's six of ten. Further, the proportion of miners in the male working population had increased in Grass Valley. Nevada City's mining population had decreased proportionally, partly because of depression and partly because of the growing importance of hydraulic mining. In 1857 Amos Laird, considered one of the largest hydraulickers in the state, used six to eight men on his claims above the town of Nevada City, where two years previously he had employed 200 pick-and-shovel miners. Although the proportion dropped in the 1860's in both towns, the high percentage of the population in vulnerable mining work explains the nearly fatal impact of the depressions of the early 1860's.

The growing maturity of the towns had nonetheless produced major changes in their occupational structures. The augmented demand for social services and amenities, the technological sophistication of local enterprise, and the growth of farming and trade all tended to create a much more elaborate system of work identities. The old society of miners and traders, largely interchangeable, no longer existed, and for many in the towns a job classification meant a much more permanent commitment to a trade or profession. Arriving in Grass Valley from Mineral Point, Wisconsin in the mid-1850's, Cornishman John Coad pursued hard-rock mining, even when times were bad; and instead of shifting to another job when quartz failed, he expected to return to Wisconsin or move on to where his specialized skills would count. C. C. Abbott, in the dairy business when Nevada City burned in 1858, moved west to Marin County rather than turn to a new trade or wait for his customers to recover. While in 1860 most miners continued to be at best semi-skilled workers, and while many continued to labor in small groups on placer sites, the number of highly skilled men like Coad rapidly increased, especially in Grass Valley. In that town, "quartz miner" began to denote an experienced, expert hard-rock man.[14]

The variety and number of artisans and craftsmen expanded with commercial diversification, particularly in Nevada City. In Grass Valley, the proportion of artisans appears to have increased only slightly between 1850 and 1860, largely because the camp's economy in 1850 had been highly speculative as men followed other pursuits in the absence of good mining. A comparison between Grass Valley in 1860 and Nevada in 1850 is more informative; the one, a successful mining town in 1860, contained twice the proportion of artisans the other had had in 1850. The increasing importance of commerce to Nevada City manifested itself in part in the dramatic increase in artisans, clerks, and craftsmen to more than three times their proportion in the first town census and almost twice that in quartz-oriented Grass Valley, despite Grass Valley's dependence on the crafts related to mining. In Nevada City, artisans composed the second largest occupational classification.

Another indicator of the increasing economic complexity of the two towns lay in the numbers of unskilled laborers. Nevada in the boom days of 1850 had had only a handful, because mining paid well and required little arcane knowledge; Grass Valley had contained more, because it lacked paying placer sites. In 1860 in both towns almost one in ten employed males worked at some variety of unskilled labor: on road maintenance, in shipping, or even in domestic service, jobs not even listed in the first census.

Changes in the proportions of businessmen demonstrate the effects of the same economic changes on a different social level. The percentage of men engaged in merchandising was reduced in both towns, spectacularly so from the barely viable Grass Valley of 1850, where commerce had attempted to make up for lack of gold. Most of the small-scale traders had departed, replaced by men frankly called peddlers and more importantly by fairly substantial if still financially vulnerable merchants, fewer in number but with much more specialized and sophisticated stocks. In Nevada City, Hagadorn and Bowley and their competitors, Joseph Brothers, offered French cassimere pants, plush vests, Peruvian hats, gaiters, mantillas, and velvet cloaks to town swells and their ladies, while Muller's "fancy goods" store sold lithographs and engravings from France for their homes.[15] As one might expect, Nevada City contained a higher proportion of merchants, men who, according to assessments published in the newspapers, held a greater total amount of property than those of Grass Valley.

The proportions of professionals in both towns hardly changed between 1850 and 1860. As county seat, Nevada City had twice as many attorneys as Grass Valley, which contained more mine professionals. In 1850 a few men had combined claim holding with water interests and sometimes legal expertise to form the base for real financial power in the town; by 1860 similar combinations also included banking, milling, mining, or investments in civic and business endeavors such as the Henness Pass road to the Comstock country. Both towns had small, interconnected, and mutually dependent groups of locally very powerful men of capital. Men with multiple interests were more numerous in Nevada City; wealth in Grass Valley tended to be concentrated in quartz development.

Combining the numbers of artisans, professionals, and merchandisers gives a good picture of the occupational results of the towns' evolution; more than one Nevada City man in five filled a commercial or service-oriented job, while one man in seven did so in Grass Valley. In 1860, Nevada City had a larger population that could be called middle class, as well as a larger group of nonmining craftsmen than did Grass Valley, which was more a laboring-class town. In 1850, the occupational structures of the two towns had differed because Nevada had been the site of the first major gold discovery in the area; by 1860 the occupational divergence instead reflected economic orientation.

In 1860 the census takers included statements of real and personal property claimed by the inhabitants of the two towns. (Since the census materials were confidential, and guaranteed not to be used for tax purposes, there was little reason for an individual either to hide wealth or to claim holdings he did not actually possess.) Nevada City residents generally claimed more value in real and personal property at all occupational levels, including miner (Table 10). Despite the varying uses of the term "miner" to denote placer worker, expert hard-rock man, or even, through reverse snobbery, mining entrepreneur, the relative position of most miners, and therefore men in the towns, becomes obvious in these reports. To be a miner in 1860 was to have given up any hope for wealth, and to accept wages or returns roughly equivalent to those for unskilled labor: over nine miners out of ten in both towns reported no real estate or personal property, and despite the importance of miners to the towns' survival and the increasingly skilled nature of their work, an unskilled laborer would do as well financially. A miner had a slightly better chance to hold over $1,000 in property than a common laborer primarily because some large operators preferred to call themselves miners. Any man with a skill other than mining could expect to accumulate more property than a miner. In this context, the attractions of the new gold and silver rushes become obvious. The success of hydraulic works gave little opportunity to the average miners of Nevada City; both wages and employment had dropped in comparison to those in the old coyote mines. Wages in quartz were going down all over the state in the late 1850's. Warren Ewer's Grass-Valley-based *California Mining Journal* argued that although pay had fallen from $6 per day to $3, quartz miners still had more income because they worked year-round rather than for the four months of the old mining season. Employers pointed out that prices had declined along with wages. Nevertheless, the "reduction in the value of labor" convinced some skilled miners to prospect for themselves. But neither the mining salaries nor the returns from individual claims gave miners any surplus with which to acquire property. Any interruption in mine production would be impossible for a man on miner's pay to withstand.[16]

Artisans also reported little property. Eight of ten in Grass Valley and seven of ten in Nevada City reported no real property; seven of ten and six of ten claimed no personal estate (Table 11). But both towns clearly offered opportunity for craftsmen and the chance to build up a business; one artisan in 10—compared with one miner in 50—attained over $1,000 in real or personal property. Moreover, artisans had a considerably better chance than miners to amass small amounts ($100 to $1,000) of real and personal property. Farmers and saloon keepers, necessary adjuncts to town society though not necessarily part of it, were even more likely to report some property.

Grass Valley's and Nevada City's economic conditions in late 1860, when the census was taken, were very uncertain and a businessman or professional could not count on future security, but he was still much better off than the rest of the towns' workers. Any Gold Rush notions of occupational equality or equal opportunity to get rich by mining or selling had long disappeared. Nearly half of the two towns' businessmen and professionals reported over $1,000 in both real and personal property (Table 12). Simply filling an occupation such as haberdasher or dentist obviously could not ensure financial success; business depression, hard luck, personal incompetence, and the low pay in the ministry and teaching together resulted in over four of ten professionals and businessmen claiming no real property and over three in ten having no personal property. But in spite of threadbare lawyers, failing storekeepers, and rank beginners of all callings, a Grass Valley merchant was 22 times as likely to hold over $1,000 in personalty as a fellow citizen trying to make a living in mining.

Golden dreams and local boosterism to the contrary, most of the inhabitants of the two towns were by national standards very poor. Only professionals and businessmen were likely to hold more real and personal estate than the national average for all occupations, while average property holdings in Grass Valley and Nevada City did not even approach national norms. In part this was because mining claims were not held by deed; nationally, the high proportion of farmers pushed up real-estate figures. In part the relative poverty reflected the financial straits of the largest single group, the miners, who in Grass Valley were seven times less likely than the national average to hold personal property. The hard times after 1859 also contributed. But simple demography was an important factor; maturing and staying put both favored individual property accumulation, whereas the two towns' populations were young and extremely mobile (Table 2). As long as Grass Valley and Nevada City remained mine towns, they would share a relative poverty despite their growing economic divergence.[17]

The most visible sign of this divergence around 1860 was in their populations; quartz mining, placer mining, mill work, and merchandising attracted different ethnic groups, and since out-migration remained as high as it had been in the early 1850's, the ethnic composition of the towns changed rapidly and in different directions. During a time of large-scale immigration to the United States, mining wages remained higher than those for unskilled labor in the East, and rapid population turnover meant constant openings in the mine and mill forces and continued opportunities to open businesses, except during the worst periods of the depression. By 1860, the foreign-born made up over half of Grass Valley's male working population and approached half in Nevada City.

The two largest European groups, the Irish and the Cornish, were looking for work as mining laborers and hard-rock miners and therefore gravitated more to Grass Valley. In 1860, 22 percent of Grass Valley's male workers had been born in Ireland, and 20 percent were from Great Britain, mostly from Cornwall (Table 8). The labor force in the quartz mines and mills was heavily Irish, especially at Allison Ranch, where Irish-born owners hired their countrymen in all capacities from labor to management, forming a nearly all-Irish community in the midst of Grass Valley township. The necessity for deeper works, water pumps, and better-made shafts and hoisting equipment that accelerated the demand for mining expertise attracted ever-increasing numbers of underground miners from Cornwall. Emigrating because of an extended mining depression at home, the Cornish constituted a mobile group of mine professionals who went where their skills were in demand. They were, therefore, both a vital and a volatile segment of the population, their stay made even more uncertain because many had come to Grass Valley by way of the Wisconsin and Michigan copper and iron mines where they had established homes and families before venturing on to the quartz region. Most Cornish miners took their place as the most skilled laborers in the most productive quartz mines. Some, like John Coad, ran small independent quartz companies, and a few managed to buy major lodes and return them to production. Grass Valley mining survived the chaos of the Comstock era in large part because of the presence of Cornish engineers, superintendents, and hard-rock miners. In 1861, Warren Ewer in the *Grass Valley National* proclaimed the town "the Cornwall of California," as "mining is for the most part carried on by Cornishmen," whose opinions on the extent of gold still to be mined in the township were eagerly quoted.[18]

The Chinese were the next largest group in Grass Valley, the great majority working in the old placer creek diggings. Germans appeared in much smaller groups, concentrated in merchandising and crafts. Scatterings of other nationalities including Frenchmen, some of whom were very prominent in town banking and mining investment, and a few Italians and Canadians, commonly laborers, contributed to the foreign tone of Grass Valley. By 1860, only one "Spanish" person was enumerated in Grass Valley.

In Nevada City, where the American-born remained the majority in the population rather than the mere plurality as in Grass Valley, the Chinese were the largest single foreign group, a fact that reflects the state of that township's mining in 1860. Excluded from quartz works, the Chinese had no important mining role in Grass Valley, but they numerically dominated Nevada City's non-hydraulic placer industry, often taking over where others gave up. Men from Great Britain came next, forming just over half the proportion they did in Grass Valley and clearly demonstrating the relative unimportance of hard-rock mining in Nevada City. Nevada City Germans, together with a handful of Scandinavians, numbered almost exactly as many as the Irish. As in Grass Valley, the Christian Germans concentrated in crafts or manufacturing, the German Jews in commerce, and the Irish in mine labor. The Germans made up a much larger proportion of the population than in Grass Valley, the Irish a much smaller proportion. The Catholic church in Nevada City was a mission of the one in Grass Valley, while the German and Hebrew social institutions serving both camps were based in commerce-oriented Nevada City. A few French, Italians, and Canadians and a single "Spaniard" made up the rest of Nevada City's foreign-born working population.

Nativists, still vocal in the early 1860's although weakened by the demise of the American Party, commonly claimed that the foreign-born had replaced American natives by undercutting wages. The accusation, usually aimed at the Chinese or less often at the Irish and Cornish, contained little truth. The Chinese often worked claims whose returns would satisfy few whites; charges that Chinese labor forced out whites at times coincided with newspaper pleas that idle whites take up unworked claims. As for the

Cornish, they could simply do some tasks better than anyone else owing to their experience in underground mining, and in many cases the jobs they held would not have existed without their presence in the towns. The high population turnover meant that slowing native in-migration quickly showed itself in the ethnic proportions of the towns. In the eyes of many Americans, California offered fewer attractions in 1860 than in 1850. With the Gold Rush days long past, those who dreamed of instant riches would gravitate toward newer mining areas. Industrialized mining might offer opportunities for Irishmen or Cornishmen, but wage labor in general would be less attractive to the American-born than to recent immigrants, especially those, like the Irish, who were discriminated against elsewhere. Within the American-born group, the greatest decline took place among Southerners and men from the old frontier, particularly Missouri (Table 4). Southerners and Westerners were less likely to be able to take advantage of Nevada City commerce or Grass Valley quartz than other Americans, being overwhelmingly farmers. The foreign-born did not drive out the native-born, but their in-migration increased while that of Americans decreased. Their skills and needs fitted the towns; more and more those of the native-born did not.

Economic Peace, Political War

In 1852, Grass Valley's economic problems had contributed to the violent response to Governor Bigler's "Special Message." In the early 1860's, once again in both towns, depression and increasing foreign migration appeared simultaneously, but this time little ethnic conflict resulted. Although nativist sentiments surfaced from time to time, these appearances, as usual, coincided with elections and were occasioned by Irish Democratic voting habits. In part, peace reigned around 1860 because all groups suffered in the depression, and all groups, native investors and Irish miners alike, joined the Comstock rush; footloose miners could not be blamed for work stoppages. The Chinese could be blamed for the Nevada City fire of 1858, but no group could be claimed to have caused the floods and drought. The problems of the 1860's did not stem from dives catering to lonely miners but from the shortage of work for miners to do; middle-class images of order and prosperity were not relevant, and middle-class moral crusades against the foreign-born did not take place.

Challenges to town quiet did not come from poor miners or the foreign-born either. With one exception, unemployment, food shortages, or rushes to new gold fields did not result in attacks on the mine operators or the capitalist system. When new finds like the Comstock Lode offered the opportunity to start over, populations as mobile as the ethnic miners would rarely stay where economies offered them little. But just as importantly, the foreign-born who stayed in Grass Valley and Nevada City during the hard times had access to most existing forms of occupational opportunity. The growing split between owners and managers of mines and wage-earning miners, the development of mercantile interests and an unskilled sector, and the arrival of Irish and Chinese together created the potential for a simple two-class structure based on ethnicity with the foreign-born in the lower echelons of society and the native-born dominating its upper reaches, and with ethnic and religious differences widening social gaps. The occupational structures of the two towns, however, suggest that social reality was more complicated. The majority of the foreign-born, like the majority of the native-born, engaged in mining (Table 14); foreigners made up a slightly greater proportion of the mining work force than in the total population (Table 8). In Nevada City, the proportion of unskilled laborers among Americans roughly equaled that in other national groups; the Chinese proportion was smaller, because of their concentration in placer mining, and the Irish proportion was greater. In Grass Valley, where the Irish and Cornish worked in quartz and the Allison Ranch offered opportunities for the Irish, the American-born had proportionately more unskilled laborers than either of those groups. The Chinese also included fewer common laborers than the native-born, although in Grass Valley, where placers were relatively scarce, the Chinese were likelier than in Nevada City to turn to handyman jobs or to be servants. The French and Italian immigrants reflected occupationally their town of residence, being miners or unskilled workers in Grass Valley, and merchants and artisans in Nevada City. In sum, the foreign-born were not overrepresented in the least prestigious occupations.

At the other extreme, the American-born did not monopolize the professions and merchandising. Journalism and the law, because of their demand for familiarity with traditional American usages and their partisan political orientation, were the nearly exclusive preserve of the native-born, but in other prestigious occupations the foreign-born were important, even dominant (Table 15). A few foreign entrepreneurs owed their prominence solely to the social segregation of their people; Chinese merchants usually supplied the Chinese, and some English hotelkeepers housed only other Englishmen. Most of the foreign-born in commerce, management, and the professions, however, served the people of the towns at large. The Germans, about half of whom were Jewish, were not prevented from entering and succeeding in large businesses (Table 14). The German Jews played a vital role in merchandising, controlling the dry-goods trade by the mid-1850's, while Christian Germans controlled brewing and were very important in meat and grain processing. Germans had the largest proportion of professionals and merchants of any national group in either town, including the native-born, with the exception of Nevada City's small circle of French bankers and investors. The growing commercial orientation of Nevada City only increased their importance. German butchers and blacksmiths and German Jewish clerks and bookkeepers also made up a disproportionate share of artisans. The Cornish involvement in mining obscured the relative occupational position of those born in Great Britain; men of wealth, influence, and professional training often listed themselves simply as miners. Still, in Grass Valley, their concentration in prestige occupations equaled that of the native-born, and, of course, as mine officers and engineers the British dominated their fields.

Among the numerically significant ethnic groups, the occupational status of only the Irish and Chinese suggests a prestige structure based on national background. The Irish, concentrated among wage-earning miners, held more low-prestige jobs in proportion to their numbers than any other major European ethnic group. Despite the owners and managers of Allison Ranch, they also had a lower proportion of artisans, professionals, and merchants, even in Grass Valley township. The Chinese occupied the bottom rungs of the social ladder. They maintained their own social structure, ruled by the merchant representatives of the Cantonese companies. Only in their case did occupational structures seem linked to the social ostracism of the group, and even with them the dominant role of the merchants resulted more from the processes of Chinese migration than from serving, without competition, a segregated community. White merchants still sought Chinese customers. The leading members of the Irish community held their positions through wealth and political acumen, and although Allison Ranch created opportunities inside an Irish community, most prominent Irishmen had won their success, especially political success, in the towns at large, just as had the Jewish dry-goods merchants, the Cornish mine engineers, and the French bankers.

The American-born tended to hold more property than the foreign-born, but except for the Chinese, who reported almost no assets, only the Grass Valley Irish lagged dramatically in real estate claimed (Table 16). Access to prestigious occupations meant access to potential wealth for the foreign-born as well as the native-born, and while Americans in general held somewhat more property than the immigrants, both towns had wealthy foreign-born citizens. The German merchants and artisans in Nevada City were likelier to claim over $1,000 in personal assets than any other group, and the wealthiest men in either town were the Irish owners of the Allison Ranch. Ethnic identity was not reinforced by class or occupation; Irish spokesmen called on their countrymen's support as Irishmen, not as poor, oppressed Irishmen, and in 1860 they acted as a group almost exclusively within the Democratic Party. The Chinese, alone at the bottom of society, were powerless and perhaps too tied to China and its institutions to mount a protest.

Peace was interrupted only once, during the Fraser River excitement of 1858. The bulk of Grass Valley's emigrants were Irish quartz-mill workers, and a number of those who stayed in town immediately struck for a return to the higher wages of 1854. Owners responded by closing the mills. Pointing to the high costs of deep-shaft mining and wasteful milling processes, they announced that the mills would remain shut down until they could hire labor at wages they felt justified by returns from the mines. After threatening to break the resulting impasse by hiring Chinese labor at wages they could dictate, the mill operators finally decided to employ unskilled American-born workers at the pay scales of 1858. The episode had generated an outburst of nativism, the use of the Chinese against other ethnic groups, a temporary Americans-only hiring policy in opposition to a consciously Irish strike, and the devaluation of skill in milling. Both owners and workers had clearly made the connection between national origin and occupational status. Despite the brevity of the strike—the Irish had no recourse against the new hiring policy—the potential for future labor violence between ethnic groups had been shown to exist during times of outward peace between peoples and classes.[19]

Depression and the growing numbers of the foreign-born did not together produce economic conflict, but they did contribute to a turbulent political period. As usual, much of the impetus for partisan strife came from national politics: the final party crises before secession and then the intense bitterness over Union Party war policy. But the diverging occupational and ethnic compositions of Grass Valley and Nevada City added to the possibility of conflict by tying each town to a different party loyalty, placing them on opposite sides, it seemed, in the Civil War itself.

Secession crystallized political sentiments in the two towns. Before that the Democrats had usually carried both towns; the late 1850's had seen a struggle in the Democratic Party to hold itself together locally in spite of national fractures. After the formation of the Confederacy, Republicans briefly held unchallenged sway, although pro-Southern sentiment remained a constant undercurrent. In the gubernatorial race of 1861, the pro-Southern Democratic candidate lived in Nevada City, but Republican Leland Stanford carried both towns. He won only a plurality in Grass Valley, however, as the majority split between Union and (pro-Southern) Peace Democrats. During 1862 Nevada City turned firmly Republican, as pro-Union Democrats forced their party to accept an official fusion. But in the Grass Valley town election of 1863, after organizing for a traditionally nonpartisan polling, Peace Democrats assumed control over town government; in the township, Allison Ranch stood overwhelmingly anti-Republican.[20]

As the war dragged on, as opposition to emancipation and disappointment over Union military failure became more vocal, and as partisan rhetoric reached new heights of vehemence, editors and politicos began to take the enmity of the two towns for granted. Military imagery became common; after the Peace Democrats carried Grass Valley in 1863, the Republican *Nevada Daily Transcript's* Edwin G. Waite reported that "the rebels made a guerrilla raid on Grass Valley yesterday and took it." During the presidential campaign of 1864, a group of Nevada City Unionists "invaded" a Grass Valley saloon, singing Republican songs and nearly precipitating a riot. When the Democratic Grass Valley marshal attempted to silence them, the report spread in Nevada City that he had threatened to jail men for singing Union airs, and several members of the town militia tried to organize a march on Grass Valley. Partisans seemed to feel that speaking their piece on hostile ground was an admirable act of bravado, and carried weapons when they went to do so. On at least two occasions, bloodshed was only narrowly averted. Before the election was over, pro-Southerners had made a covert attempt to take over Grass Valley's newspaper, the *Union,* and reverse the political allegiance of its masthead, and both sides had reported electioneering by bribery and threat. When the results were in, Lincoln carried 87 percent of the Nevada City vote, while McClellan won 54 percent of the vote in Grass Valley proper and 100 percent in the Allison Ranch precinct, giving him 65 percent in Grass Valley township.[21]

In the aftermath of the election, several Unionists, including Waite of the *Transcript,* erupted over the Allison Ranch returns, demanding that in the future no polls be opened there because "it is not safe for a white man to vote in that precinct," as "no civilized beings feel safe in going to such a barbarous place to challenge the brutes who come up to the polls there" to vote "the rebel ticket whether naturalized or not." Perhaps a more telling comment appeared in a letter written by a Union voter from Grass Valley complaining that the considerable Union strength there had "no leaders worthy of the name," as the party elite resided in Nevada City. Whether the Unionists lost Grass Valley because of illegal Irish votes or because of their organizers' Nevada City orientation, the closing of the polls did not cool political temperatures or quiet intertown partisan rivalries; the old Know-Nothing denunciations directed against Grass Valley's immigrant electorate continued to deepen the fissures between the towns throughout the 1860's.

After the election, editor O. P. Stiger and William Beggs, his second at the *Nevada Daily Gazette,* began to allege, and shortly take as proven, treasonable activity in Grass Valley. Specifically, they accused their most prominent opposite number, pro-Southern John Rollin Ridge of the *Grass Valley National* of organizing and leading a unit of a secret secessionist "army." They identified this army with the Copperhead Knights of the Golden Circle, who were resisting Union war efforts in the mid-west, and its manpower with the Irish of Allison Ranch. Their fears reached a climax in January 1865, when rumors of a planned invasion of Nevada City by Grass Valley Irish "secesh" led the Nevada Light Guard to spend a nervous night patrolling the streets, at one point sending out skirmishers toward Grass Valley and ordering an abortive evacuation of the town's women and children. According to the Union sheriff of Nevada County, the Allison Ranch "Knights" planned to assassinate Union leaders and plunder and burn the town. When the phantom Irish failed to materialize, Nevada City briefly became the laughingstock of neighboring towns.[22]

Only the final Confederate defeats of that spring, culminating in the surrenders of Lee and Johnson, stilled town partisanship. At its height, voices calling attention to the importance of the intertown trade that was endangered by civic partisan emotion were overwhelmed, though in fact no disruption in commerce took place. But ominously for the future, the nativist and ethnic partisanship evoked by Civil War politics served notice that the strike of 1858 was not a completely isolated event. Ethnic occupational identities lay quiescent, but could always be called on when circumstances warranted.

Shared Values

FAMILY LIFE AND THE FOREIGN-BORN

Social peace accompanied economic peace in Grass Valley and Nevada City through the early 1860's, despite population fluidity and growing numbers of immigrants. The moral institutions of the respectable seemed safely rooted, so reform movements withered. Family neighborhoods strengthened their special identity even though their residents often did not linger long. But the conspicuous success of traditional family life obscured some basic realities. For single miners, the old days lived on in the form of saloons, brothels, and all-male cabins. And the wives of men of all occupational levels continued to work to supplement family income. But common values prevented these Gold Rush survivals from creating open discord. All European groups shared attitudes toward home and family, the most volatile concerns of the mid-1850's. Married miners tended to behave in family matters like married merchants, German Jewish professionals like their native-born Protestant peers. Those who seemed to challenge the beliefs of the majority were hidden from sight. Segregation, shared values, and the continued health of family life and family institutions provided civic peace, even in the face of political hysteria and economic hardship.

A Compartmentalized Society

Life in Grass Valley and Nevada City in the late 1850's and early 1860's continued to reflect the dichotomy of town and township. But the prime social determinant—the essential cause of peace—was a different division, the cloistering of family neighborhoods from vice districts. During this time, partly through coercion, the functional differentiation of town sections became fixed. Topography had determined the initial locations of the business districts; the little grassy valley and the flat above Deer Creek were about the only practicable, easily developed areas for commerce. The red-light regions and the slum tenements they sheltered had grown up in close conjunction to the downtowns, in cheaper buildings in less successfully developed locations. Industrial enterprises, chiefly quartz mills and sawmills, were scattered throughout the townships, located for easy access to their raw materials. The Nevada Foundry, located in a low-lying area of Nevada City, was the lone major manufactory within either town proper. Its immediate environs took on an industrial character as the foundry attracted blacksmith shops, while close by on Spring Street stood a slum area bluntly called Washerwoman's Valley.

In both Grass Valley and Nevada City the late 1850's saw the further development of residence areas for the families of merchants and professionals. In Grass Valley a new family neighborhood developed by 1860 in an area east of the business district, principally along the east side of Auburn Street, similar to the somewhat older region on Church and School Streets. In Nevada City an area already called Piety Hill, across Deer Creek from the bulk of the town, rose to be an avowed rival of the Aristocracy Hill neighborhood. School, Church, Piety, and Aristocracy: their names reveal the intentions of their people. When the Nevada City town directory of 1856 is compared with the census returns of 1860 and the directory of 1861, a growing specialization of residential areas by occupation becomes apparent, although artisans' shops and miners' cabins were interspersed among the homes that gave the neighborhoods their identity. Nevada City observers could easily perceive a growing spatial separation by 1863 as the hills above the business district on both sides of Deer Creek began to be developed and Prospect Hill, Boulder Hill, and the upper reaches of Main Street and Broad Street—later called Nabob Hill—attracted more and more families despite the Broad Street neighborhood's close proximity to Chinatown. The hills contrasted sharply with areas like Washerwoman's Valley and "Aristocracy Hollow," as a black area was mockingly called.

Grass Valley's merchants and professionals were fewer and often poorer than those of Nevada City, and their homes were not on the slopes of highly visible hills, so their family residential areas were not as distinctive. In addition, the mining orientation of Grass Valley created a more obvious continuity with older housing arrangements. Miners and mine owners alike lived close by the scene of operations; some of the wealthiest mining entrepreneurs in the town, André Chavanne and the Watt brothers, lived in isolation, surrounded by their workers at the site of the mine or mill. Families of town merchants and bankers lived like their Nevada City compeers on predominantly middle-class streets. But even for the prosperous in both towns, some of the old living conditions still prevailed. Many single merchants still lived in the back rooms of their stores, and a majority boarded in hotels. And on the middle-class streets, fires revealed the persistence of the old canvas-walled houses alongside homes furnished with imported materials worked by master craftsmen.[1]

To townsmen of the time, the women and children living in the neighborhoods represented the most fundamental social change taking place. But as the influence of wives seemed more firmly grounded in both towns, there was a gradual, subtle change in attitudes toward at least some women. The anguished pleas for women died away, and a less romanticized image of them appeared in the newspapers. Before, only fallen women, by definition not to be accorded the respect due "true womanhood," had been spoken of in the sardonic, contemptuous, condescending editorial tone commonly used to describe blacks and Indians, but now spinsters and women in menial jobs were also referred to without the rhetoric of respect. A woman, either old maid or prostitute, who lived out of her expected place in society could, like any inferior, be made an object of fun. On the other hand, honest and open accounts of the realities of women's work also began to appear, along with testimonials to the skill and good nature of a seamstress or a milliner. And now an editor could calmly assert that while in the "early days" women, "due to scarcity," could convince "men [to] buy for them, regardless of price," now California was settled and women were no longer catered to, but were "left behind as they had been in the East."[2]

This newly relaxed attitude toward women suggests an extremely narrow awareness on the part of those who had been vocal over the need for stability; very few men were actually living with wives. In Grass Valley, only 7 percent of the male laboring population were married or living with a woman in 1860, in Nevada City 13 percent. Families seemed to demand a stability and an amount of money beyond the reach of most inhabitants of both towns. In general, to have a family was an indicator of success, often of occupational class. For although some families lived in penury, a merchant, attorney, or physician was far likelier to have a wife and children than a miner or manual laborer (Table 7). In Grass Valley, one out of every four of the business and professional class lived with his family in 1860; one in 25 miners did so. To put it another way, storekeepers, attorneys, and the like had four times "their share" of town families. Nevada City had twice as large a proportion of married men as Grass Valley, professionals and miners alike being more likely to be married. In Nevada City, the merchant, professional, and artisan groups together accounted for over half the marriages.

The relationship of stability and prosperity (the favorite words of earlier town boosters) to marriage becomes more strikingly evident when holdings in real property, land and homes, are correlated with marriage (Table 17). In Grass Valley in 1860, a married miner was ten times more likely to claim over $1,000 in real estate than an unmarried one. Only 4 percent of miners reported any real estate at all, but almost half of those married did. Married artisans were four times as likely as unmarried ones to hold appreciable real property. But among professionals and businessmen, where both wealth and wives were more common, there was less difference between the unmarried and the married. It seems that in Grass Valley for men in the less prestigious occupations, marriage was a mark of male success. The same relationship between marriage and success held in Nevada City. And, to a somewhat greater extent than in Grass Valley, the inhabitants of the family neighborhoods were, as a group, stronger financially, both in real and personal estate, than the bachelors of the same occupations who lived in hotels or in their stores. The married merchants and investors of Piety Hill and Aristocracy Hill were the richest subsociety in either town. A highly visible portion of middle-class men had families, enough to create the appearance, at least on their streets, of secure, orthodox styles of living.

Safeguarded by the family neighborhoods, churches, schools, and respectable social clubs now proliferated in the two towns. Like fire companies and militia units, they were vulnerable to poverty and population turnover; the clubs died each spring, private schools typically failed, and churches often lacked ministers. But more importantly, they or others like them always revived. Institutions, like individuals, disappeared, but the values that produced them remained constant. Furthermore, in polite society, only rarely did reminders of the old days impinge on daily lives. Some practices survived; an unmarried man leaving "for the states" after "making his pile in quartz" was treated to a "high old time" by the boys "seeing him off." Both the event and its description hark back to the early 1850's. Letters published in town newspapers inquiring about men once reported to be in the area, written by Eastern friends and relatives, were constant reminders of the individual burdens inherent in migration to the gold regions; going to the mines could still mean losing all contacts with home and the past. Cautionary tales of the dangers of sudden wealth and the lack of social controls still were deemed worthy of publication. The discovery of the Allison Ranch mine proved to many that the exaggerated expectations of 1850 still could come true, but the reaction of the lucky discoverers supplied ammunition for town moralists as "they spent their money as such men will," one man presenting "sets of diamond jewelry to the amount of $12,000" to "a woman of ill-fame in a noted part" of Grass Valley. In the end, he died of drink. The moral of this tale was that the rich Irishman perished because he could not transcend his background and adopt the values of the new moral order. He was an anachronism, a throwback like the Allison Ranch discovery itself, to the great days of 1851.[3] And like his gold strike, he was thought exceptional in 1862.

By the late 1850's, the middle class had established its own recreational world; the number of affairs "got up" by proprietors of hotels and "resorts" declined, and saloons ceased to be the locales of catered parties. A distinct winter social season evolved, sponsored in the main by organizations and institutions rooted in the middle class. Many of these affairs were intended to raise funds; churches, schools, fire companies, and militia brigades staged an almost unbroken cycle of donation dinners, bazaars, and dancing parties. Not only did the middle class's social round reflect its newly secure position in the towns, its entertainments contributed to the support of the institutions thought necessary for that position. More frivolously, several men's clubs existed solely to give parties and balls. Coming together for a winter's season, they put on one or two affairs and then dissolved for the next year. Typical of these groups, Nevada City's Bachelor Club drew its membership from the "unmarried well-to-do," and had organized "for the purpose of having pleasant soirees." Lyceums and debate clubs also flourished briefly in each winter's season during these years. Like similar clubs in small towns all over the country, they provided for the intellectual and moral self-improvement of the ambitious young lawyers and storekeepers who joined, but additionally for the conscious introduction of traditional middle-class values to the frontier.[4]

When compared to the cosmopolitan amusements available during the Gold Rush era, especially the touring dramatic companies headed by luminaries such as Edwin Booth, the recreations of the early 1860's seem makeshift and homely. They were also innocent in accordance with national small-town norms. And when a club, E Clampus Vitus, surfaced that seemed to undertake to turn back the clock by a nostalgic evocation of the lost early days of mining—its first public affair in Nevada City was a benefit for the ladies of a touring dramatic company—it attracted immediate public opposition. Despite the rapid growth of the burlesque fraternity, the inevitable prosperity and respectability of its leaders, and the innocent, almost embarrassed boisterousness of its members, charges that it was an "obscene society" that degraded women and committed the "grossest indecencies" soon silenced the Clampers. Editorial members countercharged in vain that the ministers and old maids who opposed the Clampers harbored "secret foul thoughts." In towns where the business and professional groups seemed dedicated to putting the Gold Rush behind them, the Clampers were too much a part of middle-class society to wish to challenge that intent. And in towns where the Clampers were too raucous, "respectables" had successfully set social boundaries for themselves.[5]

Society was further compartmentalized; the tiny group of the very wealthiest families in both towns, whose property holdings were based on investments in ditches and mines and connections to

Eastern and foreign capital, formed a private, self-defined elite circle. The Grass Valley Club, organized in 1860 and limited to 24 members, all quartz investors, met twice yearly for dining and conversation. The Rev. R. F. Putnam, brought to Grass Valley by men of this class to revive the Episcopal Church, described their banquets, held in new elaborate private homes or behind closed doors in the leading hotels of both towns, as equivalent to those of the Eastern rich. And Joseph R. English, the young nephew of a Nevada City banker, in rejecting an invitation to a "fire laddies' party" in order to attend a private dance at the residence of a Grass Valley physician and mine investor, illuminated the sharp differences among respectable entertainments—between homes and hired halls, family connections and stag lines, spoken invitations and public announcements, diary recollections and newspaper accounts.[6]

The moral institutions counted on by the middle class to bear much of the burden of civilization in the towns were quieter, more secure, and more segregated than before. Probably the greatest success gained by the two towns in the face of depression-caused institutional instability was maintaining public education. These years saw an increase in the number of children through family migration and natural increase—by 1861 over half the school-age children in Grass Valley had been born in California. The most obvious impact was on the schools; in 1857 Nevada City had a potential school population (children between four and eighteen) of 287, and in 1863, that group numbered 480, with an additional nearly 300 children below school age, despite the depression that had lowered total population. In the early 1850's educational systems had collapsed upon occasion, as their admitted importance had not inspired adequate civic support in towns where, even for the business community, the need for schools was chiefly abstract. Now with the help of direct state funding, variable tuition payments, and the proceeds of school exhibitions, the schools stayed in operation, although often reducing the numbers of classes offered during difficult times. The towns, responding to a greater amount of middle-class parental pressure, simply had to be more successful in maintaining education.[7]

For those who found the public schools too secular or too democratic, private schools had a new function. Previously, private schools had filled the gaps in public education. Inexpensive and often ephemeral, they attempted to teach children from all social sectors. But after the successful foundation of public schools, some secular private schools became "select schools," teaching courses beyond those usually offered by their rivals. There were "infant schools" and one college preparatory for the few middle-class young men expecting to enter college, but the most noticeable were the schools for young ladies. The Grass Valley Seminary and the Nevada Female Institute, both (as their advertisements carefully pointed out) conducted by Eastern ladies, taught languages, art, dancing, and the manners of "polite society." Such schools catered by design to the family neighborhoods where most of them were located, but evidently the two towns did not contain enough of the right kind of potential scholars; most private schools received notice in the press for only a short time before disappearing.[8]

By the early 1860's there also existed a juvenile version of the social round of the respectables, centered in the churches and schools. Besides the school contests and shows, the high points were the by now traditional Sunday-school picnics on the first of May and the Christmas-tree parties in the Protestant churches. These activities, highly publicized in the newspapers, seem to have been largely limited to Protestant children, and thus tended to separate them from their peers among other groups just as their parents' clubs segregated adults. Catholic children had parallel institutions, Sunday schools, and sociables and at one time a temperance club, all dedicated to the same sort of morality as the Protestant ones.[9]

Of all town institutions, organized religion was probably the most vulnerable to the calamities of the period. In 1857 William Kip, California's Episcopal bishop, accused Nevada City in his denomination's national press of having regressed spiritually since the fire of 1856, because the churches had not been rebuilt and the town had "given up to the world and the devil." But the churches did refinance themselves, largely through the efforts of the "ladies of the congregation," and all survived except Nevada City's Methodist Episcopal Church, South. No one had ever publicly denied the importance of the churches' place in the towns, and temporary closings certainly did not mean the collapse of religion, as Kip professed to believe. When R. F. Putnam came to Grass Valley to take over Emmanuel Episcopalian, the church building had been closed for over twelve months, the congregation was scattered, and the sanctuary was in great disrepair, construction having been hastily begun and then cut off by depression. However, as soon as he arrived, he related, "a goodly congregation was immediately gathered . . . [and] services [were] well attended." Through the generosity of a few "very liberal" persons and the church ladies, the debt hanging over the church was soon liquidated. Putnam, it is clear, was welcomed by potential parishioners already committed to reviving the church, and their interest and Grass Valley's incipient recovery in 1862 made this possible.[10]

The churches and church-based groups remained the focus of reform, of course, especially temperance and Sabbatarianism, but the willingness to reconstruct buildings and reorganize congregations was not accompanied by any wish to resurrect the moral fervor of the mid-1850's. The churches openly admitted to having influence over only a portion of the towns' populations; the majority of miners and mill hands remained unexhorted. Moral campaigns tended to be directed and inspired from the outside, by state and national associations that were themselves weakened by the onset of the war. State laws had the greatest effect on the outward posture of morality in the towns; newspaper- and church-inspired crusades were noticeably absent, and attempts to start them, such as an 1858 editorial excitement demanding the enforcement of laws against disorderly houses, proved abortive. In 1858 a state law briefly closed saloons and restaurants on Sundays but it was found unconstitutional, and editorial hopes that citizens would keep up the practice availed little. Then in August 1861 another state law shut doors on Sundays, and "not a yard of tape or a pound of soap could be bought," giving Grass Valley, Warren Ewer boasted, quite a "New England Sunday aspect." Hotels, the resorts of the respectables, could still do business and serve drinks; crowds there increased. On the second Sunday the law was in effect, saloon keepers, who had naturally opposed its passage, ignored it, while retail stores, whose owners had supported it, remained closed, waiting to see if the law was constitutional. In October the law was found constitutional by the California Supreme Court, and once again the saloons shut down, soon to reopen despite arrests of barkeeps and saloon owners. In December the towns gave up enforcing the law; there were too many people ignoring it, and many questioned the fairness of a law that closed saloons but allowed hotels to serve whiskey. Even while the law was in effect, its value had been openly questioned; editors commented that at least the saloons kept idle roughs off the streets, doubted that morality could be forced, and exposed cases where men had turned the law to their own financial benefit.[11]

Responses to Sunday closing were related to newly relaxed attitudes toward temperance. The Good Templars led a revival of anti-saloon sentiment, but editors, not taking them quite seriously, implied that the organization owed its growth to social, not moral interests. Edwin Waite of the *Transcript*, while soberly noting the presence of 93 retail liquor shops in Nevada City, laughingly reminded "our bachelor and maiden friends" that the Good Templars welcomed both sexes as members and officers. Whatever social function the temperance clubs had in Grass Valley and Nevada City, they did not promote any direct efforts to close the saloons in either town; Nevada City's Temperance Hall, the scene of most of their activities, was safely placed in one of the family neighborhoods. In the late 1850's and early 1860's, the meetings, elections, and parades of the anti-drink corps were reported in the press as any club's activities would have been, with little more than perfunctory expressions of support. At the same time, the newspapers recounted convivial male gatherings at obviously respectable saloons and made publicans the heroes of tales of toleration and good times. There were two kinds of saloons and two kinds of drinkers in the towns: downtown, businessman-oriented bars whose owners took full part in civic affairs and whose regulars seemed to be solid citizens, and the dives where gamblers and whores congregated out of public sight, whose owners came to public notice only in court cases, and whose customers tended to live in the cabins around a major quartz lead or hydraulic site. This secure separation allowed some men to be both moral and moderate drinkers.[12]

The towns, or at least the editors, also seemed willing to acknowledge the presence of gambling dives—fights in places of dubious repute were the staple of "locals" columns—and even to admit that many residents did not share middle-class mores. Waite noted matter-of-factly that a dogfight in Nevada City would outdraw a sermon. The lurid career of Nevada City's Arcade Saloon, with its knifings and robberies, its monte games and available "senoritas," was well covered in the newspapers. What was going on in the Arcade was against state law and town ordinance, but neither the town trustees nor the marshal attempted to shut it down; the only interruption of its illegal activities came when the owner was stabbed by his mistress. The California anti-gambling law of 1857 had little impact, other than to make poker more popular at the expense of the bank games specifically forbidden. In 1862 in Nevada City, jeweler A. P. McConahy shrewdly deduced in his diary that although illegal or questionable businesses flourished openly, the presence of uniformed policemen on the streets provided a semblance of order, and that was adequate for the comfort of the citizenry.[13]

The segregation of the demimonde, of course, not only meant the safety of moral institutions and families but also implied a tacit recognition that the demographic structure of the Gold Rush, and a demand for that era's illicit entertainments, still existed. More than nine men in ten residing in the towns and townships were unmarried—or had left their families elsewhere. Although as a group the townsmen of 1860 were older than those of 1850, most of them were in their twenties and thirties (Table 2), and in both towns the largest part of these men mined. The great majority of miners (88 percent in Grass Valley, 75 percent in Nevada City) still lived in parties of two to five men (Table 18). In the early 1850's their cabins had been placed for convenience to the claims they worked, but by 1860 many of their dwellings clustered around industrial mines. As before, areas in the townships of 30 to 40 residents might contain no men who were not miners or mine laborers and no women. Many cabin-mates still shared a common regional or ethnic identification or were obviously relatives, although not as many as in 1850 (Table 3). Among the American-born especially, residential links with home had weakened. Grass Valley lived, as one might expect, closer to the old ways; more Nevada City miners, although still few, lived with their families, or boarded with other families or in boarding hotels. Very few miners lived alone, and not many in company-owned barracks or boarding hotels. The single miners around major mining sites attracted camp followers in the persons of gamblers and prostitutes; some boarding hotels had saloons attached to them. This produced a handful of miniature versions of the towns' vice districts scattered around the townships, areas where middle-class mores did not apply. In Grass Valley and in Nevada City small percentages of couples living together were not married. In a disproportionate number of these cases the man was a propertyless miner, living in the townships. For most miners, then, life had not appreciably changed from the days of the Gold Rush, with one obvious exception: the romance was gone. No longer living in camps, hoping to strike it rich, they now dwelt in embryonic industrial slums, hoping for a living wage. The gap between miners and the rest of society was more than spatial; they were much less likely to own homes, have families, or accumulate possessions. In 1862, James Whartenby, an officer of the South Yuba Canal Company, fitted up his bachelor's suite of rooms in a "style of luxurious elegance," causing T. H. Rolfe of the *Nevada Democrat* to comment that the "poor miner" in "his uncarpeted and unfloored cabin" could hardly imagine that Whartenby's style of living was "among the realities of life in Nevada."[14]

The miners, like their dives, were safely hidden by the compartmentalized society. And as long as town respectables and their opposites at the miners' saloons did not come into contact, each was safe from the other. Only one case of moral vigilantism occurred during this period, but it placed middle-class community attitudes in sharp relief. In 1862 the already notorious Bed Rock Saloon on Broad Street, Nevada City, introduced a corps of Hurdy Gurdies, German dance-for-hire girls. The saloon immediately attracted a large and enthusiastic clientele, which to the horror of some townspeople included young men from the business and professional classes. The Hurdies' dancing was not illegal, but newspapers debated their potential adverse effect on "the rising generation" who were being exposed to "vice and dissipation in its most alluring mode." After the town trustees had refused a petition to have the Bed Rock declared a nuisance, the fire companies took it upon themselves to "wash out" the saloon, using a faked alarm as an excuse to pump in streams of water that wrecked its contents and somersaulted its denizens out the doors. The charge leveled against the Hurdies was that they "led *our* young men astray," and the middle class, in the persons of the young shopkeepers who manned the fire brigades, intended to protect its own; an earlier troupe of Hurdies based in a saloon attached to a Boston Ravine miners' boarding hotel had been ignored.[15]

Women, Children, and Work

Just as the perception that Grass Valley and Nevada City were safely traditional family communities ignored most of their populations, the image of women as the successful tamers of society ignored the ways the Gold Rush persisted in their lives. During these times of economic hardship, women played a much greater part in supporting their families, helping ensure sheer survival, than any contemporary stereotype would suggest. Town newspapers applauded maiden ladies for keeping "stocks of fashionable millinery and fancy goods" or for starting seminaries for young women, or widows for pluckily continuing to run boarding houses after their husbands had died, but disregarded the great majority of working women in the two towns who were married and aided their families by taking in boarders. To be sure, there were spinster schoolmarms, widowed shopkeepers, and women who maintained their dead husbands' businesses, one evidently inheriting and operating a mine.[16] In Nevada City 6 percent of all white households containing women were headed by women in 1860, in Grass Valley 11 percent were. Of course, some of these families might have been supported by a man at work in the Comstock mines, for example, but in most the woman clearly had to fend for herself. Eighteen out of 22 white female heads of households in Nevada City listed occupations, and 21 out of 28 in Grass Valley (Table 19). A similar situation existed for single women boarding in households where they were not related to the family (Table 20). Both women heads of households and women living alone would be expected, even constrained, to work. But in both towns three-fourths of all white women identifiable with occupations were married or at least living with a man.

The census takers of 1860 proved reluctant to label a women occupationally unless she lived alone or was the sole support of her family, and unless the occupation was socially acceptable; prostitutes or dance-hall girls did not appear as such. Prostitutes can sometimes be identified from living arrangements or from the conspicuous absence of an occupational label, but conclusions as to their numbers are obviously questionable. More importantly, married women who helped their families by sewing, tutoring, running shops, and the like can rarely be identified and listed, especially in

Grass Valley, where the census taker tended to list only one occupation to a household, the man's. Women who helped support their families by taking in boarders were also not noted as having an occupation. For the purposes of this study, in all married households including additional working men and women other than servants and obviously dependent relatives, the wife was taken to be employed caring for boarders. Taken together, the census taker's practices sharply reduce the figures for female economic participation, especially for married women, below what they should be.

Despite census biases, the fundamental point is simple; among white women in the two towns reported in the 1860 census, slightly less than half solely kept house. Townswomen listed fifteen occupations, most of which attracted only a handful of practitioners. In Nevada City, 13 percent of all employed white women were servants and 9 percent were prostitutes. In Grass Valley, 17 percent were prostitutes and 9 percent were servants (Table 21). The figures for prostitutes are of course problematical, but the proportions do fit with the character of the towns, Grass Valley dominated by single male miners and Nevada City tending somewhat more toward marriage and middle-class status. The other occupations with even fractional representation were schoolteacher, milliner, seamstress, baker, and cook, all trades usually identified with single women. But by far the largest occupational category for employed white women (66 percent in Nevada City and 70 percent in Grass Valley) was caring for boarders. Nearly two out of five adult white women in Grass Valley, nearly twice the national average, took in boarders, as did one-third in Nevada City. Some few families actually ran boarding houses, that being the principal occupation of both husband and wife. But most opened their homes to single men while the husband worked outside the home, leaving his wife to supplement the family's earning power, either directly from payments for rent and board, or indirectly from a wage reduction for a boarder employed by the husband. The responsibility for lodgers (I use "lodgers" and "boarders" interchangeably) fell on the wife; even if she had the aid of a servant, she still had to manage a complex household.

The small group of mining families in Grass Valley were the most committed to keeping boarders; over half did so (Table 22).

Slightly more than one in three of the wives of Grass Valley's artisans, farmers, merchants, and professionals cared for lodgers. In Nevada City, the proportions of mining and artisan families that included boarders were roughly similar, at over one-third, but the women likeliest to care for lodgers were the wives of merchants and professionals; over four in ten did so. The wives of the un-skilled were too few to generalize about.

Since keeping boarders was the most common way women aided their families, their work rarely resulted in property being report-ed in their names. Women in households that contained boarders in fact were less likely to report property than women who simply kept house for their immediate families (Table 23). Because board-ers' fees came completely within the family context, these women could not have accumulated property for themselves. Many of the occupations open to single women paid low wages; servants, seam-stresses, and milliners all earned notoriously little, and prostitutes lived a life that discouraged property accumulation. The net result of these conditions can be seen in the fact that in Nevada City, women who did not work were just as likely to have real or person-al property in their own names as women who worked. Among white employed women in Grass Valley in 1860, only two reported real property holdings. In Nevada City, where census takers listed more property holding in general, more women, but still only a handful, reported property.

Because earnings from rent and board disappeared into family funds that were reported in the census in the husband's name, it is very difficult to estimate the monetary importance of accepting boarders. Figures for the amount of rent paid by boarders are almost nonexistent. Reverend Putnam paid $45 a month to board himself and his wife on Auburn Street, Grass Valley. Some measure of the value of women's domestic work is shown in this figure, since it was three times the rent Putnam later paid for a "large and well furnished" house. A single Cornish miner in 1864 paid $1 per day, and even if that was an exceptionally inflated figure, boarding obviously could make an important difference to a household headed by a miner who made $3 per working day.[17]

The importance of boarding is clarified when the assets of fam-ilies serving boarders are compared with those of the other families within the same occupational classification (Table 24). Miners' families in both towns held similar amounts of real estate whether or not they took in boarders. In both towns, artisan and business families with boarders were likelier than those without to hold between $100 and $1,000 in real property; in Nevada City the advantage of having boarders, while not as strong as in Grass Valley, also extended to families with over $1,000 in real estate. No occupational group was so secure that it could ignore the profits gained by keeping boarders. But boarding and, therefore, women's contributions tended to be most important to the families of small merchants, less prominent attorneys, less established artisans, families with less than $1,000 in real property. Here the woman's help seemed vital in taking the first upward step into property ownership or perhaps in keeping a small enterprise afloat. Women's work also seemed indispensable for the small group of miners' families (to judge from the large proportion in Grass Valley with lodgers) not to advance, but to endure hard times and low wages.

There were also unrelated boarders in the households of well-to-do merchants and professionals, especially in Nevada City, even among the most prosperous family men (Table 25). It could be argued that here women functioned not so much to support the family economically as to transmit its values and respectability to the single men it sheltered. In such cases the traditional roles, not traditional skills, were what mattered. The wife of a merchant, for example, by providing for respectable boarders, could extend her influence and the influence of the family neighborhoods. And in some cases this obviously did occur; merchant families accommodated clerks, lawyers' homes sheltered law students, and craftsmen's wives cared for apprentices. Grass Valley mine developer Edwin Morse entered into several business deals with the man in whose house he boarded, and finally married his host's daughter. Nevada City lawyer Thomas Caswell's household, on the other hand, included, in addition to a servant, a bookkeeper who may have worked for Caswell and a miner who probably did not. Caswell and his miner were typical; for most, even among the merchant and professional families of Nevada City, accepting boarders was less a matter of social control than of income.[18]

Most boarders in businessmen's and artisans' households could not (to tell from their occupations) have been the partners or employees of the host, and their ages suggest that they were not dependents of the host family. Among miners' households, the great majority of lodgers were themselves miners, whose exact work relationship with the host would be impossible to determine. But the number of households involved and, again, the reasonably close approximation in age between boarder and male head of household—guests and hosts were similar men—suggest that these men paid rent, not homage to family ideals.

Women's work thus occupied a reasonably definable position in the two towns' social structure. While almost no seamstresses or dressmakers were married to professional men, wives among the most prestigious groups in the towns provided for boarders; a woman and her family would not lose caste if she used domestic skills to help the family by taking outsiders into the household. Single men boarded with families in both towns' vaunted neighborhoods, under the eyes of the elite occupational classes. A reputable woman could not easily leave the home, but the home and "homemaking" could be used for the economic betterment of the family. This had been true since the first women arrived in the camps, and in part this survival from the Gold Rush was linked to another; the overwhelmingly male mining society produced obvious demands for domestic skills. But still another persistent condition in the towns—economic instability—was more basic. As long as men's work remained uncertain and the towns poor compared to the rest of the country, women would work, usually by taking in boarders.

The relative poverty of the two towns, including their middle classes, was also apparent in the use of servants. Middle-class families nationally could be nearly defined by the presence of servants, and certainly no mythology of frontier democracy retarded their use in the two mining towns. Newspaper complaints of the shortage of suitable servants hint at the prestige involved and suggest a reason for the increasing employment of Chinese males to join the Irish girls more commonly hired in the East, but the laments also imply that servants had a very practical role in towns where so many women had boarders. Compared to middle-class Eastern communities, the towns contained few servants (Table 26): in Grass Valley in 1860, 3 percent of family households had live-in help, in Nevada City 8 percent. But in Nevada City, where boarders were present at all occupational and property levels, 11 percent of the houses with boarders had resident servants (Table 27). Naturally, middle-class families were most likely to have hired help; in Grass Valley all of the households that contained servants reported real property of over $1,000, and in Nevada City eight of ten did so (Table 26). In Nevada City, while the numbers of households with servants and their limited distribution across occupational and property lines reflect the desire for prestige in a town that prided itself on its respectable character, they also suggest the need for help in a town where boarding was economically important. Respectable ladies with boarders at least had some expectation of professional help. In Grass Valley there were too few servants to support any generalizations.

When one subtracts the number of households headed by women, as well as those that included boarders, live-in help, and dependent relatives, from the total number of white households including women in the towns in 1860, only 45 percent of Grass Valley households that contained women were families composed solely of parents and children, as were only 49 percent in Nevada City. And when all living units are considered, only 9 percent of the households in Grass Valley and 17 percent in Nevada City contained simple families. Practical considerations—rent from lodgers or assistance for working wives—went a long way in determining the composition of households. Families could symbolize affluence, perhaps, although it is not clear whether they were the product or producer of a man's success; what is certain is that their connection with prosperity did not arise primarily out of creating "associations of home" for Grass Valley and Nevada City men.

The depression in the mining industry perpetuated much of the old miners' society with its transience and entertainments; it also allowed economic interests to shape households. Observers saw both results as menaces to children. The fears of the "evil influences" of mining camp life current in the mid-1850's surfaced again in the apprehension that boys and girls might be induced to grow up too soon, acquiring adult vices. Segregation could not sanitize the towns, and no one claimed they were gentle moral environments. But editors found town poverty even more worrisome, because less avoidable; they warned that youth would take a precocious interest in money because of the sometimes frantic economic atmosphere in the towns. Anyone in Grass Valley and Nevada City around 1860 lived constantly with the fact of depression, the subject of making money, and arguments over ways to ensure the future. Boarders brought these concerns within the circle of the family. Editorial misgivings seemed justified by the boys who were caught robbing flumes, or the boys sent to reform school after being caught stealing iron stoves, breaking them up, and selling them to the Nevada Foundry. But editors also stressed a more insidious, even socially acceptable threat to children: that they might quit school or their parents might remove them and put them to work. The newspapers showed little concern over and no understanding of the real economic role of many women in the towns, but they knew that family needs during the hard times might shape children's lives by depriving them of school training, both practical and moral. Evidently one reason the children's clubs and celebrations received so much newspaper emphasis was that their very existence reassured citizens that "real" childhoods, innocent and unsullied, were possible in the mining towns.[19]

There can be no doubt that a child would be constantly exposed to its family's economic function. Married women had children whether they worked or not; in both towns, women who cared for boarders tended to have only slightly smaller families than women who simply "kept house" (Table 28). Given the frequency of homes with boarders, this means that about half the towns' children lived with unrelated people and were accustomed to the idea that they shared the household for financial reasons. And their mothers, who used "women's skills" to help their families, had in addition the responsibilities toward children taken for granted by society. If mothers commonly had dual roles, why would not the children also be expected to take up part of the family financial burden?

But little evidence in the census records connects women's work and children's work in the two camps. The populations of the towns were young, and most families with children had only one or two, who were too young to have jobs. So relatively few children were listed as working in the census of 1860 (Table 29). In each town, less than 10 percent were employed while living at home, and there was little meaningful difference between those whose mothers worked and those whose did not. Obviously in households where boarders stayed, children's duties may have related more directly to family finances than their usual chores, but they did not work outside the home in disproportionate numbers. There simply were not jobs for children; the mining industry had no places for girls and very few for boys. Maternal occupations did not noticeably affect children's school attendance, either. There were no consistent differences, in proportions of children in school, between households where women kept house and where they took in boarders; children were not held from school to help at home. In both cases—boarders or none—and in both towns, the majority of the children were not in school; in Nevada City, where boarding was important among the middle classes, families with boarders were slightly more likely to have children in school. Working mothers do not seem to have impaired the protective, child-rearing function of the family, which may be one reason why women's work was acceptable.

The father's economic status, likewise, usually did not determine family views on childhood. Although family size differed somewhat with the father's occupation (Table 30), there was little correlation between his occupation and the proportion of his children in school (Table 31). In both towns, miners' children were at least as likely to have attended school in the past year as children of merchants and professionals. Family property holdings also were poorly correlated with the proportion of children attending classes (Table 32). Families that reported no real property had fewer children, and lower proportions of children in school, than propertied groups; but at the same time, families with less than $1,000 in real estate were likelier to have children in school than those with over $1,000, even though the more well-to-do had more children. The wealthier families obviously had no special commitment to education. There was little connection between the father's occupation and child labor. As one might suspect, the children of miners more commonly held jobs than the children of businessmen or artisans, but the degree of difference was not great enough to suggest a real difference in attitudes toward children and work and was not nearly enough to reflect the greater need of mining families (Table 31). There was also no consistent correlation between the family's amount of real property and the likelihood that a child would list an occupation; in Grass Valley, families with over $1,000 were most likely to have a child working and in Nevada City, those with under $1,000. In neither town were those with no real property the likeliest to have working children (Table 32). The same general result holds for personal property holdings. The relationships, then, of family wealth and parental occupations to a child's work or school attendance suggest that families of all classes shared similar attitudes toward children. Boys might drink and swear, but economic necessities did not seem to be depriving them of a normal childhood.

The Gold Rush necessarily survived in the two hard-pressed mining towns, but the simultaneous sense that attitudes toward schooling, lodgers, and children's work were held in common across occupational lines could help quiet fears. Townspeople duly noted the harsh realities of mining life, but with children, families, and neighborhoods seemingly safe through segregation, these realities could be tolerated. Most men lived outside families, and the families themselves had been shaped by poverty and depression. Still, the editors who had celebrated their establishment were essentially right. Traditional family values prevailed in Grass Valley and Nevada City.

The Foreign Presence

Peace prevailed between ethnic groups during the hard times, just as it did between classes. By 1860, some groups who had seemed fearsome to the native-born had virtually disappeared. References to "greasers" still occasionally appeared in print, but few Hispanics still lived in the towns, and the term "Sidney Duck" was an anachronism. The facts that all suffered from the depression and that the foreign-born could gain prestigious jobs and wealth usually maintained economic concord. And the white foreign-born seemed to have the same commitment to family, stability, and prosperity as the American-born. At a time when the foreign-born were beginning to dominate the towns numerically, tensions between them and the natives relaxed. Among whites, shared beliefs could help keep the peace, and with other races, segregation would be enough to accomplish the same end.

The surviving Nisenan posed no threat to white communities that had long since reduced them to dependence. Peace was secure enough in the late 1850's that Waite of the *Journal* and Roberts of the *National* could solemnly and safely agree that California Indian wars were nothing more than "schemes to plunder" and that in nine-tenths of the disputes, whites were at fault.[20] Attitudes toward the Chinese, often lumped with the Nisenan as harmless inferiors, served more clearly as a barometer of white social disquiet; the Chinese were always vulnerable, as the expulsion from Nevada City in 1858 proved, but were usually left alone. The characteristics of the Chinese populations in the towns did not change (Table 33). The census of 1860 shows nearly all the inhabitants of both Chinatowns to have been young male miners and lists only five possible families and only three children. The few Chinese women were not identified by occupation, but their living arrangements, several women living together in one house or with one man, would suggest that many were prostitutes, as whites would have taken for granted. At best, few Chinese lived in ways acceptable to the white majority; the threat to white morality perceived in the mid-1850's had not been dissipated by changes in Chinese living patterns. But emotions clearly had cooled, primarily because of the confinement of the Chinese to the Chinatowns, and the grudging acceptance by whites that some sections of town would be Chinese territory.

The Chinatowns themselves had changed little in outward appearance and were still indistinguishable from the white slums that surrounded them, but they had developed a greater variety of traditional Chinese social institutions to serve their inhabitants. To whites, the Chinatowns were the abode of alien institutions, especially later in the 1860's when whites became aware of the importance of the regional companies in Chinese community life. More importantly, they were slum areas, noisome centers of crime and vice, but not dangerous if they were confined to one area of town. Citizens complained about noise emanating from the Chinese quarter, especially at the Chinese New Year when "the night was made hideous by the incessant rattle of firecrackers." Newspapers repeated continual accusations of odor pollution: "Their homes, if that sacred name can be degraded to mean the abode of a Chinaman, are surrounded with all the stenches that animal or vegetable decomposition can produce." Whites identified the Chinatowns with the health hazards of dirt, refuse, and overcrowding, but cleanup campaigns allayed fears of plagues, and disease never became an important issue between the races.[21]

Anti-Chinese feeling throughout most of the decade focused on crime. Burglary replaced gambling or prostitution as the most common accusation; any unsolved crime was routinely blamed on the Chinese, who were considered innately larcenous. Racial contempt helped influence whites to treat Chinese crime differently from that of other ethnic groups; Chinese caught pilfering were commonly administered corporal punishment on the spot. And since a few white officials claimed that some Chinese preferred jail to trying to find work during the winter when mining was closed, alternative punishments—primarily cutting queues—were used, and the whipping post was advocated, for Chinese only. Chinese crime was seen as an annoyance, not a major disruption of white society. The only serious crime against whites was stealing gold dust, and whites knew that the Chinese rarely offered them violence except in self-defense. An important part of the towns' image of the Chinese showed them as timid, easily frightened, and passive. Although the Chinese commonly did repulse robberies and assaults, the belief that they were cowardly reduced, in white eyes, the potential danger of crime originating in Chinatown. The white community treated Chinese criminals with more disdain than fear, never considering them as potentially dangerous as the "Spanish" had once been; no vigilantes moved against Chinese bandits. On the other hand, white officials never recognized, as they did in regard to other ethnic groups, that Chinese unemployment resulting from dependence on seasonal placer mining might underlie the petty theft that whites identified as characteristically Chinese. They saw Chinatown as a vice-ridden, dirty eyesore, but not as desperately poor or overtly dangerous to whites, unless they entered the Chinese districts looking for trouble.[22]

In the 1860's, then, most whites accepted or were resigned to the presence of the Chinatowns, but when there was any attempt to expand them, to buy or rebuild in areas outside the downtown slums, whites resisted. In 1860, when the "Celestial population began to colonize" in a Nevada City district previously occupied solely by white merchants, a building the Chinese erected was torn down and when rebuilt, torn down again with the implicit approval of the white population. At least one other attempt to expand met the same response. Although Chinese were not physically assaulted in these incidents, editors made it obvious that extralegal activity to keep the Chinatowns penned in one area was acceptable to the white business community. Newspaper reactions echoed the amused "boys will be boys" tone used for the raids of the mid-1850's on Chinese brothels. Public opinion would not approve gratuitous assaults on Chinese, but keeping them in their place was commendable.[23]

During these years, increased contacts between whites and Chinese also helped reduce tensions. One source of interaction was increased employment of Chinese domestic workers, especially those few who lived in white homes and businesses, as most did who lived outside the Chinatowns. Perhaps more important was the beginning of social relations between the Chinese community leaders and their white counterparts. The Chinese merchant elite initiated these meetings, apparently as part of a deliberate attempt to defend their own interests by promoting peace. Several banquets were given by the Chinese to white business and political leaders during the 1860's; they were attended by men only, white families were not involved, and the whites did not reciprocate with invitations to their homes. The guests, particularly newspaper editors, responded by publicizing previously unknown and favorable aspects of their hosts' culture. Whites, however, carefully distinguished merchants from the rest in the Chinatowns; descriptions of cultured merchants coexisted with stereotypical references to Chinese crime. In one instance a merchant, Ah Sing, had been murdered while trying to stop a fight between a drunken white and a Chinese prostitute. His funeral was well covered by the Nevada City press, which eulogized him as a "worthy and valuable citizen" who knew English and had a great and good influence on his countrymen, acquainting them with American laws and customs. But the account of his funeral also noted the presence of his wife with other women considered his concubines and condemned his marital arrangements. Some cultural gaps could not be bridged, and even though the newspapers mentioned merchants' wives and even suggested that some Chinese had "real" families, they were still usually contemptuous of Chinese women. Chinese merchants, as individuals, could win respect and could clear up white misconceptions and gain powerful acquaintances, but they could not raise the estimation of their poorer compatriots among whites, nor change the common image of Chinese women. And all their efforts had to take place in the Chinatowns.[24]

Blacks, separated less by culture from the white society but more by race, occupied in many ways a similar place in the towns. They came to public attention usually when they were in trouble: brawling in dives, being tried for theft, caught in adultery. Some blacks were the targets of boyish and not-so-boyish pranks; one "child-like" old alcoholic was temporarily driven out of Nevada City by children taking advantage of his credulity. Later, he died when someone mixed croton oil into his whiskey. The color line was carefully drawn; 84 percent of Grass Valley's black population lived in one area near Chinatown, and while Nevada City's smaller black population was not as narrowly distributed, "Aristocracy Hollow," Manzanita Ravine at the foot of Aristocracy Hill, contained several black homes and saloons. Segregation of facilities was taken for granted; the *Journal* held up to ridicule a hotel-keeper who had rushed to convince the agent of a touring minstrel company to board them at his place, only to find that they were black, not blackface performers. Churches were separate as were most social events, although disorderly whites sometimes made their appearance at formal black affairs and in black dives, and white ministers might take part in black religious gatherings. Some celebrations were uniquely black; in the early 1860's there were annual commemorations of the anniversary of emancipation in the British West Indies. But most public, nonreligious meetings involving blacks also had white participants, such as the Republican churchmen present at Emancipation commemorations after 1863.[25]

The structure of the segregated black community resembled that of its white counterpart. Most blacks lived in cabins in groups of two to five young, single men. A somewhat higher proportion of black men were married than of whites (Table 34), even though most were unskilled laborers (Table 9). Although black families took in boarders less often than whites, black women were likelier than white women to be listed in other occupations such as seamstress or washwoman (Table 35). Without boarders and servants, black families tended to be simpler in structure than those of their white contemporaries. Black children found little opportunity in the towns; the few young blacks were excluded from the schools and evidently were not hired at menial or part-time jobs. Family structure, then, in the main, belied the reputation for loose living

imputed to blacks; in appearance they hewed closer to the orthodox national values of the time than the whites in the two mining
towns. There was also more interracial contact than some whites
were comfortable with, and not always on white terms. Segregation was not absolute; blacks were partially diffused throughout white areas, especially in Nevada City, some as live-in cooks
or handymen, others living alone in white areas. At least two miners lived in houses or barracks with white miners, and there were
two interracial couples in 1860. But in the main, like the Chinese, blacks were limited by segregation and stereotyping. They
were imprisoned, if protected in a way, by the compartmentalized
society.

The white foreign-born, mostly Cornish, Irish, and German, still
maintained separate identities in the two towns. Stereotypical ethnic images—sly Jews, brawling Irishmen, clannish Cornishmen—
had not dimmed. And as the numbers and wealth of the foreign-
born increased, distinct ethnic organizations began to function:
B'nai B'rith for Jews, Wallace Monument Clubs for Scots, Gesäng-
verein for Germans. Cornish wrestling meets and commemorations
in 1859 of Burns's and Schiller's centenaries shared newspaper
space with accounts of the High Holy Days, Chinese New Year,
and St. Patrick's Day—all visible evidence of the cultural diversity
of the towns. Cultural differences and prejudices still led to violence. Irish and Americans shot it out over mining claims at least
once, and the Irish fought pitched battles with both Cornish and
Germans. One man drunk enough and fool enough to shout that he
could lick any Irishman in the house in an Allison Ranch saloon was
beaten to death. At the same time, there were conscious efforts to
promote understanding and good relations. The particular festivals
of each people, like those of the Chinese, served to educate Americans about its beliefs and practices, or at least to build bridges
between groups. Editors were invited to Jewish rites, even the
family ritual of circumcision. The German Glee Club sang at public events, and the men of both towns turned out for the Cornish
wrestling. And St. Patrick's Day acquired a new atmosphere as in
1862 and 1863 drinking and politicking took a back seat to the
religious aspects of the holiday, provoking Warren Ewer of the
National to comment on the respectability of the Irish portion of
the towns.[26]

It was no accident that the most publicized of the ethnic rituals often were family-oriented. Possibly the most important reason for the calm between Americans and European-born was that all the major white ethnic groups seemed to share the basic family values that they believed conducive to town prosperity. The white ethnics had slightly greater proportions of married men than the American-born (Table 36). Even the Irish, of all white groups least able to penetrate the professions, had a higher percentage of married men than did the natives. The difference in rates of marriage between American-born and foreign-born was not great. Most of the foreign-born, like most natives, still lived as single men with other men, but at the least, living patterns looked roughly the same among all white groups and outwardly suggested shared values.

Ethnic households took the same basic shapes as those of the American-born. In Grass Valley, accepting boarders was most common among the Irish, and more common among the English (mostly Cornish) than among American-born (Table 37). The Germans were the least likely to have boarders. In Nevada City, where boarding was more common, differences among ethnic groups were smaller, and the Nevada City Germans, unlike those of Grass Valley, commonly had lodgers in their homes. The practice of boarding, then, was more closely tied to the towns' economic structure than to ethnicity; in Grass Valley, mine families, and therefore Cornish and Irish, took in boarders, but in Nevada City, where storekeepers and professionals took in miners, clerks, and law students, the merchant-oriented Germans often took lodgers into their homes (Table 38).

The foreign-born who were married and living with families resembled their American-born compeers in numbers (Table 39) and other particulars, although in both towns the American-born were overrepresented at the top of the property hierarchy. German families had approximately the same quantity of property as the American-born, while the Irish had considerably less (Table 40). English families kept pace with natives in Grass Valley but not in Nevada City. Although among all males the American-born held an edge in occupational prestige, foreign-born men with families approximated native ones in job status. In Grass Valley, where the American-born made up 42 percent of the male population, they headed 40 percent of the merchant and professional families; British men made up 20 percent of the working population and headed 32 percent of the middle-class families, while the proportions among Germans were 3 percent and 16 percent respectively. Only the Irish lagged in this respect, as would be expected. Among married men, a slightly higher proportion of British than American were professionals and merchants, and among the German-born the proportion was twice as great as among the American-born. In Nevada City, where they were a smaller part of the general population, foreign-born families were not as occupationally successful. American-born men constituted 54 percent of the working men and 64 percent of the heads of merchant families. The Germans made up a disproportionate number of middle-class families, as usual, while the English lagged (their hard-rock management skills were less important here) so that the Irish proportionately had as many middle-class families as they did.* In Nevada City, where county court business helped create a native professional elite, about one-third of all middle-class families had foreign-born heads, and in Grass Valley, where the foreign-born dug and developed quartz gold, they were as likely to be middle class as American families.

The well-to-do households of the foreign-born resembled in structure those of wealthy native families. As a general rule, American-born merchant and professional families were likelier to contain boarders than families of the foreign-born, except that in Nevada City, German merchant families were just as likely as natives to have boarders and the tiny group of Irish merchant families more so. Well-to-do American-born families were slightly more likely to have servants and provable relatives in their households than the foreign-born, but again, the small difference does not suggest any opposition of values.† In sum, the families of the

---

* In Grass Valley, the Irish supplied 22 percent of the male population and 12 percent of the middle-class families. In Nevada City, the British supplied 12 percent of the working males and 4 percent of the middle-class families, the Irish 7 percent of the working males and 4 percent of the middle-class families, and the Germans 7 percent of the working males and 18 percent of the middle-class families.

† In Grass Valley, 55 percent of the American, 31 percent of the British, 33 percent of the Irish, and 12 percent of the German merchant and professional households contained boarders; in Nevada City, 43 percent of the American, 25 percent of the British, 75 percent of the Irish, and 50 percent of the German did so. The small number of families, especially the British in Nevada City and the Irish in both towns, make these figures at best only suggestive. In Nevada City, 16 percent of the American-born families with more than $1,000 in real estate had servants; 12 percent of similar foreign-born families did so. As usual, German families in this category, 21 percent of whom had servants, were the exception. There were too few servants in Grass Valley in 1860 for the figures to have any value.

white foreign-born seem to have been somewhat more well-to-do and traditional in appearance in Grass Valley than the native families and somewhat less so in Nevada City, a situation that reflects the foreign-born's relative economic importance in each town. And certainly, in neither town were their families so different from the American-born as to pose any possible outward threat.

Attitudes toward children, as reflected in family structures, also followed no obvious ethnic lines. There were no really consistent differences in family size between groups (Table 39). Most mothers of all nationalities were in their twenties and thirties, so the similarity in numbers of children cannot be explained by the argument that the foreign-born women, with the possible exception of the Irish, were younger than the American-born but had a higher birthrate.* As a matter of fact the Irish had smaller families than the British in each town. The well-to-do had more children than those reporting no real property (Table 40), so possibly the size of Irish families reflected poverty. And ethnicity, like paternal occupation and wealth, did not affect schooling. In Grass Valley, no consistent difference between the American- and foreign-born showed itself in the number of children in school; the same holds true of Nevada City, where the absence of Catholic schools in 1860 might be expected to have reduced the numbers of Irish children being educated. Since all families, native- and foreign-born, were roughly the same size and had members roughly similar in age, similar numbers of children in school suggest a similar commitment to education. Ethnicity apparently made little difference, either, in attitudes toward child labor.† Slightly fewer children worked in Nevada City than in Grass Valley, but in either town the Irish children seemed no more likely to work than the children of

---

* In Grass Valley, 68 percent of all married women were between 20 and 40, 82 percent of the British, 72 percent of the Irish, 60 percent of the German, and 61 percent of the American. In Nevada City, 79 percent of all married women were between 20 and 40, 66 percent of the British, 80 percent of the Irish, 84 percent of the German, and 82 percent of the American.

† In Grass Valley, 25 percent of the American, 25 percent of the British, 22 percent of the Irish, and 13 percent of the German families had one or more children in school. In Nevada City, 28 percent of the American, 32 percent of the British, 31 percent of the Irish, and 15 percent of the German families had children in school. In Grass Valley, 6 percent of the American families, 9 percent of the British, 3 percent of the Irish, and none of the German had children listed with jobs. In Nevada City, 3 percent of the American families, 11 percent of the British, 3 percent of the Irish, and 3 percent of the German had children employed.

proportionately wealthier German- or American-born men. The British were the exception; in both towns their children were somewhat more likely to be listed as employed. The amount of real property held by the father also made little difference.

The similarities in the family structures of the European- and American-born, and the occupational status and financial success of some of the white ethnics, opened the family neighborhoods of the two towns to them. Both Nevada City and, less clearly, Grass Valley developed complex forms of social and spatial segregation based in part on wealth (Aristocracy Hill), in part on race (China Street), and also in part on family respectability (Piety Hill). The blacks and the Chinese who were racially distinct, poor, and stereotyped as immoral, were kept apart although servants, cooks, and very occasionally a skilled craftsman might live among whites. Other ethnic groups were not segregated; if few Irish lived on Piety Hill, few Nevada City Irish were professionals or merchants. Few areas, surprisingly few in view of the numbers of Irish and Cornish and their mutual enmity, had definite white ethnic identities, the obvious exception being the Allison Ranch district of Grass Valley. Marriage, wealth, and occupational status were better predictors of where a white man might live than ethnicity and even these criteria were not absolute; some propertyless, single miners lived on Aristocracy Hill.[27]

Other factors obviously entered into the economic and social concord of the late 1850's and early 1860's. As long as the Cornish supplied necessary mining expertise and Irish Democrats voted *en bloc*, overt attacks on them would remain unlikely. As long as Chinese and blacks "stayed in their place," attacks on them would seem unnecessary. Still, the foreign-born's access to business and professional status was central. Economic success and the creation of families meant that the middle-class foreign-born could live respectably within the family neighborhoods, and could share in their reputation and their protective functions.

Only once during these years did ethnic differences between American and foreign families receive an airing. The crisis was precipitated in April 1859, when an unsuccessful candidate for a teaching post in Nevada City named Stratton charged that he had not been hired because he wanted to use the Bible in class, contrary to the wishes of the school commissioners. D. A. Dryden, the minister of the Nevada City Methodist Episcopal Church, which, led by trustee Aaron Sargent, had been at the heart of mid-1850's reform, intruded himself on Stratton's side, making accusations basically anti-Catholic in import, demanding the teaching of credos he saw as specifically Protestant and American, and in effect invoking the worst tendency in the town's reform tradition: the imposition of the views of part of the population on all others. In the course of the controversy, it was also claimed that the female teacher hired at the same time was a Catholic. Despite hints of "Jesuitical intrigue," and Dryden's insistence that America was a Protestant republic, the Catholic teacher was not removed. Ianthus J. Rolfe, the school commissioner most under attack, defended secular education and argued that it would be a "gross outrage" to prescribe "religious qualifications for teachers." As a Democratic party chieftain and as publisher of the *Democrat*, he could marshal partisan, particularly Irish, support for his cause. Jews also had a stake in the affair; Irish political and Jewish economic importance probably contributed largely to the outcome. In the end, the Bible remained available in class to those who wanted to use it, Stratton remained unemployed, and although it was obvious that the Protestant majority assumed that its values would dominate the schools, there was also some recognition of Catholic and Jewish rights. Dryden emerged from the battle with the anonymous epithet, "Calvinist roaster of unbelievers."[28]

Toleration triumphed, but the Stratton affair reinforced the lessons of the Irish mill strike and Nevada City's expulsion of the Chinese in 1858. If the conditions that maintained peace were to break down, the potential for conflict across occupational and ethnic lines still existed. And as the fate of the Clampers, the Hurdy Gurdies, and the Chinese houses in the "wrong" section of town attested, the middle class was willing to defend itself.

PART III

TOWNS DIVIDED
BY QUARTZ

1863-1870

Quartz Comes of Age

THE RISE OF INDUSTRIAL TOWNS

In the mid- and late-1860's the long-awaited boom in quartz arrived, bringing unprecedented economic stability, but also revolutionizing social and work relationships in both towns. Centered in a half-dozen mines in Grass Valley township, the quartz industry made Grass Valley predominant in population and gold production and widened ethnic and occupational differences between the two towns. It also completed two processes operative since the first discoveries on Deer and Wolf Creeks: the progressive sophistication of mining technology and the separation of mines and towns. The highly industrialized quartz mines generated a mine population of wage earners, both skilled and unskilled. Small-scale mining, except among the Chinese, largely disappeared. The largest mines were the foci of employee settlements peopled by the Cornish and Irish, who supplied the bulk of the new mine forces. This resulted in a new, *de facto* occupational and ethnic segregation. The influx in the late 1860's of mine labor, usually Cornish, meant that white ethnics tended to become concentrated at the lower levels of job prestige, and that gaps in wealth and status reinforced ethnic identity and residence to divide the foreign-born from the native-born. And as the mines became heavily capitalized corporate entities, ownership shifted to San Francisco, New York, even Paris. Locals enriched by quartz often left town, and townsmen, with notable exceptions, no longer had important investments in the mines. Alien in ownership and work force, supporting settlements separate spatially and occupationally, industrial quartz mining heightened divisions between town and townships as well as between Grass Valley and Nevada City.

The Quartz Boom

While most of the nation suffered through war and rebuilding, in Grass Valley the long-delayed expectations of quartz wealth finally were fulfilled; in the mid and late 1860's the town was easily the most important gold producer in California. Nevada City's placer and revived quartz works barely maintained its 1860 population, but even stasis was remarkable in a state where most gold towns were decaying. Among California's mining counties, only Nevada gained residents during the 1860's; Grass Valley quartz had been responsible for the bulk of this increase. Grass Valley mining had begun to free itself from depression in the summer of 1863, even though the drought was still disrupting most placer operations. In essence, the resurgence of production came with the successful opening of four quartz leads—one in 1863 and three in 1864—long known but inefficiently worked. The investors behind this upsurge in mine development, men like Jules Fricot, André Chavanne, William and David Watt, Edward and John C. Coleman, Miles P. O'Connor, and Thomas Findley, had in almost all cases been established locally for several years, although evidently some of the capital involved was newly raised in San Francisco and New York. The chlorination process that reduced gold sulfides effectively enough to make the refractory ores of these leads pay had been successfully modified for Grass Valley mineral conditions by Maltman and Deetken in Nevada City in 1860; by 1864 Grass Valley contained two chlorination works. And in 1862 an iron foundry capable of fabricating some of the equipment necessary for deep-shaft mining was opened in Grass Valley. The stock crash that ended the speculative glory years of the Comstock Lode rerouted workers with important experience back to Nevada County and redirected part of the flow of investment to the quartz industry, but the developers, the companies, much of the technology, and the important mining sites were already part of Grass Valley mining.[1]

The Eureka, the first mine to boom, had been worked intermittently and with mixed success since 1851, when it had been located during the town's first quartz excitement; the company responsible for the strike in 1863, organized by the Frenchmen Fricot, Ripert, and Pralus, had owned the site since 1857. During 1863, the owners sank a new deep shaft, aided by Comstock-trained expertise in underground work and by additional financing from the Watt brothers. The new shaft opened up a very rich lead in the winter of 1863, and the following spring the mine was in full production, with immediate repercussions on the town's economy. At the Massachusetts Hill Mine, where Michael Brennan had failed to find gold and been driven to murder and suicide, the Watts and their partners had been working since 1860 on a lease from Chavanne. Brennan's old employers, the Mt. Hope Company, tied up work in 1862 and 1863 with a suit against Chavanne, which since it halted one of the steadiest producers of gold in the early 1860's may have hurt Grass Valley as much as the drought, but Chavanne won in court in June 1863. Work recommenced in November 1863, and in April 1864 the Watts struck the gold ledge that had eluded Brennan. On Lafayette Hill, the Coleman brothers had bought the old French Lead in 1860 and renamed it the North Star. They started sinking a new deep shaft in 1862, and like the Watts reached the ledge in 1864. The Empire Company had worked on Ophir Hill with reasonably steady returns since 1852. In July 1864, the company reorganized, brought in new San Francisco money, and commenced more thoroughgoing, technologically advanced, and profitable operations. In all four mines only the shafts, using techniques from Comstock mining, and some of the capital, from San Francisco, were new.[2]

The year 1864 was one of massive resurgence in Grass Valley mining and 1865 the year of a full-fledged quartz craze, an excitement not seen since the collapse of 1852. Nevada City was affected as well with a speculative enthusiasm that seemed to bring back the flush times. Everyone, as William Beggs of the *Daily Gazette* put it, seemed to "talk quartz, dream quartz, eat quartz, drink quarts." Miners, many from the Comstock country, rushed back to Grass Valley, small operators searched for new leads all over the township, and smaller, already known ledges began to be reworked with new hope. The township areas around the large works filled up with the cabins of wage miners; the Massachusetts Hill mine above Boston Ravine generated an expansion that made the settlement contiguous to Grass Valley proper, although under a separate town jurisdiction. Grass Valley citizens and journalists, often complacent in the past about town government, now demonstrated a civic consciousness previously more evident in Nevada City, a spirit that blended pride with demands for immediate improvement.

But the new prosperity and accompanying expansion, while revolutionizing the town economy, did not seem to change the townspeople's self-image. In 1865, editors still employed the same images of family, home, and village they had always used to describe life in Grass Valley. New wealth had maintained apparent peace; in good times, town streets were virtually empty during the day, as the men were underground, and steady wages allowed some miners to bring in their families. Outside observers Ross Browne and John Hittell recorded what boosters had argued all along, that the quartz industry brought with it a unique stability, and editors boasted that theirs was the quietest as well as the richest of all California mountain towns.[3]

Obviously, not all was peace and prosperity in Grass Valley; the greatest success lay with a handful of the largest concerns. Independent miner Edwin Morse, working on the Essex Mine on Mill Street in the heart of town, profited little from the quartz excitement, despite sinking a shaft that ran under the street for some distance. No major new leads turned up, and some of the overflow of miners hopelessly turned to working the sites of old cabins for gold lost there by previous tenants. Grass Valley began to be plagued by ledge jumpers, described by John Rollin Ridge in the *National* as men who never worked until they heard of a new strike and then, rushing to the site, claimed prior work on the lead and threatened suit unless bought off. The same thing occurred on a large scale as unsuccessful companies sued successful ones, and litigation at one time or another idled nearly all of the largest operations in the township. But in the main, the quartz business went smoothly. In 1865, editor William S. Byrne counted 19 quartz mills and 38 dividend-paying mines in Grass Valley, and estimated for his town directory that the population had risen over 2,000 since 1860 to 6,000, of whom 2,500 were men working in one way or another in quartz mining. He also illuminated an important result of the quartz boom in reckoning that 1,500 of these men were employed by the large companies. On the assessment rolls, the value of real and personal property liable for taxation in Grass

Valley passed that in Nevada City in 1865, and that year Nevada County claimed larger incomes for its fortunate sons than any other California county except San Francisco. The highest incomes reported were those of major quartz operators. Estimates of annual gold production in the towns ranged from $2 to $4 million. In October 1865, a portent of the towns' economic future appeared, as San Francisco capitalists, attracted by such sums, bought out the Eureka for $400,000 paid in gold coin. And in November, after a boiler explosion that killed a woman living near a mill, W. H. Miller of the *Union* bitterly condemned the "numerous deaths" caused by carelessness or ignorance because companies insisted on hiring incompetents "who will work at low wages." The quartz boom had brought not only wealth and employment but also outside ownership, a hazardous new technology, and a usually submerged distrust of the motives of mine owners.[4]

Like Grass Valley, Nevada City was usually peaceful; the word editors commonly used to describe conditions was "dull." For most of 1864, Nevada City newspapers could only report with envy the resurrection of Grass Valley while the drought continued to grip their own township's hydraulic operators and agriculture. Much of the business community's capital was tied up in rebuilding and restocking after the fire of 1863, and vacant lots and shells of buildings still bore witness to how close Nevada City had come to failure. Editors noted as a hopeful sign the influx of miners from the Comstock country, but the decline of the silver district also meant the decline of the trans-Sierra commerce; hopes that spring trade across the mountains would restore prosperity remained unfulfilled. Nevada City remained in "impecunious circumstances" well into 1865. Quartz mania spread to Nevada City, but although major town investors such as George Washington Kidd helped reopen the old Banner Mine and the older Gold Tunnel, no mine achieved a breakthrough in production comparable to those at the Eureka and the Massachusetts Hill leads. Still, everyone had "quartz on the brain"; even businessmen, fleeing the merchandising recession that lingered into 1865 in both towns, hopefully scaled the hills in search of ledges. But the quartz excitement did not change Nevada City's basic economic dependencies; as good weather in late 1864 revived agriculture and allowed placer mining to return to full production, Nevada City began to shake off the doldrums, armed now with a hard-won recognition that "fortunes are not made in a single day, nor do buildings arise by magic."[5]

During the second half of the 1860's, the long process of the industrialization of both quartz and hydraulic mining came to a fruition in the two towns, creating foreign-born majorities and new occupational structures. There had been a gradual development in these directions since the discovery of the coyote and quartz leads, but the postwar quartz boom accelerated this change so that industrial mining and the foreign-born populations became the most important and most visible components in town life. Eighteen-sixty-six was the pivotal year in completing this process. It was a good year for most of the major quartz concerns, although by the end of the year the Watts' Massachusetts Hill claims had been worked out and the Allison Ranch, troubled by management problems and obsolete mining techniques, had halted production. That year Grass Valley produced not less than $2,000,000 in gold, of which the Eureka yielded almost $600,000, the Empire $175,000, the North Star over $315,000, and the Allison Ranch $200,000, despite its difficulties and a production year truncated in October. There was a "big splurge in quartz equipment"; Marcellus Deal reported in the *Transcript* that all sorts of new, expensive systems were being "flacked and tried." Probably the most important technical advance was the construction, supervised by G. F. Deetken, of an improved chlorination works for the Eureka. But while 1866 was a productive year for the major concerns, it was a time of thinning out among the small quartz operations called into existence by the enthusiasm of 1865. The quartz business in both towns had been "overdone." Many speculators failed to find purchasers for the "two or three new discoveries" reported daily, and lacking capital to develop the ledges on their own, watched their claims fall to sheriff's sales. Miller of the *Union* argued that the excitement had been "unhealthy," but the cure, the demise of the wildcatters, accelerated the concentration of gold production into fewer and fewer hands, just as had earlier failures.[6]

In 1866, Nevada City had produced $500,000 in quartz gold, roughly equivalent, as Ross Browne enthusiastically reported, to the amount of capital invested in the business. The leading mine, the Wigham, yielded $100,000, while the Banner yielded $76,000 in nine months' operation. Consolidation proceeded apace in hydraulic mining also; that year, 61 claims in the Brush Creek district were joined into one operation and yielded $32,000. In Nevada City total placer production roughly equaled quartz yield, and their returns together ended the depression. Concrete evidence of good times appeared in the building of new residences for merchants and miners and the elimination of empty downtown business sites. Nevada City's return to mining prosperity ensured a common interest between the two towns; major investors transcended political and civic jealousies to operate in both towns, and Nevada City and Grass Valley mine owners combined to take stands on questions of land and labor policy. In 1865, for example, Nevada City's Sneath and Clay mine had been purchased by the "Grass Valley and New York Company." In 1866 mine owners met and agreed to support legislation permitting permanent deeds to be taken up for mining lands. And in both towns mine owners shared a recurring problem: while there was a surplus of mine promoters, there was a shortage of skilled labor. In June, perhaps emboldened by the scarcity of skilled workers, the miners at Nevada City's Banner Mine struck for a raise from $3.00 per day to $3.50. The strike failed, because the continued influx of men from the Comstock mines eroded the miners' position and allowed the owners to hire new crews at the same wages as before. But the strike of 1866 had made clear the common interests of mine owners and the fact that labor saw these interests as contrary to its own.[7]

The mine owners' point of view was increasingly being expressed from San Francisco. In part this simply reflected a constant in the lives of all mining towns; the successful entrepreneur expected to live elsewhere "to enjoy the money made," as Marcellus Deal sourly put it, "in our mines." Transience had always been the journalists' favorite civic villain, but now this "bane of progress and improvement" showed itself most clearly in the actions of the wealthiest class as "the heaviest taxpayers of one year are not known upon the assessment rolls of the next." During the late 1860's several of the most important mining men departed, including André Chavanne, David Watt, and G. W. Kidd. If, as usually seemed to happen, they sold out their holdings, the purchasers also tended to live in San Francisco, and gradually the proven mines began to be incorporated there. In 1867, a majority of the owners of the North Star, the Eureka, and the closed Allison Ranch lived in the Bay area. Kidd operated the Banner and the Gold Tunnel with San Francisco partners, as S. W. Lee did the Empire. By 1870, the quartz developers' Grass Valley Club was almost moribund; its membership now lived in France, Sacramento, and San Francisco as well as in Grass Valley. Quartz mining had elevated Grass Valley and Nevada City to first and second among California gold producers, but little of that wealth seemed destined to develop the two towns.[8]

Hydraulic mining underwent the same process. The consolidated hydraulic outfits that had permanently altered the landscape of Bourbon, Wet, American, and Manzanita Hills in Nevada City were dependent on massive supplies of water; during the 1860's, two giant water companies, one (the Eureka Lake and Yuba Canal Company) owned in New York, and the other (the South Yuba Company) owned locally, dominated the county's supply. At the same time E. F. Bean reported in the *Gazette* that the smaller hydraulic companies were disappearing—there were two-thirds to one-half as many in operation in 1868 as in 1860—because more capital for more water pressure was now necessary to reach bedrock; as gold dwindled and cuts had to deepen, expenses mounted, returns declined, and small men went under. That year was a bad one for the lesser hydraulic companies in general; a severe winter and a water shortage interrupted work. Even a few quartz companies shut down.[9]

The tag "dull times" was attached to 1868; the Gold Tunnel had failed in late 1867, and now one of Nevada City's major quartz mines, the Sneath and Clay, ceased work. Before the year was out, the White Pine excitement of east-central Nevada state had begun to draw off population, to the usual accompaniment of editorial warnings and sneers at the prospects there. For a brief time it appeared that the combination of bad weather and rival mining towns that had depressed the towns in the early 1860's had returned. White Pine, however, was not the Comstock Lode, inclement weather lasted only one season, and the major mines did not seem to be greatly affected—indeed, 1868 was the first year of full production for the Idaho mine, on the same lead as the Empire and a site of equal importance. By now Grass Valley had 6 large mining operations and 24 others that at least paid dividends, and the town showed no sign of losing its dominant position in California mining. In 1869 depression gripped the entire state, and mining was adversely affected, at least in part because of difficulty in obtaining working capital. Nevada City editors, as usual, blamed their problems on the money situation in the rest of the state, insisted that their mines could produce indefinitely, and urged further development in quartz. In Grass Valley, the quartz industry seemed at first immune to the state's troubles, but in May major mines were closed by the Cornish miners' strike against the introduction of dynamite. After the strike dragged to its end, production resumed at former levels. In 1870, Grass Valley was again prosperous and still growing; Nevada City mining was still in slack times.[10]

Industrial Mining and Social Structure

The traces of mining lay all about, in the very appearance of the towns as well as in their social structures. John Hittell reported in 1866 that Grass Valley did not suffer as much from "dirt and boulders piled up as placer towns," but the country around Nevada City seemed to the admittedly jaundiced eye of a Grass Valley observer to consist of "hills which had been worked out and shafts that had not struck the ledge." The towns had been located among "hills once laden with the most magnificent forests imaginable," but now the ridge between the towns, like the hills for miles around, was denuded. The mines and mills required vast amounts of fuel and lumber, and by the late 1860's the "great American plan of cutting down every tree" was beginning to cause concern; timber lands had been preempted, wood had to be hauled great distances, and prices were high. At times events forcefully illustrated the all-pervasive presence of mining, as when flumes flowing underneath Nevada City streets stopped up and flooded businesses, or when the planking on Main Street settled about a foot, undermined by parties tunneling underneath it for gold. The mines may have been increasingly owned by outsiders, but they still literally shaped the towns.[11]

Industrial mining molded more than the landscape; the type and relative success of mining in each town had immediate and far-reaching effects on its society and its social values. The constantly growing importance of deep-shaft quartz mining, the consolidation of placer claims into hydraulic operations, and the abandonment of many mining sites as not profitable enough to work caused major changes in the occupational structures of Grass Valley and Nevada City. At a time when mining was booming, the proportion of miners in the towns' male working population declined. In Grass Valley, more prosperous and more mining-oriented, the proportional loss was much more drastic. In 1860, 76 percent of Grass Valley's men had been miners; in 1870, only 54 percent were (Table 5). Nevada City experienced a decline from 66 percent to 53 percent, so that at the end of the 1860's it had proportionally almost as many miners as its larger and richer neighbor. This change is in part merely semantic, and in part the result of advances in mining technology in the late 1860's. Deep-shaft mining called for a body of highly skilled men to remove the ore from the earth, plus numerous men to do the unskilled work above ground, such as breaking up the ore before processing. The quartz mines also required a large number of skilled artisans to refine the ore, as well as many blacksmiths and carpenters to construct and maintain mining equipment and buildings. Therefore, in a quartz economy, the proportion of miners decreased, as the word "miner" took on a more specialized meaning, but the proportion of men involved in the mining industry probably increased.

The different occupational structures of the two towns demonstrate the effect of the quartz mining economy. In Grass Valley, the quartz town, the proportion of miners in the population declined more sharply than in Nevada City, whose mining economy was based equally on quartz and placer mines. Part of this decrease reflects reduced work forces as hydraulic operations took over much of the placer production. Both towns had higher percentages of unskilled labor than in 1860; Grass Valley's increase was slightly greater than Nevada City's. In 1860 Nevada City had had a much larger proportion of artisans than Grass Valley, largely because of its greater commercial interests, but by 1870 the demand that quartz mining made for many kinds of craftsmen reversed this situation. Nevada City's proportion of artisans increased slightly, but Grass Valley's more than doubled.

The spread of technology and increase in population altered only slightly the proportion of the male population who were professionals or businessmen. Nevada City's middle class slid from 10 to 9 percent of the population, while Grass Valley's edged up from 6 to 7 percent. The decline of the Comstock region cost Nevada City some of its commercial importance as a regional center, and, evidently, this loss was accompanied by a small withdrawal of merchant interests from town. County prosperity led to a small gain in the numbers of lawyers and related professionals, however, since Nevada City remained the center of legal business as county seat. Grass Valley did not attempt to rival its neighbor as a trade center. There was an influx of businessmen to take advantage of the growing markets, but the slight growth in the proportion of businessmen and professionals did not mean anything more than increased services for the town. The energies of Grass Valley's investors were directed toward quartz, not toward developing a commercial center.

The great expansion of industrial mining during the 1860's did not alter the relative financial positions of the occupational classes within the two towns. All occupational groups were slightly more prosperous than they had been in 1860 (Tables 10–13), probably in part because the mild depression of 1869–70 was not as damaging as the Comstock rush had been in 1859. There was a clear reversal in the relationships of the two towns; Grass Valley had become the wealthier town during the 1860's, because of its quartz mines. Its citizens reported greater amounts of real and personal property at all levels. In 1860 there had been little difference between the towns in the wealth of miners; by 1870 Grass Valley's miners were somewhat better off, because a greater proportion of them were skilled, salaried quartz miners (Table 10). While miners had made gains, there had been no revolution in status; in Grass Valley more than seven in ten owned no real estate; a similar number had no personal property. In Nevada City the number with no real and no personal property was over eight in ten. Miners and mine-related workers did become more prosperous than common laborers during the 1860's, but a miner was not any likelier to have property than a surface worker at the mines and was usually not as prosperous as, for example, a teamster. There was some increase in the number of miners who had over $1,000 in real and personal estate, and there was a large gain in miners who had less than $1,000 in realty and personalty. Although a few more Nevada City than Grass Valley miners reported over $1,000 in holdings, many more

Grass Valley miners had property valued between $100 and $1,000. There were more small, independent mine operations in Nevada City; mining there was less likely to be controlled from somewhere else than in Grass Valley. A placer operator had a better chance at affluence, a quartz miner at a sufficiency. A quartz miner's wage, however, was not commensurate with his skills; a blacksmith or a carpenter could expect much more.

The fortunes of mining affected the towns' entire economies. The improved standard of living in both towns was shown in the increased holdings of other laborers, who made gains almost as great as did the miners. Much of this gain must have come because of the relatively good times of the late 1860's as compared to a decade before; jobs in general were more available and more permanent. There was no difference between the towns in the extent of the holdings of the unskilled population. Taking all laborers and including miners, in Grass Valley there was a sharp increase between 1860 and 1870 among men with at least some real and personal holdings, and in Nevada City a lesser, but real, increase.

Artisans in Grass Valley, as part of their overall gain in importance, made a more spectacular financial gain than either artisans in Nevada City or miners in Grass Valley. Many artisans had small holdings, and several had over $1,000 in both real and personal estate. A few were among the richest men in each town, mostly those who had started out as artisans and had become the owners of large concerns—butchers who acquired their own markets, for example (Table 11). Professionals and merchants made a proportionally smaller gain in property value than did the other classes. The Grass Valley business community made extensive gains in the amount of personal property held, and Nevada City businessmen made a small advance. However, real-estate holdings in both towns showed little change, possibly because there were fewer small investors in mining now (Table 12). Nevada City had a definite edge in the growing number of men who reported real estate over $10,000, many of Grass Valley's major owners having left town (Table 13). In personal property, meanwhile, the number of men who held over $10,000 was the same in both towns, but Grass Valley had an edge in the numbers of those who held over $1,000. Grass Valley's mines, even though owned by outsiders, created a much stronger economy than Nevada City's; conditions for business were much better in the larger town. The expansion of the quartz industry had reversed the financial standings of the two towns and had improved the position of the hard-rock miner in relation to his less skilled fellows. But miners still did not earn in proportion to their importance to the towns, and the size of the elite populations did not grow in proportion with the wealth produced by the mines because many of the most fortunate mine owners left town; quartz fortunes were enjoyed in San Francisco.

Although the quartz boom had resulted in gains in wealth, both towns still lagged behind national levels of property holding. Since the national proportion of men who held real and personal property remained nearly constant between 1860 and 1870, the townsmen more closely approached American norms for free men. But even in Grass Valley, where quartz had appreciably widened the property-holding base, residents were less than two-thirds as likely to claim $100 in real or personal estate as the average American. The reasons remained similar: recession, low pay for miners, and low persistence rates. Unlike those of 1860, the male working populations were slightly older than in the nation at large (Table 2); youthfulness was no longer a cause of low property accumulation. Only a small minority, however, had aged in the towns themselves. The White Pine excitement was brief, gold production in the towns was steadier than in most rivals, and families increased in number among all ranks, so the rate of out-migration slowed during the 1860's although neither town, by any stretch of the imagination, warranted the images of stability applied to it by civic boosters. Only one man in twenty who had been in either town in 1850 was still there in 1860, while one in eight of the men of 1860 was there ten years later. As in the 1850's the probability of moving on was higher in the first years of a man's stay; eight out of ten were gone before five years were up (Table 41).

In the 1860's the professionals and merchants continued to demonstrate greater persistence than those in less prestigious occupations, while miners were the most mobile group. Except for the miners, status and persistence are directly related. One in three Grass Valley businessmen was there for the entire decade, one in four artisans, one in fourteen unskilled laborers, and one in seventeen miners. In Nevada City, because of its less prosperous economy, persistence was slightly lower than in Grass Valley. One professional or merchant in four who was there in 1860 remained in 1870, one artisan in five, one unskilled laborer in fourteen, and one miner in twenty. Professionals and merchants could expect a more stable life, as well as a much better prospect of earning a comfortable living, than any other occupational group. Industrialization had only confirmed a reality established since the Gold Rush.

But even though by national standards the towns were poor and small, the growth of quartz and hydraulic mining had pushed Grass Valley and Nevada City further ahead of all other California mining towns. Grass Valley, including the township, numbered 7,063 and stood sixth in population in the state; no other mining center approached it. The quartz boom had reversed the relative positions of the two towns, but Nevada City, with 3,986 people, still placed eleventh among all California towns and was second only to Grass Valley among mining towns. Through quartz bust and quartz boom, depression and industrialization, their importance as mining towns had never been in doubt.[12]

Ethnicity and Social Divisions

The quartz industry of the late 1860's did more than make Grass Valley preeminent among California mining towns and change the definition of "miner"; its greatest impact was on the relationship of the foreign-born to the rest of society. During the quartz boom and after, the differences in ethnic composition between the towns, clearly evident by 1860, widened and solidified (Table 8). The expansion of quartz mining meant the continued influx of Cornish miners into Grass Valley. The two were inseparable and mutually dependent; mining techniques advocated by Cornish miners helped the industry develop and created a need for more Cornish miners. By 1870, the British-born, at 39 percent of the working male population, constituted the largest ethnic group in Grass Valley; only one-quarter of employed townsmen were American-born. The number of Irishmen decreased slightly during the 1860's, although not as sharply as that of the natives, and the proportion of French, Germans, and Chinese increased slightly. The Chinese were the fourth largest ethnic group, behind the British, native, and Irish. Three-fourths of the adult male population of Grass Valley was foreign-born, and slightly over half of these men were British, mostly Cornish.

While Grass Valley already had a foreign majority in 1860, Nevada City had been over half American-born. By 1870, although the American-born were still Nevada City's largest ethnic group, they constituted only 38 percent of the town's male workers. Three men in ten were Chinese; the other major groups were the English, Germans, and Irish. The Chinese, sequestered along China Street, did not, despite their numbers, greatly affect the town's way of life. In Grass Valley, on the other hand, the Cornish deeply influenced the town's identity. The rate of growth of the foreign-born population during the ten years was almost the same in both places; it was the economic prominence of the Cornish that made Grass Valley seem to become more foreign.

The camps' ethnic composition continued to reflect the forms the mining industry took. Deep-shaft quartz mining was carried out by the Cornish. When mining had been unskilled and unorganized, the miners had been American. They gradually gave way to the Irish as mining came to be more and more manual labor for wages, and then to the Cornish as it became more and more specialized. Where mining did not become a skilled trade, and the placers grew less valuable, Chinese gradually became the largest ethnic group involved. The two towns demonstrate this clearly (Table 15). In 1870, Grass Valley was largely a quartz town, and 60 percent of its miners were British. One miner in ten was American-born. Nevada City was part quartz and part placer, and more nearly played out than Grass Valley; Chinese were the largest group of miners, followed by the native-born and British. In 1860 nearly eight out of ten men in Grass Valley were miners, and seven of ten in Nevada City. By 1870 miners were that important proportionally only among the Chinese of Nevada City and the British of both towns (Table 14); the American-born, especially, turned away from mining in general and quartz mining in particular. Only one in four of the American-born of Grass Valley was a miner, while four in ten of Nevada City's native-born were. Germans, both Christian and Jew, had always been less involved in mining than the other major groups, and their involvement continued to decline in the 1860's to where in Grass Valley barely more than one German in ten mined. Even the Irish, often unable to compete with the Cornish in skill, were turning to other jobs, although proportionally less so than the Germans and native-born.

Changes in mining deeply affected the black communities, too. The most damaging discrimination faced by blacks was exclusion from quartz work; the shift to deep-shaft mining in Grass Valley drove out black miners. In 1860 there had been almost as many black miners in Grass Valley as unskilled laborers, but in 1870 eight in ten blacks were unskilled, and only one black man called himself a miner (Table 9). The proportion of black people in Grass Valley's population was cut in half. In Nevada City black numbers grew slightly, and while somewhat fewer blacks worked the placers than in 1860, now several were artisans and two owned farms; Nevada City's mercantile-oriented crafts offered opportunity to blacks, while Grass Valley's mine-based artisan occupations did not. Occupationally as well as numerically superior to those of Grass Valley, Nevada City's blacks dominated relationships between the two black communities.

As Grass Valley mining became San Franciscan in ownership and Cornish in work force, the American-born tended to concentrate in other occupations. A disproportionate number of them were professionals and merchants; one-quarter of the population supplied nearly half of the town's businessmen (Table 15). To a lesser extent they also dominated the ranks of artisans. At the other extreme, the American-born were slightly overrepresented among the unskilled laborers. Native miners who left as a part of the towns' normally high flow of out-migration were replaced by a much smaller group of merchants, professionals, and artisans. And new arrivals without specialized skills would end up as common laborers, since opportunities in mining had declined for them. The native-born community had become polarized. Nearly half were professionals and artisans, over twice as many as in 1860 (Table 14), giving the more prestigious occupations a native tone in a town where the bulk of the population was foreign-born. Even more than the American-born, immigrants from the Germanic states, Christian and Jew, were clustered in professional, merchant, and artisan roles as they had been in 1860. Six out of ten were in higher occupational groups, especially as merchants and clerks, while the Germans were almost unrepresented among the miners and had approximately the same proportion of unskilled laborers as the general population. In 1860 the British had been as well represented in the professions and crafts as had the American-born and the

Germans (Table 15). By 1870, however, while their representation in the population doubled, their representation in the more prestigious occupations had grown only slightly and had declined in the ranks of businessmen and professionals. British immigrants to Grass Valley during the 1860's had been largely miners. The majority of Irish continued to be miners, and a large number worked as manual laborers. Irishmen were underrepresented in the upper occupational groups, as they had been in 1860. The great majority of the Chinese were placer miners or unskilled laborers and occupied the lowest level of prestige in the town.

The influx of Cornish miners and the flight of the native population away from mining had combined to produce a new ethnic social structure in Grass Valley. In 1860 the population had not been so overwhelmingly foreign-born, and although the Irish and Chinese had not figured in the professions, the number of British and German professionals and merchants had prevented the creation of a native occupational elite. The American-born had played roles in all occupations proportional to their numbers. But by 1870 the American-born, only one-quarter of the population, were concentrated in the most prestigious occupations and played a much more important role there than did the other groups. Since the foreign-born (except for the Germans) were disproportionately miners or laborers, the social structure of Grass Valley exhibited a native-born minority apart from an immigrant majority. This condition prevailed at Nevada City also. The American-born were disproportionately employed in the professions and in business; 38 percent of the population supplied 62 percent of the merchants and professionals and 59 percent of the artisans (Table 15). As in Grass Valley, Nevada City's Germans were heavily involved in trade, and were underrepresented among the miners, although to a lesser extent than in Grass Valley. The absence of overwhelming numbers of Cornish miners, and lower levels of mining technology, meant that the representation of other nations among the miners was greater, and that there was a lesser tendency for the natives and Germans to concentrate in the professions. The Chinese and Irish, as well as the English, were heavily employed as miners (Table 14).

The arrival of large numbers of Cornish miners during the 1860's was primarily responsible for an apparent lowering of occupational status among the foreign-born; the Irish, Chinese, and Germans held roughly the same places in the occupational hierarchy that they had in 1860. The real-estate holdings of ethnic families offer further proof of this (Table 16). In both towns, German and American-born households were proportionally most likely to hold over $1,000 in real estate, as they had been in 1860. Likewise, the Irish lagged behind at both ends of the decade. But the British, whose real property had been only slightly less than that of the native-born in 1860, lost ground until they were only slightly ahead of the Irish, despite the fact that the number of Britishers with over $1,000 in real estate in Grass Valley had almost tripled. Many of the very wealthiest men, the owners or part-owners of the major mines, were foreign-born; André Chavanne was French, the Watt brothers were Scots, the Coleman brothers of the Empire were English, and the Allison Ranch partners were Irish. The Cornish also produced a large and important class of mine engineers, superintendents, and small quartz operators who were well-to-do by town standards, but the vast majority of their numbers were rank-and-file miners.

The influx of Cornish miners also contributed to another new phenomenon: the segregation of white ethnic groups. For the first time, in the late 1860's, two European-born groups, the Cornish and the Irish, began to congregate in distinct areas; previously Allison Ranch had been the only exception to a rule of white integration. Occupational status or wealth still transcended ethnicity; the family neighborhoods attracted the successful of all European groups. Jewish merchant Jacob Rosenthal dwelt with the "Nabobs" on East Broad, and English mine owner John Coleman built a house on Church Street. And since well-to-do areas could not bar the modest homes of workers, either man could have had a poor Irish neighbor. No Cornish homebuilder ever faced a mob intent on defending its exclusive living space; whites faced no physical sanctions. Furthermore, the most distinctly white ethnic areas were Irish Allison Ranch and the Cornish environs of major quartz mines in Grass Valley township, in both cases a separation based on hiring practices for mine crews. Ethnocentrism did have a part, for at mines where both groups worked, although some Irish and Cornish shared quarters, the cluster of cabins and boarding houses around the site tended toward division by birthplace.

In the towns proper the rising rents or purchase prices of houses caused by the rapid expansion of mining, together with newly strengthened ethnic occupational identities, also resulted in a slight increase in residential segregation. The middle-class areas became slightly more native-born—again, German merchants and Cornish mine superintendents limited this segregation. Speculative cottage developments intended for sale to married miners composed much of the new building in booming Grass Valley, and given the Cornish preponderance among arriving miners, these clusters of small houses on the outskirts of town tended to promote the new tendency of ethnics to live apart.[13]

Quartz also affected black residential patterns. Exclusion from hard-rock mining broke up the concentration of black miners in Grass Valley, and the subsequent turn to service jobs meant that blacks were much more dispersed throughout the white community than in 1860. In Nevada City, where segregation had been less rigid because black waiters, servants, and barbers had lived where they worked, the black artisans and restaurateurs served mixed clienteles, and at least one black craftsman, a blacksmith, employed white journeymen. Despite reduced spatial segregation, residential color lines had not been erased, as even the reduced numbers of Grass Valley blacks lived largely on "Hayti Hill." The popular definition of a slum stressed the intermingling of races. W. H. Sears described one such Grass Valley area as a "small edition of New York's Five Points . . . a sort of moral sink hole where brutal blacks and degraded whites mingle together in a common mass of reeking corruption."[14]

These changes in ethnic structure, by sharpening existing differences between Grass Valley and Nevada City, made permanent the political antagonisms of the Civil War period. Not only was Grass Valley, with its foreign-born miners and laborers, the bastion of Democratic voting power; the party leadership concentrated there, too, since the old Nevada City elite had either left town or turned Unionist during the war. The American-born Republican plurality in Nevada City managed to dominate town politics; the largest foreign-born group, the Chinese, was disenfranchised. Republican directorship remained based there. Thus, each town contained within it most of one party's oligarchy, composed in each case of some of the town's principal merchants, mining entrepreneurs, and attorneys. In this situation the minority parties found it necessary to recruit activists from occupations previously not largely represented in party circles. More miners and artisans became politically active, in each case especially so in the weaker town party. Each county party was dominated by the town with more activists and leaders of higher status.[15]

The quartz boom had produced far-reaching changes in almost every aspect of town life from jobs and wealth to population and political activism, and townspeople were very aware of some of the changes. Editors noted the growth and the concentration of foreign-born populations, and after 1865 hints of reviving nativism on the part of the outnumbered American-born appear scattered through the newspapers. Journalists also reported snobbery and increasing concern with social distinctions, sometimes with a certain nostalgia for the "democracy" of the Gold Rush. But the central editorial response to industrial mining was one of disappointment in its economic consequences. Although unaware (at least in print) that they trailed most of the nation in wealth, townspeople knew that they were not receiving the full benefit of locally produced gold. Many of the mining boosters' dreams had come true, but the towns still had not achieved stable prosperity. Some of the old panaceas—most conspicuously industrialization and the establishment of families—had been tested, and security was still problematical. Some of the old ills, especially the intent to leave after finding success, also remained and seemed endemic. In the course of editorial responses to economic conditions in the late 1860's, industrial mining was held up to dispassionate study. These analyses focused on one fact: absentee ownership. Nonresident owners would not consider diverting some of the massive capital tied up in mine development to improve the towns themselves. No mine worked uninterruptedly all year; the seasonally underemployed miners lived in the towns while the wealth generated by the mines was spent elsewhere.[16]

The most prominent spokesmen for this point of view, Nevada City editors E. F. Bean and M. S. Deal, returned to the argument of the early 1850's that if local economic interests were to prevail, agriculture would have to be developed to the point where it could ensure a locally owned and oriented source of permanent production. They promoted experiments in viticulture and winemaking, in silk culture, and in orchards. Jobless miners were urged to take up farms, not to open unworked leads. The progress of various agricultural undertakings was reported with care, and failures were played down. Edwin Waite, former editor of the *Transcript*, planted a thousand grape vines. Bean and Deal were active, along with several large farmers, in organizing the Nevada Vinicultural and Distillery Association and intended to make wine and brandy —"the American Chambertins, Burgundies and Clarets." The high-water mark for grape growing was 1870, and the association soon broke up. Silkworms, grapes, and peaches all proved unrewarding, although some orchard enterprises supplemented incomes on already established ranches. Still, an important new attitude had emerged—a rhetoric of boosterism apart from, even alienated from, mining.

A similar sense of estrangement appeared in the history of the two towns compiled by Bean in 1867. The historical portions were written by Bean, William Byrne, and Waite, all veteran local editors, and stressed the achievement of townspeople, not that of township people. Mining and the history of prominent mines were extensively covered but were kept separate from the stories of the towns themselves, which were treated largely in terms of their commercial successes and hard times. *Bean's History* did not trace connections between town merchants and mining, and seemed to consider the histories of mines after they fell into San Francisco hands of less import than their early, much less valuable days. To the editors, the history of Grass Valley and Nevada City was the history of local businesses and businessmen. And a prominent group of long-established spokesmen for town promotion concluded—as two of them, Aaron Sargent and Edwin Waite, had in the mid-1850's—that mining was less important than the now-successful establishment of "the comforts of high civilization" in the towns.[17]

Residents also recognized that industrial mining had dictated different social structures in the neighboring towns. Grass Valley and Nevada City editors, like other small-town journalists, customarily marked the turning of a new year by evaluating local prospects. During the first week in January, the press intoned its standard litany for prosperity, giving thanks for "inexhaustible mines," "vine-covered cottages," "enterprising businessmen," and "saintly mothers." But in 1868, the *Grass Valley Daily Union* attempted something more ambitious and more revealing; its editors, William Byrne and Charles H. Mitchell, published a comparison of the social values and, indirectly, the social structures of the two towns. The Nevada City newspapers reprinted the short essay without comment. What the *Union* actually undertook, in the course of weighing civic characteristics, was to contrast a middle-class town, Nevada City, with a workingman's town, Grass Valley, and to find consistent class-derived value differences in every sort of social behavior. The editors grounded their argument in the most visible economic activity of each town; Grass Valley, "almost exclusively a mining town," was "hard working," while Nevada City, "a center of law," affected "greater learning and more taste." It followed that Grass Valley would be Democratic, Nevada City Republican. Nevada City was inventive; Grass Valley adopted "useful machinery." Men in Nevada City, because of "habitual sitting on juries," looked more to evidence and facts; those of Grass Valley had more faith. Nevadans supported a public library and plumed themselves on reading the *Atlantic Monthly;* Grass Valley had no library, and its people read *Harper's Magazine.* Nevada City was more "polished in its politeness," Grass Valley more hearty; hospitality flowed more freely in Nevada City, but was more sincere in Grass Valley. In religion Grass Valley had "many neutrals," while Nevada City contained only the "strongly religious" or "open deniers." Grass Valley residents were never fooled for long; Nevadans sometimes "flew off the handle." The editors, both Democrats, were comparing what they saw as the solid virtues of a working class with the more sophisticated if more volatile values of a middle class. They were also asserting that mining and miners shaped the actions of Grass Valley's well-to-do citizens, who despite their new affluence were still pragmatic and adaptable and without cultural pretensions.[18]

Several further inferences can be drawn from the *Union*'s New Year column. Nevada City, inferior now in numbers, gold, and, at times, political influence, still saw itself and was seen by its neighbor as intellectually superior because it was the home of the area's largest group of liberally educated men, its attorneys—the *Union* did not allude to its merchants. The most cosmopolitan and wealthy group in either town, Grass Valley's mining entrepreneurs, were not visible in this social analysis attempted at the close of their most successful year, 1867. The column is also evidence that the towns were becoming class conscious and more alert to class-based differences in values. Byrne and Mitchell were right; social distances had increased both within and between the towns during and after the Civil War, primarily because of the changes in mining. But the editors had missed, or ignored, the really vital change. To Mitchell and Byrne, lawyers and miners, not Americans and Cornishmen, had created separate civic identities. They did not seem to notice that in Grass Valley especially, lower prestige occupations had become tied to ethnicity, that groups lived apart, and that a new ethnic hierarchy had grown from an in-migration of American-born professionals and Cornish miners, while in Nevada City the presence of the Chinese in humble positions exaggerated ethnic and occupational differentiation. Social distances were probably greater in Nevada City, which contained a larger wealthy white group as well as larger Chinese and black populations, but the situation was potentially more disruptive in Grass Valley. Unlike the Chinese, the Cornish had both a political voice and, as always, a basic economic role. They also had a strong sense of self and a high estimation of the importance of their skills; if segregation should be accompanied by attempts at subordination, they could and would resist.

Miners Against Merchants
RACE AND REGION COME TO THE FORE

Industrial mining widened social fissures in the late 1860's not only by strengthening the bond between ethnicity and occupational status, but also by heightening group self-consciousness through the money and the labor disputes it generated. Women and children accompanied prosperity to the towns, and the expansion of family life bolstered the institutions of the middle class. A more secure middle class demonstrated a sense of class separateness missing since the crusades of the mid-1850's. Its clubs and benevolent organizations transcended ethnicity by including the families of foreign-born merchants and professionals, but at the same time its charitable societies carefully distanced themselves from the indigent, stressing the notions of stewardship and the "deserving" poor. Women's work became less acceptable and less common as it was identified with economic necessity: the presence of boarders now seemed respectable only if it signaled moral instruction by the householder. This sense of separateness and the influence of the middle class both were more apparent in commercial Nevada City. Grass Valley's native middle class was neither large enough nor rich enough to determine town mores.

At the same time, most ethnic and racial groups developed a greater self-consciousness, often because of national events like Emancipation. But with the Cornish, and to a lesser degree the Irish, this sense of national identity was linked to a recognition of the group's occupational role in the towns, and to perceptions of its own unique interests. Among the miners, this feeling came to a head in 1869, when the threat of attacks on Cornish traditional skills and ultimately on all white mine labor, through the proposed introduction of dynamite and Chinese work forces, inspired a Miners' Union and a strike. The strike pitted Cornish and Irish miners against native and other ethnic merchants and professionals. One result was a renewed Sinophobia, as a statewide Democratic Party campaign against the Chinese in the name of labor meshed with local miners' views of the Chinese as potential tools of the mine owners. More importantly, the strike's success and the concurrent outburst of political activity by Grass Valley miners demonstrated that Grass Valley, unlike Nevada City and the great majority of American towns, was not under the unchallenged sway of American-born merchants and professionals. It had become, by virtue of their numbers, ethnic pride, and a monopoly of skills, a Cornish miners' town.

The World of the Family

During the late 1860's family life began to be common, if not the norm, among all occupations and nationalities, always excepting the Chinese. Relative prosperity had brought an influx of Cornish miners, and steady wages had also resulted in slower rates of outward migration; together stability and solvency allowed miners and laborers to establish families. Nearly one Grass Valley man in three was married and living with his family in 1870; in Nevada City the ratio was one in four (Table 7). The proportion of married men in Nevada City was over twice as great as it had been in 1860, while in a Grass Valley revolutionized by the quartz boom, the proportion had grown more than fourfold. A professional was still much more likely to be living with a family than an artisan, miner, or laborer, but the proportional difference was far less than it had been in 1860. Then, for example, a merchant had been over nine times as likely to be married as a miner; in 1870 he was less than three times as likely. Marriage was no longer as sure an indicator of occupational status as it had been in 1860.

Marriage, family, and relative prosperity still went together, but the difference between the amounts of property held by the married and the unmarried had become much less during the 1860's. In 1860 a married Grass Valley miner had been ten times as likely to claim $1,000 in real property as miners in general; in 1870 he was two and one-half times as likely (Table 17). The property gap between the married and the unmarried was greater in Nevada City, especially among miners, than in Grass Valley, reflecting the higher working-class income of Grass Valley's wage-based mining economy. On average, married men were relatively less well off in 1870 than they had been in 1860, as more men had acquired a sufficiency to support wives and children; again, this was most true for Grass Valley quartz miners. Adult working males had constituted 85 percent of Grass Valley's 1860 population; in 1870 women and children made up over half the residents of both towns. And while single men still numerically dominated, young men no longer did as half the men in both towns were over 40 years old (Table 2). Certainly in the towns themselves, the most common male would be a family man of middle years, but even including the mining townships, demographically these were no longer Gold Rush towns.

This change most affected—and comforted—the middle class in both towns. For the first time, a solid majority of merchants and professional men lived with their families, as did nearly half of the artisans and farmers. Family life could finally be seen as the norm, as it was in most of America. Moreover, the moral values of middle-class families seemed to dominate the towns. Churches seemed secure; they gained notice usually through the constant round of church suppers and an occasional revival, and only rarely as vocal moral guardians. The new Cornish miners were loyal Methodists, and the Irish Catholic churches taught the same morality and followed the same round of fundraisers as the Protestants; editors lauded their salutary effects on Irish miners. And while social clubs, fire companies, fraternal organizations, and militia units flourished, the old reform and moral clubs languished. Temperance groups went through cycles of brief sudden growth, usually when a new organization with a novel ritual appeared in the towns, but invariably a rapid decline followed. The strongest new moralist organization, the Young Men's Christian Association, which arrived in Nevada City in the fall of 1869 accompanied by extensive newspaper enthusiasm, did not survive through the following spring. Individual uplift was no longer the major concern of a comfortable middle class.[1]

The school systems failed to provide uninterrupted public education, but that resulted from overspending in Nevada City to meet new needs, not from the lack of interest that had characterized the 1850's. The number of potential scholars grew, while the education they needed became more sophisticated and expensive. The state of California in 1866 reduced the number of children counted in the school census by raising the entry age from four to five and dropping the leaving age from eighteen to fifteen. Nevertheless, the number of school-age children expanded in both towns, rapidly in Grass Valley, more slowly in Nevada City, until the onset of depression in 1869. The proportion of school-age children who attended classes also increased during the decade, again until the trend reversed in 1869. In Grass Valley in 1864, seven school-age children in ten were enrolled; in 1868, more than nine in ten; in 1870, more than eight in ten. (Comparable figures do not exist for Nevada City.) Simultaneously, private schools gave way to public education. In Grass Valley in 1864, over half the children attending classes did so at private schools; the figure had declined to 30 percent by 1870.[2]

The scope of education offered in the two towns had been greatly expanded during the 1860's. In the early part of the decade, Grass Valley had contained one primary and one "unclassified" public school, while by 1867 it had a high school, an intermediate school, four elementary schools, and four private academies. The Grass Valley high school boasted of its Latin class, its literary magazine, and its impressive edifice, and professed to prepare students for the new University of California at Berkeley. Grass Valley's populace was large enough and solvent enough to finance this necessary expansion; Nevada City's evidently was not. The latter's school board had exhausted its funds in 1867 by buying one schoolhouse and building another, so students had to pay monthly charges to keep the school doors open. Town officials deemed Nevada City's high school inadequate, so in 1869 they erected a $15,000 brick school, but the following March, lack of money for teachers' salaries shut the public system down. Teachers operated the schools as private academies for the rest of the term. When debts still prevented the opening of the public schools for the autumn session of 1870, a lottery promoter, trying to win public favor, donated $500 toward reestablishing free schools.[3]

The desire for education, as in 1860, permeated all levels of society in both towns. Neither the father's nor the mother's occupational status made an appreciable difference (Table 31). Professional families did not have a consistently greater commitment to education; in 1870 in Grass Valley, the proportion of school-age children actually attending classes was larger in the families of the unskilled, and in Nevada City the families of miners and artisans had higher rates of school attendance than those of storekeepers or attorneys. Similarly, family wealth made little difference in rates of school enrollment (Table 32).*

Nor did a father's poverty or low occupational status force his children into the job market. In Nevada City, the families most likely to have employed children had $100 to $1,000 in real property, while in Grass Valley they had more than $1,000; proportionately children of the propertyless were less likely to work (Table 32). Artisan families proved most likely to have a child at work in both towns, then merchants and professionals, miners, and finally the unskilled (Table 31). In part, this simply reflected opportunity, as the son of a blacksmith or storekeeper could assist his father, while a quartz miner or a common laborer could not easily place his son at his side. Boys who worked tended to take their cues from their fathers; miners' sons toiled as miners or quartz mill hands, farmers' sons as farm laborers (Table 42). Sons listed as apprentices usually had artisan fathers; sons employed as clerks came from merchant families.

In family size, just as in school attendance and children's work, growing separations between occupational classes did not seem to be accompanied by divergences in family values. A married professional or merchant was no likelier to have children than a blacksmith or miner, although the unskilled had fewer children (Table 30). In the same way, a man who reported no real estate proved, in both towns, slightly less likely to have children, and decidedly less

---

* In Grass Valley, 74 percent of miners' school-age children attended school, as did 81 percent of merchants' school-age children, and 65 percent of artisans' and 82 percent of unskilled workers' children. In Nevada City, 88 percent of miners' school-age children attended school; the figures for merchants', artisans', and unskilled workers' children were 76, 82, and 71 percent. In Grass Valley, 79 percent of school-age children whose parents had no real property attended school, as did 75 percent of those with holdings of between $100 and $1,000, and 76 percent of those with realty worth more than $1,000; in Nevada City the corresponding figures were 80, 85, and 82 percent.

likely to have several than a man with holdings (Table 32), in part possibly because he was younger. And the differences in numbers of children were not great; the household of a propertyless miner resembled that of a wealthy storekeeper.

By the late 1850's seasonal, legitimate, social recreations had been established in both towns; during the late 1860's the clubs that were central to town amusements were strengthened and expanded to include a wider segment of the population, and, at least in part, became more family oriented. Social clubs still tended to last for only one winter season, to be resuscitated for the next, but their transitoriness had as much to do with their rules as with mining town instability; by 1869 only one original member of the Young Men's Social Club of Nevada City was still on the rolls, the others having left the county or been expelled—for marrying. Other organizations began to serve the entire family. For instance, the Nevada Literary Society, a forensic club and lyceum that functioned intermittently during the late 1860's, had prominent townsmen as its officers and sometimes pitted them against each other in debate over major social and political issues: Fenianism, spiritualism, or women's suffrage. The speaker in favor of votes for women, a well-known political lawyer, defeated his opposite number, another well-known political lawyer, in front of an audience estimated at 90 persons, some of whom were women. While women did not debate or serve on the jury that decided the question in the affirmative, they did read poems and original essays at this meeting—before the main business had been called. Children also declaimed or played piano pieces, as was customary, as part of the preliminaries. The Literary Society, then, disseminated "genteel culture" for all members of the family, and while it took on controversial questions, the structure of its meetings was firmly conventional. Married professionals took over the club so thoroughly that the young clerks, law students, and storekeepers who had founded it had to start their own debate society so that they would have a chance to make their voices heard.[4]

The same range of surnames—Reardon, Finninger, Rosenthal— appeared among the performing children on the night of the suffrage debate as appeared among the active adult members of the societies, uplifting and frivolous alike. Blacks, Chinese, and "Spanish" were excluded, but among the rest, occupation and family

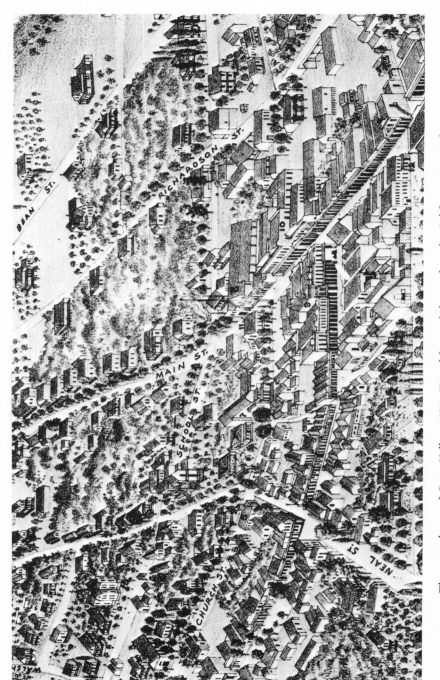

The central area of Grass Valley, 1871. (Detail from a lithograph in the California State Library.)

mores operated as unifiers more powerful than the usually divisive forces of church and nationality. However, some lines were drawn. The fact that each town's middle class was predominantly American-born and Protestant served to limit ethnic access to these clubs, and Jews appeared as officers less frequently than their importance to the merchant communities would have warranted. Probably the most durable club during the 1860's, outside the national fraternities, was the Eureka Social Club of Nevada City for young Jewish men. Possibly some elders felt that parties and dances designed to lead to marriage should be segregated by religion in a way the educational societies need not be; still, the Eureka and the Young Men's Clubs held joint gatherings, and there is no evidence that Jews and Catholics could not buy tickets to the affairs of clubs dominated by Protestants. Certainly the Eurekans' dances followed the same format and rules of decorum and received the same newspaper coverage as did Gentile balls. Even when ethnicity determined membership, the same rules and values, essentially middle-class, prevailed.[5]

The clubs also widened their scope to include a larger portion of town populations; editors preened themselves on town democracy in reporting that the season's finest balls, particularly those for good causes, had attracted all ranks of townsmen. Miners and artisans began to surface in numbers in the clubs as officers and committee members, and their families began to be more evident at church suppers and the like.* That is, sound, married, moral miners began to appear, but in the main the organized social life of the towns was still the preserve of merchants and their families.

Paradoxically, at the same time that mining and foreign-born families began to be more evident in these organized recreations, the increasing social distances that characterized the late 1860's began to be visible during the social season. Some of this was simple snobbery; "the aristocracy of wealth" at a Grass Valley ball observed by the *Union*'s W. H. Miller did not smile upon those whose

* In Nevada City during the 1860's, 55 percent of the officers of the social clubs, and 54 percent of the officers of the service clubs were drawn from professional and merchant groups. In the late 1850's 66 percent of all club officers had been merchants or professionals. A more striking change took place in Grass Valley; 39 percent of the social club officers, 53 percent of the service club officers in the 1860's, as opposed to 88 percent in the late 1850's, were professionals and merchants.

"purses did not entitle them" to recognition. More subtly and more substantially, the public dances and dinners operated at definable levels of exclusiveness. Some events, notably those with charitable intent and the subscription balls, welcomed all presentable comers. But to attend a club ball, one had to present both a ticket and the invitation to buy it to gain admission, and occasionally subscription balls followed the same format, evidently to attract a more middle-class clientele. In 1865, when this innovation first appeared, the entrepreneurs responsible attracted angry denunciations from the excluded for catering to a select group, but in spite of charges that it was anti-democratic the practice became more common.[6]

Possibly the best evidence of change in the attitude of the middle class toward others is the organization, first in Nevada City, then in Grass Valley, of Benevolent Societies. In some ways the Benevolent Societies resembled the old civic reform groups, whose place they had usurped. Women held office and took a major part in collecting funds, the societies focused on protecting the family, and much of their support came through benefit dinners and parties. But in other ways the Benevolent Societies more closely resembled the social clubs. Although a few of the wealthy mining entrepreneurs lent their names, money, and labor in support of the undertakings, most of the active officers were successful merchants and their wives. Likewise, although there already existed a Catholic orphanage and traditional Jewish mutual-aid associations, the Benevolent Societies were ecumenical in membership in a way the nativist-tinged reform clubs of the 1850's had never been. In 1870, the Nevada organization elected Father J. J. Claire president and Aaron Goldsmith vice-president, presumably because of their experience in charitable work. And because of seasonal hardships and the rhythms of mine work, these societies, like the social clubs, were most active during the winter when casual labor for the unskilled was scarce, remaining moribund during the summer.[7]

But most importantly, the members of the societies consciously and carefully divided themselves from their clients. Those who received aid had to prove legitimate need, and help was usually tendered to lone women with dependent children or to families whose man was sick or injured. Impostures would be published; Grass Valley tardily called together a society in direct response to instances of residents being "bilked by professional operators." The

Nevada City Benevolent Society claimed, as one of its successes, to have reduced the number of "outside beggars" some of whom the society believed to be on the lookout for chances to steal. In one instance, the charity gave a destitute single woman a sewing machine so that she might earn her own way. In their vigilance against impositions, the Benevolent Societies seemed far distant from the attitudes of the benefit suppers and dances sometimes tendered to victims of mining accidents and other personal disasters; the societies expected not to know those they helped, and therefore felt they had to protect themselves against fraud, while the benefits tended to be arranged by a man's friends and coworkers. Despite the lapses in support and the reorganizations that characterized the careers of the Benevolent Societies—Grass Valley's lasted less than a year and Nevada City had two distinct clubs— they had their successes; the second and lasting Nevada City group aided 55 families in a period of fourteen months, and the societies did embody a desire to regularize help to the deserving by making charitable aid the product of monthly dues and research, not emotion and chance.[8] The middle-class self-improvement of 1850's reform was gone; social distancing was now all-important, and condescension had replaced fear of aliens.

Women's Work and Middle-Class Mores

The most public and possibly the most important social change accompanying the great increase in the numbers of women and children was in the place accorded women and the standards of behavior expected of them. The presence of families at all occupational levels helped to continue taking the pressure of male role expectations off middle-class women; by the late 1860's newspaper references to woman as civilizer and to the necessity of making the towns fit for mothers had almost disappeared. Suffragism, the most publicized female reform of the time, aimed not to protect women but rather to expand their moral role into politics. During the summer of 1869, the *Gazette* published the Nevada City Suffrage Association's statement of premises, which asserted that women were "equal in all save strength" to men, and went on to request that "women's restraining influence on men's coarser nature might extend to the polls." The statement demanded that the vote be based on intelligence irrespective of sex, and specifically deplored the "rabble," black and white, that currently "disgraced our polls." Arguments published later continued to emphasize women's uplifting effect on politics; middle-class women, not men, sounded this theme. The editor of the Republican *Gazette*, E. F. Bean, taking a moderate position, doubted that the vote would either degrade women or cleanse politics, but he wished the suffragists well, hoping wistfully that a chapter in Grass Valley might "redeem it from its political thralldom"—that American middle-class women might defeat Irish Democrats. Amos Morse of the Democratic *Daily National* of Grass Valley consistently made fun of the women's movement. The rhetoric of suffragism, therefore, expressed not only the traditional view of women as uplifters and the political mistrust of the foreign-born embedded in a Whig-Republican tradition, but also a new sense of class separation: respectable women versus the "rabble." [9]

Women, inescapably, played a more visible role in the life of the two towns during the late 1860's. Voices such as that of "Old Maid," a correspondent of the *Union*, complaining that Grass Valley girls were far too evident on town streets, were balanced by others like that of H. C. Bennett of the *Union*, who argued that California's most characteristic accomplishment had been to open "every avenue of employment . . . adapted to their capabilities and habits" to women, thus preventing "the demoralization of the gentler sex," that is, keeping them from prostitution or dependency. Even "Old Maid's" letter demonstrated a new acceptance of public places for women; after 1869, women became noticeable if irregular contributors to town journals, usually commenting on the civic responsibilities of women. Newspaper advertisements by dressmakers, milliners, and servants wanting places became commonplace during these years. Officials admitted women to the county hospitals on the same terms as men—that is, if they had no relatives to care for them and were unable to work—indirectly admitting that for some women at least, the rules of survival were the same as for men. If they could not work, they must starve or become wards of the county. [10]

Ironically, the greater public presence of women coincided with a dramatic reduction in the proportion of women self-supporting or directly contributing to family income. In the census of 1870, 64 percent in Grass Valley and 76 percent in Nevada City of all adult white women "kept house" for simple nuclear households (Table 21). The proportion of working women inside and outside the home had gone down by one-third in Grass Valley and more than half in Nevada City, and in Nevada City, the actual numbers had gone down as well. Women as well as men in the towns lived more traditional lives. And this orthodoxy grew for all races; the proportion of black women "keeping house" roughly matched that of whites (Table 35), and for the first time census takers listed an appreciable number of Chinese women, one in five in Grass Valley, as housewives, not prostitutes.

Some of the specific changes in women's occupational patterns reflect the new prosperity and changing occupational structures brought by the quartz industry, and the dramatic increase in the number of families. More women and children meant more jobs for single women such as teaching school, making and mending hats and dresses, nursing, and domestic service. In Grass Valley, domestic and child-oriented job-holders were the only group of female workers to increase in proportion to the gain in adult women; in Nevada City, despite the appearance of a new female occupation, nursing, these jobs remained roughly as important as they had been in 1860 (Table 21). The proportion of women servants went up slightly in both towns, but not nearly as much as the numbers of young women and of family households offering potential employment. Grass Valley now contained only a handful of prostitutes, while in Nevada City, with its higher proportion of propertyless, unmarried men and its greater commercial traffic, the proportion of white prostitutes in the female work force increased slightly. Prosperity and more potential customers also helped produce a new group of women in Grass Valley—storekeepers, boarding-house keepers, and the like—who could be classified as merchants; in Nevada City, the proportion of merchant women remained constant over the decade. In general, women who worked outside their own homes were likelier to hold real and personal property than they had been in 1860, and also likelier to do so than other women (Table 23). Given the small number of women involved, one or two unrepresentative cases could skew the results. Still, a small body of women (97 in Grass Valley, 41 in

Nevada City) employed as servants, nurses, teachers, or dressmakers could hope to accumulate property in their own names, in a way not previously possible.

But the largest group of women workers still reported few assets in their own names. These were, of course, married women who took in boarders. Since they remained the great majority of all working women, it is they who account for most of the general decline in female employment. On the surface, the sharp reduction in the percentage of adult white women in the towns who accommodated lodgers seems to correspond to the demographic changes brought on by quartz and hydraulic mining during the 1860's. The towns now contained slightly fewer men, and considerably fewer single men. But there were still enough to supply boarders; though the proportion of Grass Valley women taking lodgers went down, the actual numbers tripled. The general "good times" probably made outsiders in the home less necessary, just as the failure of servant girls to appear in numbers proportionate to the new opportunities for them may mean that the families of young women could afford to keep them at home. But prosperity, like demography, does not completely explain why women became less likely to have jobs. In 1870, relatively prosperous Grass Valley had more working women than relatively poor Nevada City. And a wife who simply kept house in no way signified her husband's occupational prestige. In both towns, larger proportions of miners' wives "kept house" than did wives of storekeepers, attorneys, or craftsmen (Table 22).

A more complete explanation must take into account the social place of women's work and of working women in the two towns. As before, an analysis of boarding casts most light on women's employment. The move away from boarding was dramatically greater in Nevada City, but in both towns it affected miners' families more than professionals' or artisans'. The poorest group in either town, Nevada City's unskilled, had the greatest proportionate decline of all (Table 22). In 1860, boarding single men, especially in Grass Valley, seems to have been the province of families "on the make," those of middling property holdings; by 1870, it was more nearly the province of those who by local standards had made it. Households with boarders were somewhat better off than the average for all families (Table 24). Among married miners in both towns, having a boarder made little difference, but among businessmen and professionals, and artisans and farmers, families with lodgers were clearly more likely to claim over $1,000 in real property than those without.

These facts might suggest that the increasing prosperity of the 1860's had made taking in lodgers for profit no longer necessary, and that the practice had become predominantly a way in which the well-to-do taught their values and watched over single young people. But a comparison of the occupations of boarders with those of their hosts suggests that in all but Grass Valley's wealthiest classes, the profit motive remained paramount. Among laborers and miners, as in 1860, boarding relationships tended to be between equals (Table 25).

Among Grass Valley's artisans and farmers, the most likely of all groups to have boarders, only one-quarter of boarding households contained men of equal status, commonly partners in a craft such as blacksmithing or carpentry. Three in ten contained men who were roughly the same age as the host, not identifiably related to the family, and working at an unrelated trade. Four in ten contained employees and apprentices. Here the idea that boarding functioned partly as a means of social control and instruction, that hosts stood as surrogate parents, seems more likely. But only 2 percent of artisan and farm households with boarders contained apprentices, whereas 67 percent were farm families that put up farm laborers. Farming had boomed in Grass Valley township during the decade, and paying farms boarded more workers. Notoriously transient, varied in age, and often of different ethnic background from their employers, these men would not seem likely to have been under any sort of moral care, although farm owners certainly imposed a certain discipline on their lives.

Boarding for reasons other than profit would seem most likely to appear in the households of businessmen and professionals, and in Grass Valley this assumption holds; such families were the most likely to board men in some state of dependency. Six in ten of these high-status households with boarders contained clerks or other employees, students, or junior partners. Only one-third contained men whose jobs were unrelated to, and lower in status than, the business of the host. Since 1860 the profit motive had apparently declined as a reason for boarding among the majority of these and a smaller proportion of artisan households; women's work perhaps had become less purely mercenary and more an extension of their moral influence. Of course, such households made up less than 10 percent of Grass Valley homes accepting lodgers.

Nevada City's merchant and professional families tended to maintain the form of boarding they had practiced in 1860. Nearly three in ten boarded men of equal status with the host; 44 percent hosted men of occupations and ages suggesting profit motives; and only 28 percent had clerks or other possible dependents. Higher percentages of artisan and farm households contained partners and employees—again often farm laborers—than in Grass Valley. The small group of miners' and laborers' homes with boarders resembled those of Grass Valley. Motives beyond simple profit, then, also existed in Nevada City, although no group stood out in this regard like Grass Valley's merchant families. Given the much smaller number of households with boarders at all levels in Nevada City, and the greater importance of rent in the boarding practices of its merchants, the ideal of teaching social values and exercising moral leadership seems to have been less practiced than in Grass Valley.

In some ways, the connection between women's work and household structure was the same as it had been in 1860. Having a job did not exempt a married woman from the responsibilities of motherhood; more specifically, there were no significant differences in Grass Valley in numbers of children in the household between families where the mother did and those where she did not accept boarders; in Nevada City, boarding families had more children (Table 28). And just as in 1860, Nevada City women who took in boarders were twice as likely to have servants as those who did not take in boarders. There had been too few servants in Grass Valley in 1860 to support a correlation between their presence and boarding; but by 1870 the correlation was essentially the same as in Nevada City. Still, while the numbers of servants in prosperous Grass Valley during the 1860's increased, the proportion of homes with servants remained small (Table 27).

Merchants and professionals, not surprisingly, had more servants than men in other occupations; one Grass Valley merchant in five had hired household help, and one in twenty had more than one servant (Table 26). The more property a man had, the more likely he was to have at least one servant. With more servants and more boarders living as members of a surrogate family, Grass Valley merchants and professionals, enjoying a quartz-based affluence, lived closest to the mid-nineteenth century ideal of a middle-class family. But the conjunction of boarders and servants still suggests that for many the hired help contributed to family finances (lodgers paid more than domestics earned) rather than reflected them.

The general decline in the proportion of working women was rooted in the increased prosperity of Grass Valley and Nevada City, complicated by the increased power of middle-class notions of respectability. There was less need than in 1860 for wives to perform income-producing work, and the sheer numbers of them now in the towns had created communities where, as never before, orthodox family values could not merely survive but dominate. But these forces operated to differing degrees and in different ways in the two towns, and within each town among the various economic and occupational classes.

In Grass Valley, among miners, the lessened incentive for families to take in boarders was offset by the increased demand for their services generated by a growing quartz work force. The proportion of boarding families went down, but the actual numbers went up, and the patterns of host-guest relations were unaffected (Table 25). In the artisan-and-farmer class, the farm boom created a slight proportional increase in boarding (the only increase in any class in either town), and host-guest relations became if anything even more purely economic. Among businessmen and professionals, the proportion of boarding families decreased, but the decline was the smallest in either town, except among artisans. And boarding for apparently paternalistic reasons increased significantly, especially among the richest members of the middle class.* Alonzo Delano had tried to turn the town toward traditional morality for as long as he had been in Grass Valley; in the late 1860's, he had charge of a young man not his son.

Nevada City was more prosperous than it had been in 1860 but less so than its neighbor, and boarding declined more there in all

* Among Grass Valley merchants and professionals whose boarders seemed likely to be paying rent, 57 percent had more than $1,000 in real property, and all of those whose boarders seemed to be dependents did so. Of merchant families with boarders for rent, 29 percent had more than $5,000, and of those with dependents, 41 percent. No similar relationship existed in Nevada City.

classes. The decrease was most drastic among miners, where less-ened incentive to take in lodgers had not been offset by any rise in the mining work force; as with Grass Valley miners, the patterns of host-guest relations remained the same. There was also a large decline, and somewhat less boarding for rent, among artisan fam-ilies, where no special circumstance such as an agricultural upsurge offset decreased family need. In the merchant and professional class, boarding declined very significantly, but the patterns of host-guest relations remained as economic as they had been in 1860 because the very richest families, instead of turning to paternalism, simply stopped accepting lodgers. The Grass Valley elite (as the big mine operators left) were often merchants who boarded clerks; the equivalent upper stratum in Nevada City included many attorneys without law clerks to board. While the actual numbers of such very well off families were small in both towns, it seems fair to con-clude, as Byrne and Mitchell of the *Union* did in 1868, that those of Nevada City had more influence upon their fellow townsmen, and that this influence also contributed to the greater decline of board-ing there. In a community where women were, in theory, impor-tant chiefly as a source of moral influence (as the suffrage move-ment demonstrates) and yet where in practice most women who cared for boarders did so because their families needed the money, boarding was bound to become less socially acceptable with the rise in wealth. Living in a more commercially oriented town with more American-born and less ethnic segregation, Nevada City's resi-dents would be likelier to adopt the views of their merchant fam-ilies than those of Grass Valley, where the large numbers of ethnic miners lived in a separate world. The connection between board-ing and paternalism, important to Grass Valley's elite, had nothing to do with boarding in mining households. And as boarding de-clined, of course, so did women's work. Relative prosperity, then, shaped women's work, but so did the relative power of the middle class.

The New World of the Foreign-Born

The social divergence between the two towns, especially the lesser influence of the middle class in Grass Valley, was openly admitted in the late 1860's. But the ethnic content of the difference was not, nor was the increasing identity of ethnicity and occupation. The growing sense of nationalism demonstrated by some ethnic groups during the decade reflected this identity—the Cornish, for example, defined themselves in terms of mining skills. The dynamics of intergroup relations became much more complex; at times the ties of an ethnic group to a certain occupation or economic interest overrode ancient prejudices. The felt need for cheap labor to keep the mines going brought some American-born professionals and merchants to extol the capacity for work of the Chinese, while the Cornish and the Irish attempted to bury their enmities in the common cause of miners facing new challenges from absentee corporate ownership. The ethnic confrontations of the mining strike of 1869 expressed in action these new perceptions of each group's actual position in town life.

Fundamental to the growing strains between the natives and the foreign-born was the congruence between birthplace and work. Some natives, however, claimed to find the split between themselves and the immigrant population not in jobs, but in family attitudes. Editors hinted that the behavior of Irish and Cornish boys—idle, noisy, violence-prone, especially toward the Chinese—stemmed from the refusal of some foreign-born working families to assume responsibility for disciplining, controlling, or teaching their children.[11] But despite veiled editorial accusations, with two very important exceptions, national origin did not affect family structure or behavior. The Chinese men, except some merchants, did not have wives in America; Nevada City's men had a smaller proportion of wives and children than Grass Valley's in part because of its larger Chinese population (Table 36). The British (three-fourths Cornish) of Grass Valley lived closest among major European groups to Gold Rush conditions. Predominantly miners, commonly living in cabins with their countrymen, they had followed standard immigrant procedure in leaving their wives, if any, at home, in Wisconsin or Cornwall. By 1860 standards these Cornish miners lived orthodox lives, but in 1870 they stood out as the inheritors of the old ways; in Grass Valley only the Chinese and French were less likely to be married. Already known for clannishness and arrogance and subjected to a muted nativism, in Grass Valley they also seemed outside the common pattern of marriage and family life. In Nevada City they did not.

The households of foreign-born families seem to have been

shaped more by occupation and wealth than by ethnicity. When an ethnic group stood out in any way—size of family, number of boarders, working children—it was because that group was identified with a particular level of status. Its families shared attributes with other groups having similar occupations and assets (Table 43); German middle-class households looked like those of the native middle class. Families from each ethnic group in the two towns had roughly the same number of children (Table 39). Except among the American-born, the rule within each group was the more property, the more children (Table 40). The Irish likewise proved a partial exception to this rule; they had larger families than the other major groups, just as Irishmen were likelier to be married, despite their generally inferior economic situation. The wives of the foreign-born, with the exception of the Germans, were less likely to take in boarders (Table 37). In particular, Irish households contained proportionately fewer boarders than German or native households in either town, and fewer than British ones in Grass Valley. Likewise, the households of the foreign-born contained proportionately fewer servants than those of the native-born. Within each ethnic group, boarding and servant patterns resembled those of the town at large; the miners were less likely, the merchants and artisans more likely, to have outsiders in the home.* From the outside, ethnic families and households probably could not be distinguished from native families of the same occupational and financial status. No hordes of Irish or Cornish children, unsupervised by their working mothers, idled in the streets, any more than did American-born youth.

Even though ethnic family structures resembled those of the American-born, nativists might still have argued that family values differed. But the proportions of children working or going to school—and by extension, attitudes toward children—also varied little among ethnic groups. The Irish families of Grass Valley had the same proportion of male children employed as the natives, the British slightly more. In Nevada City, the American-born and Ger-

---

*In Grass Valley, 14 percent of the American-born, 5 percent of the British, 3 percent of the Irish, and 9 percent of the Germans had servants. In Nevada City, the figures were, respectively, 9 percent, 1 percent, 3 percent, and 7 percent. Among Grass Valley miners the figures were 6, 2, 0, and 0 percent; among Grass Valley merchants they were 28, 14, 17, and 22 percent. Roughly similar conditions existed in Nevada City.

mans were most likely to have working children. In both towns the foreign-born seemed to have a greater commitment to education than the natives.* Finally, the very small number of households where unmarried men and women lived together show, among whites, no differences reflecting ethnicity; each group produced its proportionate share of social outcasts. In sum, just as in 1860, the families of the white foreign-born could not be invidiously compared to native families. To the extent that they differed, that difference reflected the concentration of ethnic groups in certain occupations. Miners lived unlike the rest of society, and the people most identified with mining, the Grass Valley Cornish, were furthest outside late-1860's family norms, but even mining families lived like other families.

The essential similarity between the families of the American-born and other whites had not changed during the 1860's; commentators suggesting otherwise were indulging nativist fantasies. However, the relationship between several of the ethnic groups and the rest of town society was changing, largely because of changes in the occupational structure, but also through gains in self-consciousness, even nationalism on the part of nonwhite and foreign-born groups. Growing group identity reflected local events, often simply an increase in members sufficient to support social clubs or institutions, but also at times events international in scope, such as the unification of Germany or the Fenian movement.

The black populations of the two towns are good examples of this change toward autonomy. The quality of life within the black community did not change during the decade despite the appearance of a small group of artisans in Nevada City; blacks were a tiny, poor minority. They constituted less than 1 percent of the population in Grass Valley and less than 2 percent in Nevada City,

* In Grass Valley, 93 percent of the American families, 91 percent of the British, 93 percent of the Irish, and 95 percent of the German families had no resident children listed with a job. In Nevada City, 89 percent of the American, 91 percent of the British, 94 percent of the Irish, and 88 percent of the German families had no working children. In Grass Valley, 69 percent of the school-age children of American families were actually in school, 79 percent of the British, 80 percent of the Irish, and 82 percent of the German. In Nevada City, 67 percent of the American, 88 percent of the British, 88 percent of the Irish, and 77 percent of the German children of school age were enrolled. The number of American-born blacks was not large enough to greatly affect these results.

and few reported real or personal property. Family living gained in importance as it had in all groups, as during the 1860's black men became almost twice as likely to have wives and children as in 1860, and over half now lived in traditional two-parent households (Tables 34 and 35). In 1870, as in 1860, blacks were more likely to live in families than whites.

However, Emancipation and Reconstruction changed attitudes on the part of both whites and blacks. For the first time, newspaper references to blacks were not monopolized by deprecatory tales of low life, although these did remain current. Instead, Republican editors made a point of applauding black endeavors at self-improvement. Blacks shifted attitudes more completely, now openly seeking a part in the two towns' public life. In the late 1850's blacks in both towns had commemorated the end of slavery in the West Indies, and during the Civil War blacks had staged events in support of the Sanitary Fund; awareness of racial interests had been expressed in public ways before the late 1860's. But after January 1, 1863, each new year was ushered in by a celebration of Emancipation, the largest and most formal occasion recognizing a black identity in the two towns. Perhaps the most noteworthy facts about these annual affairs were that black enthusiasm maintained itself throughout the decade and that the role of whites as planners, speakers, and active participants diminished, not only because of the Republican defeat of 1867, blamed on anti-black backlash, but also because of strong black efforts to take over the holiday. In 1868 the Lincoln Club of Nevada, composed of blacks from Nevada City, Grass Valley, and lesser camps, organized to put on the observance. After that, Emancipation Day became a black affair, and whites acted merely as spectators. Blacks also demonstrated interest in national politics. Some had tried to register to vote immediately after the passage of the 14th Amendment, only to be turned back; after the 15th Amendment went into effect, fifteen Nevada City blacks registered the first hour the books were open, and a Grass Valley black, Jacob Saunders, announced for town trustee. Local Republicans responded gingerly, while Democratic spokesmen had a field day, but the new black voters had other things in mind than the comfort of Republican politicians. The Lincoln Club staged a commemoration of the amendment at

which white Republican politicians campaigned; at the 1864 freedom festival a white minister had urged blacks to "leave their
cause in the hands of their white friends," but by 1870 similar
speakers solicited votes.[12]

In 1864 black Methodists in Nevada City built a church with
funds raised in part at a festival supported by local whites. When
the church house was destroyed by a storm that winter, it was
rebuilt with money from a series of dances, dinners, and bazaars
that white editors admitted demonstrated a greater concerted effort than they had believed the black community capable of producing. And in 1865 the African Methodist Episcopal Church of
both towns opened schools that proved as stable as their segregated
white counterparts. Black lecturers at educational meetings taught
African history and culture; others at these black lyceums demanded equal justice and stressed the importance of blacks acting in
self-defense. At times, all-black subscription dances benefited
black clubs and churches. While the black communities in both
towns combined to support black undertakings, there were not
enough people and money for black institutions to operate completely outside white influence, models, participation, and aid.
Still, Emancipation had inspired black activities that, while they
took their shape from white practice, took their content from black
needs and racial consciousness.[13]

The white ethnic groups also expressed a new sense of their
separate identities during the late 1860's. There had been Schiller
Clubs and Burns memorials, but usually ethnic organizations had
not gone beyond cultural awareness; in the procession honoring the
murdered Lincoln, only the Hebrew Benevolent Society among the
European clubs marched as a unit alongside the Masons and Odd
Fellows. Only the French paraded as a national group, and some of
them insisted on joining "the citizens generally." In 1870 there
would probably have been a prideful nationalism displayed by
German, French, and Irish marchers and also by Cornish miners.
The French, despite their small numbers (about 40 in Nevada City
and twice that in Grass Valley), had always been conspicuously
nationalistic and remained so even though they became fewer
during the 1860's, partly because of the constant flow of migration
and return. The Franco-Prussian War crystallized their identity,

however, as hostilities in Europe inspired fistfights between Frenchmen and Germans and a series of entertainments culminating in a lottery for the relief of war victims in France.

For the French, the war simply brought into public focus an established chauvinism; for the Germans, the war helped forge a new unity. Previously divided by religion and by state of birth, the Germans had no permanent organizations to mark their common background. The Jews had seemed to have no social ties to the Christian Germans, even though the great majority of Jews were German-born. The war reversed all that; the Germans, few Prussians among them, united like the French to raise monies for the home front, with Jews prominent in the efforts. The German Patriotic Association of Grass Valley met monthly throughout the war to collect funds. Only marginally larger as a proportion of male workers in 1870 than in 1860, the Germans were much more visible as a group. The Jews who marched among the Germans in support of Bismarck's nationalistic policy had already managed through increased numbers and business prosperity to make for themselves a more complete religious life. Importing rabbis from San Francisco, renting halls for use on the High Holy Days, purchasing religious equipment, they were able to observe most of the festival calendar even without a synagogue in either town. Anti-Semitism remained quiescent, and possibly this fact, with the Jews' secure position in the towns as businessmen and their success in maintaining the practices of their faith, helped enable them to transcend religious differences to embrace the German cause.[14]

The Irish followed the common pattern: combinations of local and European events focused national feelings previously vented through the Democratic Party or St. Patrick's Day parades. In 1866 St. Patrick's Church was completed and furnished—it had been used while construction continued—and the same year the Sisters of Mercy opened their orphanage; in 1868 the sisters also founded a school. In 1868 the establishment of the Diocese of Grass Valley (although the bishop resided in Marysville) added to the new strength of the Catholic Church in the quartz township. This institutional religious growth showed itself most obviously on St. Patrick's Day. The hilarious parades of the 1850's had already been toned down, and religious charity had become one of the celebration's purposes, but after 1865 the Sisters of Mercy, the church, and later the orphanage became central; a charity ball for the orphanage crowned the day in the late 1860's. Catholicism was becoming more important to specifically Irish experience in the towns.[15]

The other agency promoting Irish separateness was the Fenian Brotherhood, which founded chapters at Allison Ranch, Grass Valley, and Nevada City in 1865. Militant refugee revolutionaries hoping, among other things, to help liberate Ireland by attacking British interests in Canada, the Fenians met enthusiastic responses in the towns that spring and summer. During 1865 Grass Valley township raised over $3,000 for the war chest; in Nevada City, although the brotherhood temporarily disbanded during the winter of 1865, Irish owners dubbed a saloon the Fenian Exchange. The abortive Fenian invasion of Canada in 1866 gave new impetus to the movement in Nevada County; word of the attack brought forth $1,000 in additional funds and twelve volunteer soldiers. Divisions in the national organizations in the aftermath of the Canadian adventure weakened the local brotherhoods, and a reorganization in 1868 did not halt their decline. But in their prime, marching as greenclad militia companies in Fourth of July and St. Patrick's Day parades, the Fenians exemplified local ethnic nationalism. And in their last major gathering, Fenians summed up the new sense of Irishness. They assembled in Grass Valley on the morning of March 17, 1868, marched to the Catholic church for Mass, and then moved on to the Mazeppa Saloon, where they were temporarily dismissed. Upon reassembling they paraded on to the Orphan Asylum, where the inmates serenaded them with Irish and American patriotic airs. They then adjourned to attend the orphanage's charity festival and ball. The church and the flag, the local religious institutions, and the trans-Atlantic revolutionary movement together created a revitalized sense of self.[16]

The efflorescence of black and European ethnic particularism was based in part on discrete events outside the towns: a war, a revolutionary movement, Emancipation. The passage of time could, and in the 1870's would, erode the public expression of identities formed in this way. The Franco-Prussian War soon ended, the Fenians disbanded, and the commemoration of the Proclamation lapsed. But the separateness of the Cornish and the Chinese, based on race, culture, and occupation, remained constant, and the treatment of the Chinese remained a good gauge of whites' sense of security. The Chinese population grew in the late 1860's; the turn to quartz reduced their presence in Grass Valley, but that loss was more than made up in Nevada City, where they increased until they constituted 17 percent of the total population. The Chinatowns evolved into more complete neighborhoods, with a wider range of institutions to serve their inhabitants. Temples and a theater supplied traditional Chinese culture, while restaurateurs, physicians, and druggists multiplied to meet physical needs. There were more Chinese stores, and also more opium dens, gamblers, and prostitutes. Buildings remained flimsy, although temples and merchant dwellings were often expensively furnished; the Chinatowns, like the white slums next door, did not assume an air of solidity or prosperity.[17]

The Chinese continued to be almost without exception male, young, and single (Table 33), and the most common living unit in the Chinatowns or at Chinese placer sites was a tenement or cabin occupied by four to six men. Industrial quartz mining reduced the proportion of Chinese listing "miner" as their occupation, although the majority still dug for gold (Table 14). Placer mining projects organized and manned by the Chinese increased in number, size, and importance as whites moved out of traditional placer works, until the Chinese owned some of the largest nonhydraulic placer operations in the two towns. For the rank and file, domestic work and common labor took on more importance—work more town-oriented than mining had been. The great majority of Chinese continued to work at jobs in which they did not directly compete with whites, but a handful worked beside whites as quartz-mill hands or skilled laborers, and could be seen as rivals to white laborers. The emergence of these men, with the rise in numbers of domestics and common laborers, meant that more Chinese earned their living at close quarters with whites than previously. While most Chinese continued to live in the Chinatowns, or at all-Chinese mining sites in the townships, the Chinese populations had become somewhat more diffused throughout both Grass Valley and Nevada City because of the turn to domestic or service work. Outside the towns, quartz mining companies that employed both whites and Chinese perforce created situations where the two groups lived in close proximity, as laborers lived near their work. In very rare cases, Chinese and whites shared the same dwelling, and of course in the red-light districts, all races lived mixed together. The Chinese, then, like the blacks, were not absolutely segregated; the nature of their work, both service and skilled, brought them together with whites.[18]

Even with seven in ten Chinese in Nevada City listed by the 1870 census as miners, the town supported a more varied occupational group than Grass Valley because its larger Chinese community generated a greater range of supporting services.* Tailors, cobblers, peddlers, and restaurant keepers catered to the Chinese miners, supplementing the wares of the larger Chinese merchants. Only half of Grass Valley's Chinese mined, while a higher proportion of the non-miners performed domestic services for whites. Although they both became larger and more complex, the relative positions of the two Chinatowns therefore remained the same between 1860 and 1870. Temples and religious festivals multiplied, but the traditional Chinese institutions that most struck white observers in the late 1860's were the hui kuan, the Chinese regional companies. Whites saw the hui kuan, the stronger Sze Yup and the underdog Young Wo, primarily in terms of street fights and assassinations—when the two companies staged a brief battle in the streets of Nevada City in 1870, together they mustered more than 150 fighting men—but whites also became aware of, and perhaps exaggerated, the companies' economic control of the Chinese. Both towns also contained tongs, which feuded over women and mining rights, and occupational guilds that set prices and attempted to regulate competition.[19]

Although a wider spectrum of the white population became acquainted with Chinese customs during the late 1860's through visits to New Year's celebrations, Chinese theaters, or Chinese stores, druggists, and doctors, white professionals and merchants showed most interest in the Chinese and had most contact with them. These middle-class contacts came in part through the growing use of Chinese servants, in part through the efforts by Chinese merchants to forge links with their white compeers, and in part

---

* Nevada City had four Chinese men who owned restaurants, Grass Valley, one. Nevada City contained two Chinese tailors, two cobblers, and two blacksmiths; only one Chinese cobbler lived in Grass Valley. Nevada City contained 22 washmen to Grass Valley's 10. More Chinese common laborers, gardeners, and servants lived in Grass Valley than in Nevada City.

through white attempts to shape the Chinese into white patterns of behavior. Several denominations had tried to teach English and Christianity to the Chinese during the 1850's and 1860's in California. Locally, the most important attempt came in 1869, when the Methodist churches organized Sunday schools to teach English in both towns. Initially, especially in Nevada City, the response was favorable among both whites and Chinese; in spite of suspicions that the Chinese might misuse their knowledge to cheat whites, William Byrne felt that educating the Chinese would "eliminate their sick civilization." Attendance at the Nevada City school grew from 9 to 45, and the Chinese proved good students. However, as one teacher explained, racial stereotypes held by whites proved too established to overcome, and after hopeful starts, the schools closed as the Chinese became disgusted and quit at the failure of enough teachers to come forward to maintain instruction. Religious efforts in Chinatown reverted to the distribution of tracts by white individuals.[20]

While at least a portion of the native middle class, including several newspapermen, defended the Chinese, the old hatreds continued to flourish, particularly among miners and laborers. American-born editors hinted that this dislike was also especially virulent among the foreign-born; their suggestions that immigrant children were not being reared properly commonly pointed to Irish and Cornish youths stoning or snowballing Chinese. More dangerous were the state Democratic Party's claims that Chinese labor, controlled by capitalists, would be used to oppress white labor, especially when accompanied by that party's traditional appeal to ethnic group solidarity. Older Sinophobic stereotypes of slave women and an intrinsically immoral culture survived intact from the 1850's, now reinforced by images of servile masses content with absurdly low pay; ascriptions of Chinese character kept them vulnerable to racial violence.[21]

The people most likely to see a danger in docile Chinese mine labor were the Cornish. No group, not even the American-born, had a greater sense of uniqueness and separateness than they did. And while other groups expressed their ethnicity through *Landsmannschaften,* through national heroes and racial history, the Cornish saw themselves as special largely in terms of their work. Methodism, wrestling and soccer, diet, and dialect set them apart, but their ethnocentrism largely centered on their assumption of the superiority of their mining methods and their insistence on working with their own. Outsiders often felt that the Cornish were attempting to create a monopoly of skilled mining by claiming a monopoly of mining skills. As a group the most recent immigrants from Europe (except for the French) and sometimes possessing only a limited knowledge of America, they had gained and kept an immediate standing in the two towns because of their deep-shaft expertise. Their acceptance was dependent not on acculturation but rather on necessary knowledge; in the late 1860's, as in the late 1850's, Grass Valley's future lay with them. Their prickly sense of self had helped involve the Cornish in ethnic brawls from their first days in the towns, and their pugnaciousness did not diminish as their numbers rose. Unfortunately for peace and quiet, their newly dominant presence in Grass Valley coincided with the Fenian phase of their traditional Irish enemies. The Cornish were quick to resent the anti-British rhetoric of the Fenians, and while other groups held silent, respecting Irish political and physical abilities, the Cousin Jacks talked and fought back. Pitched battles, ten or twelve to a side, took place on several occasions, and rumors surfaced at least once of an impending total war between the Irish and Cornish communities. The Cornish also maintained a nonpolitical feud with the Germans, staging one memorable encounter on the Germans' home ground in front of a Grass Valley saloon, with 25 to a side; only the fact that neither people habitually used knives or pistols prevented dangerous injuries and death.[22]

Accusations of violence contributed to the developing estrangement between Cornish and natives during the mid-1860's; in the Grass Valley press, encomiums on Cornish skill and diligence gave way to reports of arrogance and exclusiveness. Much of this attitudinal change stemmed from the fact that miners' Saturday nights in town had always been seen as dangerous to the towns, and now the revellers were mostly Cornishmen, made easily identifiable by their obvious group cohesion. But the change also exposed the American-born's disquiet as Grass Valley's largest ethnic group came more and more to dominate town life outside of politics. Underlying the natives' resentment was Grass Valley's dependence on the Cornish; no one argued that the town could do without them.[23]

The Miners' World

The Cornish brawled with Irish and Germans because of simple ethnocentrism; their growing separation from the towns at large, particularly the American-born middle class, had deeper, more ominous origins. Industrial mining had reinforced in Grass Valley and to a lesser extent in Nevada City one of the salient social characteristics of the towns' early history: the physical and emotional distance between the townships and the towns, the miners and the merchants. And because the Cornish supplied a disproportionate fraction of mine workers, cultural identities exaggerated the alienation rooted in occupational class.

The quartz boom had altered the living arrangements of miners. Both family homes and boarding hotels became more common, but the all-male cabin with three to five inhabitants remained the most common living arrangement (Table 18). In Nevada City, where the mining population was heavily Chinese, by 1870 only one-third lived in the old male cabins (three-fourths had in 1860). Almost one-fourth of the miners lived with their families; almost one-fifth lived alone, in hotels and boarding houses, but also in scattered cabins in the township. These solitary men, mostly white and native-born, suggest an almost pitiful remnant of the placer days, men left stranded as their companions gave up the effort of small-time mining. Another 20 percent, overwhelmingly Chinese, lived in boarding hotels, actually large, crowded dwellings, where fifteen to twenty men still fended for themselves. The remainder lived with parents or boarded in private homes.

Grass Valley differed dramatically from its neighbor. Roughly the same proportion of miners, one in four, lived with their families, but only one in twenty lived alone. Less than one-tenth lived in boarding houses, but these men, mostly Cornish and Irish, enjoyed the services of cooks, housekeepers, and resident owners; their boarding houses were not simply the old cabins writ large, as with Nevada City's Chinese. Ten percent boarded in private homes, usually with the families of other miners. And half lived in the traditional cabins; quartz mining had not changed that. Miners sharing a cabin, boarding with a mining family, or living in a miners' boarding hotel truly lived apart, and all these dwellings tended to house one ethnic group (Table 3).

Miners of all backgrounds found themselves increasingly at odds with the rest of society. Single miners living in boarding hotels, the cabins around township mine sites, or the slums of the Chinatowns maintained through the 1860's the system of illicit resorts established in the mid-1850's. In noting that the county grand jury had indicted "a couple of notorious cyprians, residing on Broad Street, Nevada City," W. H. Miller in the *Grass Valley Daily Union* demonstrated that upper Broad had not changed. But he also revealed that nothing had changed in Grass Valley, as he sanctimoniously continued: "Thank Heaven, the Grand Jury nor any other man can't find a house of prostitution within the precincts of Grass Valley. If we except the delectable Chinatown, there is not a house of ill repute in this town." That is, the "fancy men" and their women stayed in an area on Mill and Main Streets where the Chinese and the underworld had lived together, as they did in Nevada City, since the early 1850's. The forcible drawing of lines between virtue and vice also survived. The fire companies repeated the innovation of "washing out" undesirable businesses four times between 1865 and 1870, the Nevada City firemen concentrating on dives on the very upper part of Broad, next to a middle-class neighborhood. The return of prosperity and the accompanying influx of miners to the townships also brought the expansion of miners' institutions—five new saloons opened within one month in Nevada City—and renewed conflict between citizens and miners on sprees. The majority of the men committed to the county jail in 1867 faced charges of riot, and candidates for marshal routinely pledged to clear the streets of "the foul mouthed bummers." Town officials wavered, caught between the economic importance of miners' amusements—Nevada City levied a license fee of $5 per night on saloons with musicians—and the complaints of residents upset about noise and potential crime.[24]

The continuing transience of the miners also set them apart in the eyes of merchants and professionals, who judged others in terms of their stake in the towns and their permanency. Although quartz production had slowed population turnover, many miners, including those with families, continued to pursue new strikes; miners demonstrated less persistence than the middle class. Half of the Nevada City women who appeared as heads of households in 1870, unlike those of 1860, listed themselves as "keeping house," which implies that they may have had husbands elsewhere (Table 19). Some men made a practice of leaving their families behind in reasonably secure places like Grass Valley or Nevada City while they prospected or worked in raw, untamed camps. In 1869 a fire in Gold Hill, Nevada, resulted in two funerals and two widows in Grass Valley, and several of the women aided by the Nevada Benevolent Society had husbands who had died or failed while mining elsewhere.

Some of these miners on the road bore solid reputations at home, but, particularly in Grass Valley, found themselves unable to compete with corporate mining. Independent operator Edwin Morse failed to develop his own quartz claim during the boom of 1865 and shifted his promotions elsewhere, developing sites in Austin, Nevada, and Siskiyou County, California. Starting in the mid-1850's, he had been absent from Grass Valley for years at a time. His engagement to Abbie Robinson stretched to almost five years, and immediately after the wedding he went east to raise capital for a company to work the Austin strike. Morse, much luckier than most independents, finally made a killing on the Black Bear mine in the Siskiyou country. But Morse's feat was no longer possible in Grass Valley; even the expansion of quartz operations during the mid-1860's had depended on capitalizing and developing known sites. Grass Valley and Nevada City became bases of operations, where patient Abbie Robinsons waited.[25]

Prospecting trips may have divided families, but mining accidents destroyed them. E. F. Bean of the *Gazette*, commenting on injuries sustained underground in Nevada County, noted with wonder (and detachment) that no one seemed to learn by example, that people looked on injury as an inevitable adjunct of mining, outside human control. Bean estimated that a mining accident occurred almost every day. Men permanently crippled, attempting to eke out a living by peddling pictures or notions, were common sights on the streets of the two towns. A much larger proportion of Grass Valley female heads of household worked or took in boarders than did their counterparts in Nevada City (Table 19); likely more of the former were widows with dependent children. The accident rate worsened in the late 1860's. The county hospital neared financial collapse under the burden of pauperized, incapacitated miners; the county grand jury underlined the alienation between miner and town taxpayer by denouncing the practice of admitting disabled miners to the charity facility. Mining injuries, then, were a constant threat to family security and survival, the public response to them a constant reminder to miners of society's indifference to them. Typically, the miners turned to a Cornish solution. Unable to depend on the benevolent societies or benefit suppers, they followed the custom of paying a portion of their wages each month—50 cents or a dollar—into an accident fund.[26]

Industrialized, absentee-owned corporate mine companies, a largely ethnic work force, and a heavily middle-class native population had resulted in new social distances; spatial segregation had heightened them. Images of transient, pugnacious, clannish Cornish miners and of indifferent, hypocritical, Chinese-loving town merchants turned distance into dislike. The old term "honest miner" no longer described the model citizen of Grass Valley or Nevada City; the miner was an alien in mining towns, and acutely conscious of that fact.

The Miners' Strike

Distrust and enmity between ethnic and occupational groups came to bitter fruition in the spring of 1869 in a divisive mining strike that lingered through the summer, blending into an anti-Chinese political crusade that fall. Although the first walkout took place in Nevada City, both the strike and the Sinophobia centered in Grass Valley, where social fissures gaped widest. And both events pitted ethnic groups against each other. During the strike, the native merchant class counterpoised the Germans and the Chinese against Cornish and Irish miners; in the political campaign, most whites, but especially the Cornish and the Irish, opposed the Chinese and their middle-class native "protectors."

Rumors that a miners' society would be founded to promote mutual aid and standardized wages had been current for over a year when the introduction of dynamite, or "giant powder," and single-handed drilling into local mines precipitated the formation of a Grass Valley Miners' League. Up until this time "miners' meetings" or clubs had been called into being by mine owners, in efforts to protect their rights. Hard-rock miners had opposed giant powder ever since it had been introduced in California; in Edwin Morse's unsuccessful quartz mine, the Irish foreman had had to force men fearful for their health to work in a shaft being sunk by dynamite. But giant powder posed a threat to miners beyond nitroglycerin fumes. Setting charges of black powder had required two men to drill the large holes necessary to hold sufficient powder; dynamite, much more powerful, needed smaller holes that could be cut by one man. Dynamite and single-handed drilling would save owners money by eliminating miners' jobs. The innovation also obviated Cornish mine practices, which used two-man teams, and Cornish expertise underground. In response, the Cornish insisted that single-handed work had been proved inefficient years before.[27]

The debate over giant powder moved from theory to action on April 21, 1869, when the underground crew of Nevada City's Banner Mine quit, refusing to use dynamite. Mine managers replaced them, but less than a week later the new men also walked out and the Banner closed. While newspapers debated the health question (pro-owner journals ridiculed the miners' "head-aches" from the fumes, more neutral voices demanded exhaustive tests) and told miners that strikes always proved futile and that dynamite would create more jobs by permitting the exploitation of previously non-paying ledges, Grass Valley miners prepared to organize.

On April 30, a group of mining superintendents including S. W. Lee of the Empire and J. H. Crossman of the North Star mine staged a test of giant powder; on May 5, Amos Morse of the *National* reported that the superintendents had bought up all the giant powder locally available; the next day the *National* announced the formation of an informal miners' association to oppose giant powder. The miners' correspondent, Thomas Faull, was in communication with Comstock mine unions concerning the formation of a similar league in Grass Valley. On May 8, Captain Faull issued a "Notice to Miners" announcing that the Miners' League would oppose giant powder and single-handed drilling and would not "allow" any man to work underground for less than $3 per day. The League would assemble its members as soon as the by-laws were received from Nevada state.[28]

Faull's statement hardened editorial opinion on giant powder; the newspaper consensus decried strikes and violence, pointed out that miners, far from facing wage cuts, were in fact demanding raises for shovelers and carmen, the less skilled underground workers, and insisted that the miners' only legitimate issue was health. Byrne in the *Grass Valley Daily Union*, taking the strongest pro-owner stance among the newspapers, stated that giant powder had already been proved harmless to miners' health, denounced the issue as a screen for opposition to single-handed drilling, and insisted that profitability was the only real test of giant powder. In answer, the miners reaffirmed that they would use force if necessary. On May 11, Crossman of the North Star mine announced to his underground crew that he would not meet League demands, and 135 men left the mine; Lee of the Empire discharged 100 underground workers for League membership. While the mines crushed quartz previously excavated, and the San Francisco owners telegraphed their support to their superintendents, James Brew, vice-president of the Gold Hill Miners' Union, arrived to complete the formal organization of a branch league. Philip Painter replaced Faull as head of the League, and Brew assured Morse of the *National* in an interview published on May 18 that it repudiated earlier resolutions threatening violence, made health, not single-handed drilling, the basis of its opposition to giant powder, and demanded $3 per day for underground work.[29]

While League resolutions proclaimed that "the interest of the miner is equal with that of the owner; labor is the father of capital" and journalists countered with the "absolute right of ownership" and right of all men to make any wage contract they desired, the superintendents of the North Star, Empire, and Banner mines tried to recruit new crews. On May 24, Lee tried to open the Empire with a crew of 40 German and native miners. Sixty to 100 strikers met them on the way to work and, with threats of bodily harm and displays of weapons, persuaded all but twelve not to enter the mines. But the action backfired against the League. That evening a Grass Valley citizens' meeting, led by mine investors such as Dr. William McCormick, political attorneys like A. B. Dibble, E. W. Roberts, and J. C. Deuel, and merchants like B. Nathan and Rufus Shoemaker, heard statements from Lee and Crossman, passed resolutions upholding the majesty of the law, and called for a second meeting to determine a course of action. A citizens' posse was formed to protect men wanting to work. Only a week before, Nathan, a dry-goods merchant, had spoken in support of the strike at a miners' meeting, because of the economic importance of miners' purchases; now he graced a committee in support of law and order. The *Gazette* correspondent announced that "the war in Grass Valley is inaugurated."[30]

Miners attended the second meeting in force, constituting the majority of those present, but they had come to announce acquiescence. Their spokesman, George Taylor, disavowed the men who had terrorized the Empire's strikebreakers. He further repudiated Faull's League, instead calling the organization a union, a mutual aid society, pledged to staying within the law and to using moral suasion against giant powder. The meeting then passed, with union support, resolutions proclaiming the mine owner's full right to his property and the right of the worker to enter any wage contract he wished; the miners endorsed the merchants' and moderate newspapers' position. The Miners' Union had retreated to the issue of health, and had promised not to use violence against giant powder; the *Daily Union* in Grass Valley and the *Transcript* in Nevada City agreed that "nothing more could be demanded of them."[31]

The strike continued with little excitement through June and early July. The pro-owner editors, Byrne, Deal, and Bean, continued to emphasize the rights of capital and periodically reported, incorrectly, that the Empire or North Star had hired a work force and would reopen. Grass Valley butchers pledged mutual cooperation to hold up the price of meat and limit credit during the strike-induced depression; the Miners' Union threatened to open a cooperative store to fight the artificially high prices. Grass Valley, Byrne concluded in the *Union*, now stood at its lowest ebb. In early July, Lee again recruited workers and attempted to resume mining at the Empire mine; two unknown assailants attacked and beat two of them. A second citizens' group appeared, called the Law and Order Association, and only the *National* of Grass Valley stood with the miners, denying that Union members had been involved in the assaults. The excitement had no effect on the course of the strike. In mid-July, the owners finally gave way; on July 13 the Banner mine in Nevada City, where the strike had been maintained without evident help from the Grass Valley miners, re-opened using black powder, followed by the Empire and in August by the North Star. Despite lingering editorial truculence and claims that the Empire would use "whatever kind of powder it wants," the strike had successfully, if temporarily, defeated the introduction of giant powder.[32]

Ethnic enmities and identities had been inescapably entwined in the fight over giant powder from the very beginning; after all, double-handed drilling was the traditional Cornish method. Pro-owner newspapers argued that the true issue of the strike was the Cornish belief that "mining has been brought to perfection in Cornwall, and that no improvement is possible on their systems"; that is, that Cornish intransigence obstructed American progress. And in the early days of the strike, editors called on the resentment of the Cornish that had been growing in Grass Valley since the mid-1860's, mocking Cornish accents, ignorance, and arrogance. The strikers recognized their vulnerability to the claim that the Cornish only wanted to keep their monopoly on mining knowledge. Their wage demands not only tied local strikers to the wage-oriented unions of the Comstock country, they also brought the Irish carmen and shovelers, who would receive a wage raise if the strike succeeded, to the side of the skilled Cornish miners; E. F. Bean reported with evident surprise that the Irish on the Empire's underground force had joined the League. James Brew also showed that he understood the ethnic dimensions of the strike, as he led the League to reemphasize health and play down the issue of single-handed drilling, reducing the specifically Cornish content of the strike. Mine owners and their newspaper supporters promoted replacement of Cornish and Irish miners with men from other ethnic groups; at different times the companies projected hiring Australians, French Canadians who "understand single handed drilling," and natives who though short on skills claimed not to fear "giant powder nor any man." Editors discussed importing whole work crews from Germany, "the type of population needed in the mines," because they would establish family homes and gardens. Throughout the strike, pro-owner editors counted on the support of the middle-class foreign-born, particularly the Germans; the butchers who clashed with strikers over prices were commonly German. The confrontation at the Empire mine matched a mixture of German and native strikebreakers against Cornish and Irish strikers. Rumors of splits between Irish "ambitious" for League office and "selfish" Cornish organizers were cited by opposition newspapers as evidence of the impending collapse of the strike; when Irish-born Father Thomas Dalton preached against the strike, his sermon received much attention from Republican journals not accustomed to printing priests' opinions. Acting in their long-established role as spokesmen for town business, editors insisted that the town, ethnically mixed but essentially middle-class in outlook, stood united against the Cornish and Irish miners' township. But while the middle class could force the miners to disavow violence, it could not force them back to work.[33]

But the most dangerous potential ethnic conflict uncovered by the strike pitted the Cornish against the Chinese. The second day of the walkout, E. F. Bean editorialized on the merits of Chinese labor in the mines—cheapness and tractability. On May 21, the *Grass Valley Daily Union* published a letter dated May 18 from a San Francisco owner of the North Star Mine to Crossman, warning that the company might be forced to turn to Chinese labor if the strike continued. A second letter, dated May 22 and published on May 25, repeated the threat and called on owners to stand together. This implied ultimatum exacerbated the conflict in two ways: it politicized the strike, and it made Chinese once again the scapegoats for strife and fear within the white community. Sinophobia had reached a frenzy all over California in 1867 and 1869 as the Democratic Party attempted to reestablish itself after the disaster of the Civil War by allying with the depression-dogged workingman's movement. The resulting campaigns stressed that cheap Chinese labor allowed Republican capitalists to drive out unionizing whites; racist and anti-aristocratic rhetoric provided powerful weapons against a party that could be identified with both big business and the 15th Amendment. Even though the next election was a summer away, the political newspapers already knew the terms on which that campaign would be fought. Bean's Republican *Gazette* applauded Chinese labor, the independent pro-owner conservative Democratic *Union* argued that owners had the right to employ Chinese, while the Democratic *National* reluctantly and painfully had to change its stance on the strike.[34]

To Amos Morse, its editor, the strike had been "reckless and suicidal." His first response to the suggested introduction of Chinese strikebreakers was to warn the League against excluding white workers willing to use giant powder. Such exclusion only opened the door to the Chinese, whose arrival in numbers would destroy the town's economy. In an editorial published on May 27, Morse continued to argue that the miners had brought the danger of the Chinese on themselves; however, the threat of the Chinese, who saved their wages to send home and who did not patronize white storekeepers, forced him to argue that "Grass Valley lives not off the mines, but the miners," and that absentee mine owners who received the profits of the quartz industry had no concern for the fate of the town. Neither did the Cornish Leaguers, but "we are not writing of these injudicious men, but of the welfare of the town and of those white men who did not strike and who are willing to work." As a Democrat, a town booster, and a Sinophobe, Morse had to support white miners against mine owners and their "Chinese hordes." The other papers tied town prosperity to the mines, not the miners, and found submissive Chinese more acceptable than striking Cornishmen. Even Republican papers that had promoted diversification as an alternative to dependence on absentee owners forgot their anti-absentee rhetoric during the strike.[35]

The League did not formally ally with the Democratic Party, which divided over the strike; party leaders A. B. Dibble, E. W. Roberts, and Rufus Shoemaker figured prominently in the law-and-order citizen's meetings, while William Watt, Scots-born owner of the Eureka, who was both the wealthiest party boss and the most prominent mining magnate living in town, used League members and black powder in his mine. But the League certainly appreciated the opportunity for forming public opinion offered by the Chinese issue; Captain Faull wrote to Morse mocking owners so desperate to break the strike that they contemplated introducing "unfit" Chinese labor. And everyone knew what the introduction of Chinese labor might lead to; at the point during the strike when bloodshed seemed most imminent, when strikers and strikebreakers faced each other at the Empire and "citizens" called together a posse, rumors also flew that the miners would attack and destroy Chinese houses near the mines. For the first time since the mid-1850's, Chinese would be menaced by white men deterred from directly attacking other whites. As the strike lingered into the summer, spokesmen for the Miners' Union had to deny accusations that the main issue had shifted from the toxic effects of giant powder to Chinese exclusion.[36] No anti-Chinese violence took place, but the strike ended with the miners still convinced that the Chinese threatened their jobs.

In the aftermath of the strike, the Miners' Union maintained itself in Grass Valley, with between 500 and 700 members employed locally. Amos Morse, now consistently supporting local miners against absentee owners, congratulated the union for having brought Grass Valley's working class "into perfect harmony" by stilling the battles between the Irish and the Cornish. The Miners' Union lost members the following year, a year when black powder prevailed in the mines and the Democrats dominated county politics, but it had already made Cornish miners into a considerable force in Grass Valley. In late 1869, Grass Valley trustees rejected a proposed law that would close miners' resorts at midnight, and instead repealed Ordinance 14, "the terror of the miners," which had attempted to control riotous behavior; in Grass Valley, opinion had swung away from moral appearances to the side of the miners.[37]

The Miners' Union and the Democratic Party also helped to keep the inflammatory issue of cheap Chinese labor before the public. During the summer, Morse and Bean debated the economic effects of the strike and of Chinese miners, making it clear that to support Chinese labor meant to oppose Cornish and Irish miners and vice versa. In the past, political movements against the Chinese had not elicited much response in the two towns, but in the autumn of 1869 the charges of the Sinophobes seemed to mesh with recent experience. Not only was the statewide political crusade against the Chinese more organized and more persistent than its California predecessors, but in the two towns, especially in Grass Valley, anti-Chinese rhetoric tended to link the towns' future to the fate of their laboring classes, and could therefore exploit the new sense of ethnic and occupational identity demonstrated by the strike. The campaign became a vehicle for the resentments of the Cornish and Irish against the American-born elite expressed through aggression against the Chinese, the elite's potential weapon against them. In this context, contacts between native and Chinese merchants and efforts by Protestant churches to teach English did not soothe animosity toward the Chinese but inflamed it. The further fact that the same Republican newspapers that extolled the gentility of Chinese leaders supported, in theory, the use of cheap Chinese labor to open mines that would not pay with $3-a-day labor did not promote racial peace. And the complaints about the "idle boys" who made life miserable for passers-by, especially Chinese, brought retorts that the boys were willing to work but could not compete against Chinese. A pointed accusation against native Republican employers was that they preferred Chinese to Irish, both socially and as employees; the pro-Chinese were charged with covert Know-Nothingism.

Some editors, ministers, and businessmen may have developed a new and more favorable image of the Chinese during the 1860's, but the political Sinophobes employed all the old anti-Chinese stereotypes, emphasizing that of slave labor, in an effort to keep the Chinese out of quartz mining. The defenders of Chinese cheap labor and the Chinese in general soon recognized the impact of partisan racism and shifted as the 1869 elections approached to insist that they too would like to see the Chinese go but thought expulsion and exclusion illegal. For the purpose of the election, the Chinese were barbarians whose standard of living and lack of families enabled them to underbid and drive out white labor. Agitators claimed that Chinese drained off American wealth to China and put no money in circulation where they lived—arguments Amos Morse, for one, found totally convincing. Pro-Chinese statements seemed too politically dangerous, and no politico stood up to challenge racial stereotypes.[38]

The strike also brought miners more directly into politics; miners' participation increased in the late 1860's, in part because of their own gains in wealth and persistence, but also because of their recognition of their own anti-mine-owner, anti-Chinese interests. In 1869 the county Democratic Party split, and in that anti-Chinese election a Cornish blacksmith and miner, Sam T. Oates, was elected to the state legislature over the opposition of both the Republicans and an "aristocratic," mine-owner faction of the Democrats. Once in the legislature, he introduced pro-miner bills. Also in 1869, Philip Painter, the president of the Miners' Union, won election as a Grass Valley township justice of the peace; the union, then, would supply much of the government of the township. In 1870 the union put up candidates for marshal, recorder, and assessor in Grass Valley, the posts most vital to its interests. Opponents claimed that miners wanted to hold the office of marshal so that they could take "liberties when in town," and the miners obviously intended to further emasculate ordinances against their recreations. They lost the election of 1870, and Oates failed to hold his post beyond one term, but miners as miners had almost wrested political control of the town of Grass Valley from the middle class.[39]

The miners' anti-Chinese charges also outlasted the strike; the image of the Chinese as unfair labor competitors remained dominant. Long after the election, advertisements continued to appear notifying the public that firms had fired their Chinese employees. A Grass Valley Anti-Coolie club, proposing to protect workingmen by boycotting all who hired Chinese, survived the autumn of 1869 by several months. And its leadership demonstrated how Sinophobia had united white sympathies behind the miners' cause: Philip Painter of the Miners' Union stood with lawyer J. C. Deuel, once active on the anti-League citizens' committee.[40]

Anti-Coolie Clubs, boycotts, and the firing of Chinese were certainly not unique to Grass Valley; local activity drew on the state campaign for technique as well as political support. But the usual explanations for the force of the California agitations of the late 1860's do not fully account for their impact in the two towns. Simple economic arguments that may apply to much of the state do not explain the lasting local response, since Nevada City and Grass Valley had escaped the worst of the depression. Nor is a purely political explanation adequate; the Democratic Party successfully used the Chinese issue to reestablish itself in county politics as it did statewide, but the movement was most intense and persistent in Grass Valley, long a Democratic bastion, and peaked in 1869, two years after the party had already reasserted itself. Growing numbers of Chinese might explain the depth of the fears exhibited in 1869, except that Nevada City contained the larger, faster expanding Chinatown. The relative receptivity of the towns to agitation depended, in 1869 as it had in 1855, on town conditions; an outside movement prospered in one of the towns because of a situation unique to that town. Grass Valley had a smaller, less influential native middle class, larger self-conscious national groups, and a greater sense that the future of the town lay with the ethnic workers. The miners confirmed to their satisfaction the connection proclaimed by the Democratic Party between capitalists and Chinese, the merchants seemed to face a choice between Cornish customers and Chinese, and finally, of course, the resident town elite led the Democratic county organization. The simplest way to close ethnic and occupational breaches was to attack the Chinese.

When the disturbances of 1867 and 1869 are compared to those of 1855 and 1858, it becomes clear that one segment of public opinion had set limits on anti-Chinese activities. No one attempted, despite rumors, to destroy the Chinatowns. Assaults on individual Chinese did not increase, and even the leaders of the Anti-Coolie Association did not openly condone violence, although they argued that failure to expel the Chinese would lead to bloodshed. A few Chinese lost their jobs, but the leading hotels kept their Chinese employees, and laundrymen and domestics living in white areas did not suffer unusual amounts of abuse. Even at the height of the agitation in 1869, a minority quietly defended the Chinese, a minority that considered itself the social and moral elite of the towns and, in Nevada City, tended to shape society. But this defense from the American-born middle class only highlighted the ethnic and occupational differences the Grass Valley strike had made manifest. The anti-Chinese movement of 1867–70 lasted longer than the crisis of 1854–55, in part because the later agitation was more organized, and more relevant to the felt needs of part of the white population. The cardinal difference, however, was the fact that the social crisis of the mid-1850's could be resolved by the establishment of more families and family neighborhoods, while the divisions of the late 1860's could not be ended as long as the Cornish miners, and to a lesser extent the Irish, lived apart. The strike ended and conflict between whites quieted, but Sinophobic images lingered, in part because they papered over these divisions among whites.

In the coming decade, the population of Grass Valley would decline as quartz mines worked out their leads; Nevada City would gain population as hydraulic operations prospered, although Grass Valley would remain preeminent in population and production. In 1872 a second Grass Valley strike, this time against William Watt's Eureka mine, failed; giant powder had been adopted throughout the rest of the California mine industry—evidence of the unique influence of Grass Valley's Cornish—and opposing Watt precluded any newspaper or party support. More importantly, the Cornish-Irish alliance broke down, as striking Cornishmen demanded that less skilled Irish miners be fired. After this defeat, the Miners' Union decayed, though anti-Chinese organizations continued, by their lights, to defend the miner.[41] Nevertheless, by 1880, Grass Valley's Cornishness was well established. The strike of 1869 had driven home the point of Mitchell and Byrne's 1868 New Year editorial: the native middle class did not run Grass Valley. Of course, it had its spheres—certain professions, most political leadership, and its social and moral institutions—but the Cornish also controlled certain jobs and institutions. While the split between the realms of the Cornish (and Irish) miners and the native (and German) middle class was never absolute, in part because of the growing Cornish presence in middle-class spheres, it did separate town and township. In Nevada City, commerce and county business maintained the primacy of the middle class, and the smaller quartz industry did not produce the ethnic, occupational, and spatial distances of its neighbor.

Over time, ethnic identities became less important. But although the crises of the 1850's and 1860's were not repeated, images established then persisted: standoffish Cornishmen, a workers' Grass Valley, and a sophisticated Nevada City. Modern residents sometimes hint that they still hold true.

Conclusion

Both Grass Valley and Nevada City were simultaneously mine towns, frontier towns, and industrializing towns. In addition, one was a quartz center, the other a county seat. Thus many factors, from the raucous expectations of the Gold Rush to the decisions of absentee mine owners, from acculturation to capitalization, molded their development, providing them with rapidly changing, sometimes contradictory civic characters. The gold was in the ground. That fact, despite overproduction, drought, and strike, gave a kind of stability to both towns, a constancy of purpose, a promise of future prosperity. As mining towns, Grass Valley and Nevada City were almost uniquely blessed, freed from the desperate, often unavailing attempts to stave off inevitable early decline suffered by most Western gold and silver camps. And the security of their resource base likewise reduced the importance of the boosterism and factionalism that plagued other frontier towns. Although both capital and technology grew in importance in Grass Valley and Nevada City (as they did in all industrializing towns), mining, with traditional skills, no jobs for women, and a highly transient work force, set the towns apart from most of their compeers. But even these broadly similar neighbors possessed gold in different quantities and in different matrices that required different mining techniques. These natural conditions generated widely divergent ethnic and occupational structures and contrasting self-images: a Grass Valley of Cornish miners, a Nevada City of the native middle class. And of course, the towns were unique in a different sense, diverging from each other and the rest of the urban nation in, for example, the timing of economic growth and the talents of their leading spirits.[1]

Their gold and their miners made them unlike most American towns. But they faced imperatives common to many American towns in the mid-nineteenth century, whose citizens often had to build community institutions from the ground up, cope with a revolution in production, compromise among competing behavioral and cultural patterns, and maintain reasonable civic stability in the face of individual impermanence. The people of Grass Valley and Nevada City participated in national events: election campaigns, economic failures, and the Civil War itself. A constant flow of population and information traversed the sparsely settled semi-arid West, providing constant contact with the "civilized" East and its fads, crusades, and prejudices. Croquet and velocipede clubs, the Sons of Temperance and the Anti-Coolies, suffragism and Fenianism all arrived from elsewhere to elicit at least brief enthusiasms. And all flourished and faded within the context of the traditional mores and American political structures consciously established early in the towns.

The unique and local interacted with the general and national to form Grass Valley and Nevada City; it remains to place them within the context of their contemporary America, to show how they were similar to other American communities and how they differed, and to suggest why. Earl Pomeroy has long pressed historians to be more aware of the continuity of ideas from east to west; while this study has insisted on the primacy of local conditions in causing such events as the reform crusade and the mining strike, the ideologies and the organizations involved, as well as the essential structures of the towns themselves, were imported. The continuity of ideas was especially direct for urban areas, and the most useful comparisons are those with other towns.[2] During the first period of the two towns' existence, 1849 to 1856, they are most directly comparable to frontier communities; during the second, 1856 to 1863, to the small towns that dotted the landscape wherever the frontier had passed; and finally, from 1863 through 1870, to industrializing towns, east and west.

Grass Valley and Nevada City as Mine Towns

Throughout the time under study here, mining remained central to the two towns' economies. Grass Valley and Nevada City always produced at least some gold. And as men could always see returns, local investment continued, so that even after industrial mining and San Franciscan capital came to the fore, local interests remained more involved with the mines and their operation than in districts like the Comstock or the White Pine. Nor, despite the growing San Franciscan influence on the two towns, did most of the mines become subject to stock-market manipulations. Just as no company stores and relatively few barracks existed even in Grass Valley, no mines shut down merely to deflate stock prices. Also, Bourbon Hill was a pleasanter place to live than, say, Virginia City's Mount Sun: more accessible, and with less extreme weather. With a wider range of individual opportunity both in and out of mining, an easier life for miners, ownership less divorced from local concerns, and most importantly, production never quite ceasing from the days of the pound diggings on Deer Creek through the heyday of the North Star mine, Grass Valley and Nevada City were not typical precious-metal towns.

Rather than typical or atypical, the two towns, like the California mines in general, were prototypical for later western mining frontiers. Customary mine laws, like mining practices, followed the Californians back east. And the processes of social development that the two camps went through appeared again and again, as Rodman Paul says, at different speeds and with different degrees of completeness.[3] Miners in later excitements remained largely young, wifeless and childless, and remarkably volatile. During the first days of any rush, American-born whites dominated the ranks of miners, and miners heavily outnumbered all other workers. Sherman L. Ricards discovered essentially the same demographic characteristics in Butte County, California, a minor gold region, in 1850 that Duane Smith uncovered for the first half of the 1880's in the San Juan Mountains of Colorado; both resemble the Grass Valley and Nevada City of 1850.[4]

In the camps that survived their first booms, merchants, ministers, editors, and wives soon began to agitate for reform. Even Virginia

City, Nevada, went through such a movement, working, as usual in mine towns, against indifference and hostility from most miners, who unlike the middle class had little stake in a town's permanence or reputation for piety. As in Nevada City, reforms usually ended in a compromise compounded of business interests and biology, with the potentially violent gambling dives and bordellos concentrated in recognized areas and operating on the sufferance of law-enforcement agencies. Likewise, all over the mining West, the Chinese served as scapegoats, and camps carefully drew racial lines. As the flush times faded, urban problems took center stage, since the tamed camps had to be governed, supplied, and maintained. But for most camps this calm presaged death, not maturity, as worked-out placers no longer attracted miners or merchants.[5]

Nevada City supplied a pattern that later placer camps might trace, but Grass Valley set the more important precedents. As placers gave way to lode mines, the number of wage-earning miners grew, absentee owners became more common, and bankers gained power. The American-born abandoned the towns, to go home or to join later mining excitements, leaving the depleted placers to the Chinese and the lodes to the Cornish and Irish. Miners became skilled labor, looking for steady work; they were older and more commonly family men than before. In the San Juans, as in Grass Valley, the remaining American-born controlled managerial and professional positions; social distances widened. Mining became more dangerous, and amusements perhaps fewer, so that the gambling spirit and boredom that had attracted the demimonde kept its districts alive. Fears of cheap Chinese labor sustained racial enmity. A union organized and struck over Chinese labor in Humboldt County, Nevada, and miners expelled the Chinese from Nederland, Colorado; all over the West, fears of unfair labor competition led to assaults on the Chinese. Clashes between workers and owners became bitterer and strike violence more prevalent. And finally, throughout all the changes, the instability of mining life continued, as mines opened, failed, and often reopened, and there always seemed to be a new strike to attract both miner and investor.[6]

Grass Valley and Nevada City as Frontier Communities

Between them, Grass Valley and Nevada City ran the gamut of mine-town development, from the frontier placer stage to the milltown life of lode mining. The towns are further comparable, then, to communities, especially urban communities, on other frontiers, as well as to other towns experiencing industrialization.

The excitement of 1849 kindled perhaps America's gaudiest frontier movement, the usual high hopes of pioneers heightened almost hysterically by romanticized images of California and tall tales of riches. Ray Allen Billington has offered perhaps the most useful recent definition of the frontier in economic terms, seeing the frontier as both a place—an area adjacent to unsettled territory—and the process of change occurring there, fueled by a chance for the average individual to better himself by taking advantage of a low man-to-land ratio and untapped natural resources. Billington argues that this potential abundance, the frontier's main attraction, led to materialism, but also to optimism, hard work, pragmatism, and achievement. On the other side of the ledger, it engendered restlessness, a destructive wastefulness, and a lack of concern for social welfare in general.[7]

All of these frontier characteristics, positive and negative, affected life in Nevada City and Grass Valley during their first years, and lingered as ideals or problems long afterward; the tone and taste of the Gold Rush outlasted it. "Practical miner" was a term of high respect in the two camps, earned by long hours of experimentation, learning how to respond to local conditions. A miner in a gold rush did not behave simply as an economic man, as adventure was part of the attraction, but hopes for economic opportunity were real. A miner might get rich, or at least command very good wages for his work, and for a brief time in both camps, most miners had a chance to find gold. Gold also generated returns for the wide range of others who followed the miners to the diggings. Almost from the very beginning, however, many worked for others, and as in all mining strikes, miners quickly overpopulated the camps and the chance for riches became very slim. Certainly a materialism rooted in the pursuit of this diminishing main chance shaped the towns and the landscape around them; contemporaries decried the lack of concern with the well-being of the towns, usually blaming inhabitants easily lured to the newest gold discovery. Fewer noted the ravaging of the countryside in the search for gold. But the full force of the Gold Rush soon spent itself. After Nevada City's crash of 1852 a more sober mood prevailed, and by 1856, with hydraulic and quartz operations mainly responsible for the towns' futures, and Chinese, Irish, and Cornish miners starting to replace the native-born, Billington's frontier of available resources and individual opportunity had clearly passed, just as it would quickly depart from mine towns all over the West.

Merle Curti's study of Trempealeau County, Wisconsin is the classic look at opportunity in a frontier community. Since its central purpose is to test F. J. Turner's ideas on frontier democracy, much of the work is not easily comparable to this study, but Curti's book does make it possible to demonstrate how two very different frontier areas, one based on farming, the other on mining, resemble and differ from each other. First, despite early promotional speculations, Trempealeau never went through anything quite like the Gold Rush. It and other farm frontiers remained more isolated, suffered physical hardship over a longer period, and had to wait longer for schools, churches, and reliable communications. More importantly, the access to farm land, the form that opportunity took in Trempealeau, was very unlike the access to a mining claim. Before 1866 miners did not possess deeds but held their claims by working them, while buying farm land required at least some solvency. On the other hand, the holder of a mine claim was even less certain of returns than a farmer. That is, no direct comparison is possible between Trempealeau and the two mine towns, either for access to resources or for wealth, especially measured in real estate.[8]

But more general comparisons are possible, if only because Curti states that Trempealeau's economic and social structures largely echoed those of the rest of the country. The topheavy distribution of wealth in Trempealeau almost exactly matched that of farming communities in Vermont. In Grass Valley and Nevada City, both before and after large-scale mining came in, the bulk of property likewise ended in a few hands. In Trempealeau as in the two California towns, a disproportionately American-born elite surfaced quickly.[9] After the first wave of migration to Trempealeau, fewer businesses could open, and occupations became more specialized. Still, in the countryside the landless continued to acquire land, and the foreign-born gradually moved into property-holding and, later, positions of community influence. The same development took place in the towns that served the farmers; in less than a generation the foreign-born overcame stereotypes and moved into jobs previously reserved for the American-born. Trempealeau before the land ran out resembles Grass Valley and Nevada City after the Gold Rush and before the quartz boom, when levels of personal and real holdings were rising, and the foreign-born had reasonable access to prestigious occupations. As Trempealeau land became scarce, advancement slowed and the social structure became more rigid; loss of an accessible resource had, as in the mine towns, limited some types of opportunity, and nothing existed in Trempealeau equivalent to Grass Valley's new jobs for skilled miners, which replaced dreams of future riches with a higher actual standard of living.[10]

Trempealeau County, like farm frontiers in general, was a family frontier, as no mining frontier could be. Even in 1850, before settlers organized Trempealeau County, roughly 30 percent of gainfully employed men had wives, and by 1860, as farmers poured into the county, about 70 percent were married. By contrast, 2 percent of Nevada City's first comers had wives with them, and ten years later, in a town thought safe for families, 13 percent (Table 44). An excess of males peopled all the trails headed west, but from the days of Forty-nine, miners and mine excitements contributed disproportionately to this masculinity. John Faragher has shown that the Oregon-bound migration of the early 1840's had at its core young families, but after the strike at Sutter's Mill, prospective California (and later Nevada) miners, outnumbering the Oregon contingent, raised the proportion of males on the trail throughout the 1850's and 1860's. In Western states in general, sex ratios depended in large part on the economic basis of the region's frontier phase, and as the Far West had fewer farmers than previous areas of new settlement, it was more male (Table 45). In this regard, mine frontiers resembled the timber county of Manistee, Michigan, or the Anglo cattle ranches of Nueces County, Texas. Farm frontiers, from Clarence, Iowa to Kanab, Utah to Roseburg, Oregon, all were family affairs.[11]

The forty-niners were also young, and the populations of Grass Valley and Nevada City remained youthful until the rise of industrial mining. In that the two towns fit the pattern of frontiers in general, where population concentrated between 20 and 40 years of age, with an overloading between 20 and 30, and a shortage of those over 40. If frontiers represented a new chance to start in on equal terms with the rest of society, the barely mature would be especially attracted—young men looking for jobs or young couples looking for land. On farm frontiers, however, a second group also stood out: families with children old enough so that the parents had to start thinking of their futures—that is, access to land. Besides, it took time to accumulate enough money to buy a farm; in frontier Crawford County, Iowa and Bureau County, Illinois, the median ages of male householders were 38 and 39 years. Miners did not have to wait years to acquire claims, and few brought families into the gold camps; in 1850, the men of Grass Valley and Nevada City were young even by frontier standards. But the shortage of women created another, sharper difference between the mines and other new settlements: few children. This meant that while the working population was youthful, the total population was older than either frontier or national norms. And of course the recently married couples in new agricultural areas produced a baby boom in a few years, while the number of children in mine towns, or other frontiers where women were rare, remained low.[12]

These population characteristics—sex ratios, age, numbers of children—persisted in the mining towns like the survivals of Gold Rush behavior that upset the residents of the middle-class neighborhoods, and for some of the same reasons. Constant movement, poor wages, danger, the uncertainty of mining, and the felt need to tolerate the demimonde all in their way discouraged family formation. Until industrial mining was well along, wives and children, especially among miners, remained uncommon. If women and families tamed the forty-niners, they did it without appreciable strength of numbers.

What women there were in Grass Valley and Nevada City behaved, like other American frontier women, in ways that expressed the continuity of American values as modified by local conditions. The people of the two mine towns knew how women were supposed to act; the question was whether they could act that way in the camps. Women were archetypically the conservators of morality, and as such had a special obligation to reestablish traditional mores on the frontier. But they also had even more urgent responsibilities to their families, especially when husbands were off pursuing their fortunes. And women themselves found economic opportunity in the scarcity of domestic comforts resulting from the wildly unbalanced sex ratios of the mine towns. The two responsibilities conflicted; by entering the marketplace, women further endangered their claims to moral superiority, already jeopardized by their mere presence in the midst of the license associated with the frontier. The danger to women from loosened sex roles and a general loss of social restraint was a major subject of debate, especially in early Nevada City.

Julie Roy Jeffrey argues that frontier women solved this conundrum by accepting, at least temporarily, the new economic dispensation while advocating and reaffirming older versions of woman's place.[13] Certainly both processes took place in the two towns, though the real impact of women was more economic than spiritual and more a matter of family survival than of family morality. The demand for women's skills coupled with the comparative poverty of the townspeople resulted in a greater acceptance of women's working. Since mining provided few jobs for respectable married women, their contributions to family income usually came from caring for boarders. In 1860 almost twice as many families accepted boarders as in Modell and Hareven's national estimates. Households at all occupational levels took in boarders; doing so was not identified with the lower class. But the legitimacy of the practice rested on a noneconomic advantage: it resolved the tension in the lives of frontier women. It was a relatively secure way to maintain stable family incomes without altering women's accustomed places or skills.

In sum, in the two towns as on other frontiers, the traditional role of women was maintained. There was some loosening—both work and divorce became more common—but no real change in belief. Women on the overland trail drove teams when necessary, but even on the trail they spent most of their time in their constricted sphere, performing woman's work. Women on the farming frontiers filled in for hired hands on occasion, and their garden and dairy products provided cash when nothing else was salable, but as Glenda Riley has pointed out for Iowa, census takers did not list them as gainfully employed because their profits were subsumed in family income. And even the limited changes created for women by the frontier did not last long. Marion Goldman has shown that in Virginia City, within ten years of the first stampede, outside work had become less respectable and women's lives more private, centered in their homes.[14] In Grass Valley and Nevada City, this process took longer, although as in Virginia City it accompanied the rise of industrial mining. But clearly in the two mine towns, the passing of the frontier meant a narrowing of the roles of women.

Grass Valley and Nevada City as American Small Towns

Comparisons between Gold Rush Grass Valley and Nevada City and other new settlements show commonalities among frontiers in general, but also basic differences between rural frontier areas and the urban communities generated by the mines. Grass Valley and Nevada City developed like other frontier towns, dominating a local rural region, trying to establish complex institutions almost overnight, and ambitious for greater things.[15] But it is the two mine towns' irreducible Americanness, rather than their newness, that makes it easy to draw parallels between them and the frontier and post-frontier towns analyzed by Robert R. Dykstra, Don Harrison Doyle, Lewis Atherton, and Robert V. Hine, among others. Boosting editors, benevolent and fraternal associations, community celebrations, and continual formal and informal socializing all seem to have been basic to nineteenth-century small-town life on or off the frontier. So was a spatial division by class and ethnicity, and above all by race. Moral orthodoxy reinforced wealth and occupation in determining respectability, and the schools, churches, and clubs that served that orthodoxy seemed bulwarks against disorder, commanding loyalty and support accordingly. With their Sunday-school picnics, Independence Day orations, election parades, and school exhibitions, at times Grass Valley and Nevada City sound stereotypically small-town American. So did Jacksonville, Illinois, in the 1840's, Algona, Iowa, in the 1860's, and Dodge City, Kansas, in the 1880's, as soon as the first stage of settlement passed.[16]

Town leadership in nineteenth-century America also seems to have had common attributes. Grass Valley and Nevada City's trustees, like their peers elsewhere, came largely from the commercial ranks and governed with two goals: promoting business and holding expenses to a minimum. The editors and merchants of the two mine towns, like many Americans, equated peace, stability, and acceptance of social place with survival and success. And no sympathies with "frontier democracy" hindered their acceptance of social stratification and middle-class responsibilities. In their view the early gold camps escaped chaos only because many miners were businessmen and professionals temporarily disguised. And some members of the middle class were willing, if not able, to impose their code of behavior on the mining majority in the name of permanent prosperity for themselves and their towns.[17]

The same proprietary attitudes characterized merchants and promoters in the five Kansas cattle towns studied by Dykstra. These pioneer businessmen first sought personal wealth and civic greatness in the cattle trade—in commerce, not agriculture, because only commerce could create cities. But town building was complicated by intramural feuding and antagonism between townsmen and local farmers. Dykstra builds from a model designed by Allan Bogue that posits that frontier life forced settlers into more conflicts than they had faced at home, because they lacked well-developed institutions, established social customs, and an agreed-on leadership, and lived among others who might test and reject their values. Dykstra, then, looks for significant conflicts, usually factional struggles over which economic direction each cattle town would take, who would benefit most, and what moral stance the town would assume.[18]

Dykstra's Kansas trading centers have much in common with the two mine towns beyond having been initially settled and later run by coteries of merchants and lawyers who profited from enterprises employing unruly young males. Nevada City, where county business and the transshipment of goods to other mining areas at times approached mining in importance, especially resembled new small commercial towns like Ellsworth or Abilene. In popular literature, only the trailhead towns exceeded Gold Rush camps in license, and in both cases the reputation for personal violence was highly exaggerated. More importantly, the cattle towns in Dykstra's study, like many mine towns, passed through reform phases that identified morality with northeastern American Protestant mores—reform movements that ended in a common compromise, the segregation of vice.[19]

But the Kansas cattle towns and the two California mine towns produced contrasting styles of reform, as of town governance in general. The "honest miner," however short his tenure and disreputable his recreations, lived, bought, and sometimes voted in the township community; the drovers and trail bosses were Texans. Mine production never remained constant, and investment capital often came from San Francisco or New York, but the two mine towns never stood as economically vulnerable to the whims of outsiders as the cattle towns were to the favorable or unfavorable reactions of the trail bosses. Further, in spite of editorial appeals for diversification into agriculture and the opening of the trans-Sierra trade, no one really questioned the primary economic interests of Grass Valley and Nevada City. As long as the gold held out, nothing like Wichita's successful shift from cattle market to general farm entrepot could occur.

With miners a permanent reality of town life, and the economic direction essentially set, the two mine towns never faced conflicts as internally divisive as those of, say, Abilene. The reform movement in Abilene was more absolutist, less regardful of short-term financial consequences than in Nevada City; cowboys were strangers, and the cattle trade itself a transient. The compromises reached in cattle-town reform rested on blatantly monetary considerations—saloon taxes kept town governments solvent—and could be seen as temporary; as the Texans went elsewhere to ship their stock, the reformers would win by default. While editorial and clerical rhetoric was equally severe in Nevada City, reform limited itself in practice to neighborhood protection, and only against the Chinese, not all miners. Once the family streets were safe, the miners' votes and their financial importance ensured a lasting compromise.[20]

Even the divisive mine strike of 1869, although rooted in the alienation of the Cornish miners from the towns and the mine owners, was ultimately very narrow in scope. The miners and the town merchants shared both interests and values; both parties depended on miners' wages and deplored violence. Strikers could not feel as free to set themselves against the town as drovers did in defense of compatriots threatened with arrest. Miners and mine owners might disagree fundamentally over wages, the use of Chinese labor, and dynamite, but once Cornish skills were protected, and once it was clear that most of the community shared the miners' antipathy toward the Chinese, the strike could be settled with minimal actual fighting.

Another source of controversy in the cattle towns, the clash between rural and urban interests, had no real parallel in Grass Valley and Nevada City. In Kansas, farmers whose crops were trampled and whose stock was infected by longhorns bound for market could do little, at first, to protect themselves. But as their numbers grew along with their economic power, and the towns' future dependence on cattle shipping became more dubious, the angry political impotence of the early phase of farm protest changed. Farmers could ally themselves with reformers and dissident merchants to hasten the departure of the herds and cowboys. Farmers went from despised interlopers to saviors in the eyes of town businessmen. Nothing like that could have happened in the townships surrounding Grass Valley and Nevada City, where miners claimed prime farm lands and hydraulickers sluiced away roads and pastures. Agriculture was tributary to mining and could not have supported the township population had mining failed. When, in the 1880's, California farmers finally curtailed the right of the mine companies to dump tailings into waterways, the effort centered in the Sacramento Valley, not the mine counties.[21]

The factional disputes that Dykstra finds to have been the main motive force of cattle-town politics rarely assumed significant proportions in the mine towns. True, rival Nevada City business streets fought over the location of the courthouse and fire department; companies politicked for the right to supply town water; mine and merchant interests both campaigned to control the early township governments. But given the towns' commitment to mining, factionalism could have neither the importance nor the positive results that Dykstra uncovered in the cattle towns. The mine-town governments did not have the power to make essential decisions about the future, and their immersion in trivia led to moribund municipal politics, with offices often filled by default. In the cattle towns, factional disputes inspired community participation in decision-making on vital issues, most importantly the towns' future dependence on the cattle trade. All in all, Dykstra finds factional conflict usual, inescapable, and in some ways beneficial.[22]

Don Harrison Doyle has also elaborated on Bogue's model of potential internecine conflict in his study of Jacksonville, Illinois. Doyle emphasizes cultural and sectional differences among settlers and adds the complicating factor of the high rate of population turnover, but he too is essentially investigating the consequences in a frontier setting of an expansive and competitive capitalistic ethic. Doyle argues that community was the central problem of frontier capitalism—that in order to grow, Jacksonville had to order its diverse, transient population—and he focuses accordingly on elements that provided community stability. These elements (both ideas and institutions) linked Jacksonville to an older America, and to much of the frontier.

First, a booster ethic demanded that townspeople hide differences behind a campaign of town promotion, and that solidarity be based on the "ethos of self-discipline, temperance, and respect for authority" furthered by the churches, schools, and social clubs. Churches and fraternal organizations, along with political parties, were the heart of a voluntary community that Doyle argues took on a newly important function on the frontier. The voluntary community supplied much of what Bogue believed the frontier lacked; it granted its members identity and middle-class respectability, reinforced beliefs against pressures from competing views, allocated and advanced individual opportunity, and helped integrate newcomers into their ethnic or occupational groups. Institutional permanence was vital; churches and clubs remained while members passed through. The booster ethic and the voluntary community were fostered by a stable population core of middle-class families, who stayed while poorer, less trained, single males moved on. These persisters supplied a solid leadership committed to the town and, again, to orthodox mores. Doyle sees contradictions within Jacksonville's society—between community ideals and competitive capitalism, ethnic identity and town loyalty, the dependence on voluntarism and a desire for moral discipline—but he still uncovers a workable social order.[23]

In Grass Valley and Nevada City, too, early attempts to impose order coupled boosterism and morality. But traditional institutions, especially churches, had to accept the existence of other mores, and a compartmentalized society grew up. In the two mine towns, as in Illinois, although no group was completely ghettoized, spatial segregation and parallel institutions kept the foreign-born and the American-born apart. Indeed, much of what Doyle finds prevailed all over the frontier. Most notably, the voluntary community provided necessary recreation, associations with home, and middle-class status for its members in Jacksonville, in Nevada City, and in places like Portland, Oregon, Leadville, Colorado, and San Francisco. And in many new communities, the middle class attempted to defend its accustomed authority against cultural diversity and its prosperity against economic uncertainty. San Francisco's vigilance committees were only the most spectacular among many frontier crusades in the name of conformity to American middle-class mores. And in most cases—in Jacksonville, in the Kansas cattle towns, in Nevada City, and ultimately in San Francisco—a compromise emerged between an ideally unified community and an assemblage of ethnic and even red-light enclaves.[24]

In an influential work, Page Smith typed American towns as either covenant towns, colonized for essentially religious or moral reasons, or cumulative towns that grew without direction other than a drive for wealth. Certainly most frontier town planters dreamed of riches; as Billington argues, most frontiersmen sought economic opportunity. But the evidence of Jacksonville, Abilene, and Nevada City suggests that Smith's dichotomy is far too sharp. Moral and religious order were felt to be inseparable from permanent prosperity, and the protection of piety the obverse of frontier opportunity. Moreover, in these towns, people who certainly believed themselves to be members of covenanted communities, and expected to live in towns governed by the values of their particular covenants, coexisted with alien cultures and moralities, a coexistence sometimes forced by the requirements of town commerce. Covenant and cumulative communities intersected far too much on the frontier to be classified separately.[25]

A sense of community, organizations to support belief systems, and a willingness to tolerate limited cultural diversity went a long way toward solving the problems described by Bogue; Doyle's institutions and core population did reduce conflict. But some of the same factors that distinguished Grass Valley and Nevada City from the Kansas cattle towns also limit the applicability of Doyle's complex of explanation to the mine towns, and incidentally underline the uniqueness of the mining frontier. Jacksonville contained no laboring group as important as the miners and no resource base like the gold lodes. In Jacksonville prohibition could be passed, if not enforced, by the core population, aided by its institutions, against the wishes of the foreign-born and working class. In Grass Valley, the miners repealed ordinances limiting the celebration of "miners' Sabbath." And the number and economic importance of miners ensured that compromises between value systems would be more equitable than in Jacksonville.

The gold allowed Nevada City and Grass Valley to survive fires, floods, and a massive population turnover—in the 1860's the persistence rate of the two towns was slightly more than half that of Jacksonville (Table 46). The pace of out-migration meant that the institutional and middle-class stability that helped hold Jacksonville together as a community could not be as effective in the gold towns. Some institutions, such as the Masons, the Methodists, and the Democrats, maintained themselves remarkably well. But most social clubs collapsed seasonally, churches lost evangelical zeal, and fire companies disbanded. While political parties flourished, giving outlets and identity to their activists, they contributed more tension than tranquility and focused their energies on national, not local problems. Similarly, while professionals and merchants persisted longer than miners, even they could hardly be called a stable core population. And the booster ethic never eclipsed the rival Gold Rush ethic of "get rich and get out." Since wealth in a mine town depended more on mine development than on community development, ties to town, church, or club were less important than in Jacksonville.[26]

But continuity in the two mine towns was not dependent solely on gold deposits. People were transient, but beliefs were settled. Belief systems—for all groups, not just the American-born middle-class—proved much more permanent than the institutions designed to promulgate them. Individual clubs lapsed or remained small, but their duties as social arbiters continued; particular families moved away, but the dependence on the socializing, civilizing function of the family remained; the "cult of true womanhood" defined an ideal even when very few women had the leisure to live up to it. While population turnover could damage or destroy institutions, it could not deeply alter ideas.

Virginia Yans-McLaughlin, in a recent analysis of Italian family life in Buffalo, New York, emphasizes the ability of traditional beliefs to survive the pressures of physical instability and poverty. Sex roles, supportive kin networks, and loyalty to the place of nativity all continued to operate in America, shaping the ways Italian Americans adjusted to the industrial city. "New wine in old bottles," new experiences fitted into old cultural patterns, enabled the Italians to cope successfully with rapid change in their environment. Robert Doherty, studying society in five small Massachusetts towns in the first half of the nineteenth century, makes two complementary points: that young men were expected to move around in search of opportunity, and that widespread movement long antedated the symptoms of disorder commonly blamed on fluid populations. Doherty defines "excessive mobility" as involuntary mobility, movement forced upon men without jobs or the hope of getting jobs. Caroline Golab, in her work on Philadelphia Poles, supplies a connection between the points made by Yans-McLaughlin and those of Doherty, by arguing that the almost overwhelmingly high rates of movement within the immigrant community illustrate traditional cultural values; the majority returned to Europe, as they had always planned to do, using their American earnings to improve their families' financial standing in the homeland.[27]

The findings of Golab, Doherty, and Yans-McLaughlin illuminate the experience of Grass Valley and Nevada City. The mercurial young men of the Gold Rush, both native and immigrant, were within the bounds of respectable behavior for youth at mid-century, especially since they intended to invest their gold back home. Civic leaders repeatedly proclaimed that town prosperity depended on the establishment of stable populations but until the late 1860's rarely denied the legitimacy of moving on. Aaron Sargent himself, the most powerful and vocal reform politician and booster editor in either town, left after his timely conversion to the Republican Party accelerated his career toward its climax in the United States Senate; he returned to Nevada City only when his burial plot was preempted by a growing San Francisco.

The expectation that success would both follow from and result in moving on was complemented by another, that qualified men could interchangeably fit fixed social roles. Together, these beliefs allowed the relaxation of the contrary view equating order and prosperity with stability. When families came in growing number to the two towns, spatial mobility slowed down—as contemporaries assumed it would. The families of all ethnic groups that arrived proved very adaptive, both as economic units and as custodians of culture. Family neighborhoods supported schools and churches, flourishing in the midst of industrial work forces. And most importantly, family values transcended nativity and class, reinforcing shared beliefs about work and success. All this, coupled with the transmission of the American economic system and the institutions of all ethnic groups, provided the towns with a basic social coherence.

American communities in general have had high rates of outmigration; Stephan Thernstrom has argued that only between 40 and 60 percent of a town's men remain there a decade later, and that this rate holds for all sizes of communities, in all parts of the country, in both the nineteenth and twentieth centuries. The only exception Thernstrom allows is for rural communities in the earliest stages of settlement. Studies done since the publication of Thernstrom's work suggest that frontier communities of all kinds have lower persistence rates than Thernstrom's norm. The few studies of pioneer farm districts and frontier towns and cities show persistence rates clustering between 20 and 30 percent, with the rates for Gold Rush towns much lower, and those for farm communities often higher (Table 46). Trempealeau County, Jacksonville, and San Francisco all lost over 70 percent of their male working populations in the course of a decade.[28]

Fewer frontiersmen may have stayed in one place for ten years, but they stayed (or left) in the same patterns as their Eastern contemporaries. People in their late teens and early twenties were very mobile, while older people were less so. Single individuals moved more often than families. Men in prestigious occupations, especially those who had accumulated money or real estate, stayed in place more than the unskilled or poor. Ethnicity and birthplace were consistently less important. The belief that extreme transience in a town would be accompanied by disorder and economic failure was as universal as the patterns that transience took. Some of the agencies identified by Doyle as strengthening community on the frontier also had similar functions in Eastern cities and farm districts; core populations persisted and governed in Massachusetts farm towns like Pelham and mill towns like Waltham. Among the highly transient Philadelphia Poles studied by Caroline Golab, not only did a stabler core provide a continuity of leadership, but also the churches and benevolent clubs "supplied an infrastructure necessary for the survival of the community," instilling values and reinforcing ethnic identity. A common mobility created common needs and institutions; again, frontier towns share much with the nation at large.[29]

But the editors frightened by impermanence in Nevada City knew what they were talking about; the mine towns faced the problem in an extreme form. Some frontiersmen were essentially vagabonds, but more generally, frontiersmen tended to be young, unmarried, propertyless, and unskilled, and miners exaggerated these characteristics. Not surprisingly, farm communities, even in their pioneer stages, closely approached national persistence norms; they contained more mature adults, more families, and more people with enough capital to invest in land than other frontiers. Established farmers were in fact more stable than the merchants in neighboring farm towns. The gold camps during the placer era represented the other extreme from farming areas. The two towns' inhabitants, by national standards, were poor in both real and personal property. This relative lack of assets reflected in part the repeated mining depressions, in part miners' lack of title to their claims, and in part returns on mine labor that remained low in relation to local prices, but it also reflected the youth of the mining population. Further, the very character of mining forced movement when claims were depleted and inspired it when a new district boomed. The gold ensured that Grass Valley and Nevada City would survive, but it also guaranteed extraordinary levels of movement.[30]

Townspeople not only managed to adjust to out-migration, they even benefited from it in at least one way. Population turnover in conjunction with a reasonably open field of endeavor gave young, untried men a chance to exercise authority and to take important places in town economic life. Certainly that aspect of the lure of the frontier operated in Grass Valley and Nevada City, but the two towns were further distinguished from much of America in that these same conditions enabled the white foreign-born to enter prestigious occupations. Status and wealth relationships between ethnic groups roughly followed national patterns, but there was room at the top for immigrants. No miner expected to give up the amenities of life permanently, and their supplier's merchandise was more important than his religion or birthplace. Need stifled prejudice, and the lack of an established merchant class, together with the business openings forced by fire and failure and, often, the previous experience of the newcomers, eased the entry of the foreign-born into the middle class. As Peter Decker discovered for early San Francisco, a large proportion of these successes were German Jews; certainly frontier towns offered much to this group. In mining the foreign-born found opportunity even more accessible. The combination of luck and knowledge necessary for wealth in gold could not be monopolized by the native-born, and insofar as the mine business before 1860 gave preferential treatment to any ethnic group, it was based on the identification of the Cornish with expertise in hard-rock mining.[31] And of course, access to jobs contributed to community peace.

Grass Valley and Nevada City as Mill Towns

The industrialization of the mines moved society in the two towns away from frontier and closer to national conditions—for good and ill. Large-scale mining increased prosperity by establishing steadier production and wages, and that in turn promoted population stability and family formation. But while it opened new skilled jobs, industrial mining also tightened ethnic identification with certain trades, and thereby eroded the ethnic occupational integration of the early years. And while prosperity reduced the need for women to drudge for boarders, it also narrowed acceptable female roles and responsibilities.

Family life was more conventional after the industrial quartz boom of the mid-1860's. Family values had always followed American custom, and now new wealth allowed townspeople to make practice somewhat more congruent with preachment. The number and proportion of families and women grew. The proportion of households containing lodgers dropped until it approximated the national figure. Taking in boarders for income was now more suspect, and ideally a middle-class family with a boarder would make him subject to quasi-familial control and instruction. The number of children per family, the products of older, more established parents, was close to averages elsewhere. Ethnicity did not significantly affect family structure, and groups that did not conform to usual practice—the largely unmarried Chinese and those miners who continued to live in cooperative all-male or boarding households—clearly stood out from the rest of society in the two towns.[32]

The process of industrialization took essentially the same course in the mining of gold as in the making of shoes or rifles: increased dependence on technology and on high capitalization, the development of new skilled and semiskilled positions accompanied by the devaluation of older skills, and the proliferation of jobs and kinds of jobs joined with lessened worker independence. Industrial mining widened social distances by promoting ethnic occupational specialization; Americans and to a lesser extent the Irish tended to leave hard-rock mining, which became more than ever the preserve of the Cornish. The native-born concentrated in the higher status occupations but also, blacks especially, at the bottom of the job ladder. The quartz mines engendered a selective migration of Cornish miners, who not only replaced departing Americans and Irish in town populations but also, by weight of numbers, lowered the proportional representation of the British in prestigious occupations. As Dean Esslinger has demonstrated for South Bend, Indiana, industrialization in Grass Valley and Nevada City did not eliminate the British from the better jobs—the premium put on mining expertise meant that the Cornish became foremen and superintendents, and other British-born men ran hotels and stores—but the status of the group as a whole was lowered by the high proportion in mine jobs. And as in Eastern mill towns, selective hiring coupled with the requirement of easy access to work sites also added to ethnic residential segregation. Miners, that is, the Cornish and Irish, lived apart; previously only the blacks and Chinese had been separate. Likewise, the well-to-do neighborhoods remained open to German Jews and Cornishmen, but now, to a greater extent, excluded all the working class.[33]

The restructuring of jobs resulted in an ethnic, occupational, and wealth hierarchy roughly similar to those of other industrializing towns: Milwaukee, South Bend, and San Francisco. The American-born were overrepresented at the top, but because of German, especially German Jewish, success in merchandising, the native-born held no lock on elite status. German storekeepers were reinforced by brewers, butchers, and other master craftsmen and as a group stood at the top of the foreign-born prestige structure with the French financiers. British command of mining and mine management experience placed them next, while the Irish, among the major European groups, remained last, despite spectacular mining and political successes by a few of their compatriots. Non-whites and non-Europeans existed outside the status system.[34]

In sum, industrialization promoted both prosperity and social divisions. And a new sense of those divisions grew in the towns in the late 1860's, as witness the miners' societies that combined mutual aid with a strongly felt national identity and the middle-class charities that combined stewardship with careful social distancing. The Miners' League, the strike of 1869, and the anti-Cornish editorials of the late 1860's mark the results. Class consciousness was largely absent from the Grass Valley strike, but ethnic and occupational consciousness were essential to its success. Daniel Walkowitz, in a study of Irish steelworkers in Troy, New York, demonstrates how a cohesive, politically potent Irish working-class community was able to defend its established place against mill owners' innovations, and Susan Hirsch shows how a similar threat to job status in Newark cemented a union movement able to overcome ethnic rivalries. It was no accident that miners living in Grass Valley, where the split between mines and town was greater and ethnic tensions were more palpable, were likelier to support a union than the men of Nevada City. The number, group and craft identity, and residential insularity of the Cornish all contributed to the union's ability to keep dynamite out of the mines for a time. And this effort was based on an alliance between the Cornish and recently Fenianized Irishmen; even though the endangered techniques were Cornish, the threat of Chinese labor was enough to unite two groups often at each other's throats.[35]

The fact that Grass Valley and Nevada City were and remained mine towns limited the impact of industrialization upon them. As large mining companies displaced the small outfits that had worked the placers, few men stayed to undergo a personal loss of independence, and though the knowledge gained in the placers was devalued, few men had ever considered the cradle or long tom as the tools of their life work. Those who did could follow the round of later mining frontiers. In towns like Lynn or Newark machines replaced men and their training, but despite dynamite, nineteenth-century technology could not duplicate the hard-rock miner or his skills.

In general, population stability increased as communities passed the frontier stage, but if the economic base remained uncertain or continued to employ the unmarried at low wages, as the mining industry did, out-migration would remain high. In Grass Valley and Nevada City during the quartz era, changing technologies and repeated interruptions in production contributed heavily to population movement. So did the wandering bent of the men themselves; even the Cornish industrial mining elite had lived as sojourning experts since leaving Cornwall, going wherever deep mines opened. And although the two towns' working populations grew older than the adult population of the nation at large, few individuals waxed old and wealthy there. Mature successful men moved to San Francisco, or like the very successful San Franciscans, retired back home. Despite gains in average holdings and a wider distribution of asset-holding during the late 1860's, Grass Valley and Nevada City residents still owned less real and personal property than the national average. Relative poverty and economic uncertainty counteracted the family formation generated by the quartz boom, so that while the number of women, children, and families grew rapidly, the mine towns still had overwhelmingly male populations. A prosperous industrial mining town was still a mining town. And that precluded a stable population, as only one resident in ten stayed in Grass Valley or Nevada City through the 1860's.[36]

Towns other than mine towns found that the passing of their frontier stages did not necessarily bring dramatic changes in persistence rates; towns other than those in the first phase of settlement failed to approach Thernstrom's national norms. Rapid growth in the area around Jacksonville kept the population in flux during the 1850's and the Civil War resulted in even more migration during the 1860's, well after initial settlement. In Cairo, Illinois, long-term economic stagnation maintained population instability. In San Francisco, the changeover from commerce to industry during the 1870's kept out-migration particularly high among the occupational groups affected most, including well-known and well-to-do merchants. A swiftly growing or a declining economic base, or a massive changeover in that base, could maintain town persistence rates like those of a new community.[37] Again, the two mine towns shared in a national experience; nevertheless, few towns survived the population turnover that Nevada City and Grass Valley lived with.

Custom and Contingency

Grass Valley and Nevada City thrived despite transience and managed to limit potentially destructive strife between social groups increasingly separated and increasingly at odds as industrialization progressed. I have argued that this success rested on a complex of local conditions and national practices, and that like the sources of conflict, its outcomes were shaped most importantly by the local situation. Factors that operated nationally did play significant parts. Social clubs, churches, and schools contributed to stability in the two mine towns as they did in Jacksonville, Illinois and Waltham, Massachusetts. So did the middle class, taking on its accustomed responsibilities. More importantly, each group in the mine towns had come with its own customary cultural behavior and in large part succeeded in living by these customs. My essential disagreement with Allan Bogue's model of frontier conflict rests first on evidence from Nevada City and Grass Valley that social beliefs and practices arrived intact. New men became town trustees, but the same kinds of men were elected; the Clampers relived the flush times but accepted the mores of the Masons they parodied; Cornish and Irish allied under pressure but also retained St. Patrick's Day parades and wrestling tournaments. Besides, all the inhabitants of the two towns had deliberately chosen to seek their fortunes, directly or indirectly, in gold, in mining towns. The ability of all groups to make minor adjustments without sacrificing the essentials of their codes enabled the people of the two towns to confront an environment alien in part to all of them. And the compromises necessary in a compartmentalized society prevailed nationally, as did the cultural resiliency shown in Grass Valley and Nevada City.[38]

But there were other and more peculiarly local factors that helped maintain at least a minimal order. Again, the gold was in the ground; as long as that was true, the towns could survive, and ambitious individuals would promote peace and quiet. No one group was strong enough to coerce all others; mutual cooperation was necessary to keep the mines producing and local government working. Native-born merchants and politicians could not react to fears of aliens and disorder as freely as their Eastern peers evidently could; they were too close in age and income to the miners during the first years, and later too dependent on Irish votes and Cornish mine experience. For the same reasons, when the Cornish organized against the mine owners, they had to still their dislike of the Irish. Just as need forced families to accept boarders, the imperatives of political power, manpower, and expertise forced adjustments—at times grudging—in prejudices. Those with few claims on the rest of society, most notably the Chinese, suffered.

These were, after all, nineteenth-century towns, and racism was a constant in town life. Local events might call the fear of blacks and Chinese into the foreground only occasionally, but even when prejudice was quiescent, it was an important presence. To whites, peace seemed to rest on the quarantining of darker races, regardless of the strength of black families or the gentility of Chinese merchants. On this point, flexibility and compromise did not rule.

The values, then, of the townspeople of Grass Valley and Nevada City derived from a survival of their pasts, their heritages, as modified by local realities. But day-to-day concerns like jobs, wages, and strikes, as Daniel Walkowitz has well argued, depended in mid-nineteenth-century America on local conditions; national currents were still secondary. Cohoes and Troy, New York, the neighboring mill towns that Walkowitz studied, had different ethnic workforces and drastically divergent strike histories because of their different industrial bases.[39] Similarly, mining—the type pursued, its profitability or failure, and its stage of development—determined the social structures of Grass Valley and Nevada City and made them differ from each other just as mining in general made them different from most of the urban nation. Grass Valley quartz attracted more Cornishmen, Nevada City's placers drew more Chinese, and in both cases this tendency increased as mining matured. During the placer flush times, Nevada City was the richer town, but as the placers worked out and deep-shaft mining began to dominate, commerce bulked larger in its economy, and its neighbor gained financial primacy. Still, the chances of an individual success in small-scale mining were evidently greater in Nevada City, the chance for a steady wage clearly greater in Grass Valley.

Grass Valley mining demanded many proficient hands, Nevada City hydraulicking needed few, and relatively unskilled, men; again, changes in mining technology made the towns progressively less similar. The commerce and county business that augmented Nevada City's mining meant that the town would be more middle-class and American-born and, of course, more like the majority of urban places in the United States, while Grass Valley's commitment to one industry resulted in a more foreign, working-class population. Political loyalty flowed from ethnicity and class, and Republican Nevada City opposed Democratic Grass Valley.

Prosperity generated stability and encouraged families, and as Grass Valley became the wealthier of the two towns it also surpassed its neighbor in numbers of women and children. In the 1850's it contained more prostitutes than Nevada City, while in the 1860's it had fewer. Nevada City had fewer boarders and more social gatherings, while Grass Valley had weaker charities and stronger schools. Nevada City had a greater degree of moral consensus, a larger middle class, and a shakier economy; Grass Valley produced more gold and more social conflict. And when peculiarly "American" values seemed under attack, excitement centered in Nevada City; a threat to customary Cornish mining techniques elicited a response centered in Grass Valley.

As Grass Valley and Nevada City grew from Gold Rush camps to industrial towns, the essential determinants of their townspeople's lives remained the same: the continuity of customary belief and practice as shaped by local economic conditions. In that, they resembled other frontier settlements and other mill towns. Their people adjusted and the gold held out, so the two towns survived as peaceably as was possible in nineteenth-century America.

Appendix

·⊸❦ APPENDIX ❧⊷·

Demographic, Social, and Economic Data for
Grass Valley and Nevada City, 1850-1870

The relatively small size of Grass Valley and Nevada City, and the number of analytical categories I have used, mean that the populations of individual categories are small. Further, the census takers, especially in 1850, were neither free of bias nor overly careful in recording their findings. Therefore, I have attempted not to overburden the results of the computer cross-tabulations, and have avoided statistical apparatus. These are illustrative, not definitive figures. The sources of the tables, unless otherwise noted, are *Population Schedules of the Seventh Census of the United States, 1850*, National Archives Microfilm Publications, microcopy 432, roll 36, California, Yuba County, pp. 547–610, 619–30; *Population Schedules of the Eighth Census of the United States, 1860*, National Archives Microfilm Publications, microcopy 653, roll 61, California, Vol. 4, Napa and Nevada Counties, pp. 143–330; *Population Schedules of the Ninth Census of the United States, 1870*, National Archives Microfilm Publications, microcopy 593, roll 75, California, Vol. 5, Napa and Nevada Counties, pp. 142–233, 271–322. The figures for Nevada (City) in 1850 are based on a random 25 percent sample of the whole town, and the figures for the number, property, and ethnicity of miners in 1860 and 1870 are based on a sample of 20 percent. All other tables, with the exception of Table 3, which is based on samples of 50 cabins, are drawn from the total populations involved. Portions of the census data on some of the residents are missing or illegible, so that I may know a person's birthplace, for example, but not his occupation. This results in sometimes inconsistent base numbers in tables that should ideally be comparing exactly the same populations. Decimal fractions have been rounded, and a figure of 0+ indicates a positive figure of less than 0.5 percent.

TABLE 1
Township Populations and Sex Ratios, 1850–1870

	Grass Valley			Nevada City		
Population	1850	1860	1870	1850	1860	1870
Males	429	3,367	4,543	2,624	2,901	2,692
Females	25	473	2,520	59	778	1,294
TOTAL	454	3,840	7,063	2,683	3,679	3,986
Sex ratios	1,716	712	180	4,447	373	208
National sex ratios	104	105	102	104	105	102

NOTE: Additional data from *Historical Statistics of the United States;* Seventh Census, *Compendium,* Eighth Census, *Population,* Ninth Census, *Compendium.* Sex ratios are the number of men per 100 women.

TABLE 2
Ages of Working Males, 1850–1870

	1850		1860		1870	
Age	N	Percent	N	Percent	N	Percent
Grass Valley						
15–19	20	5%	24	2%	76	4%
20–29	245	64	575	49	426	25
30–39	84	22	495	42	610	35
40–49	23	6	74	6	394	23
50–59	7	2	10	1	152	9
60 and over	2	1	7	1	66	4
Nevada City						
15–19	9	1	21	2	68	6
20–29	576	63	447	41	219	20
30–39	280	31	463	43	330	30
40–49	41	5	119	11	319	29
50–59	5	1	17	2	119	11
60 and over	—	—	21	2	57	5
National[a]						
20–29	2,194,469	39	2,911,558	37	3,351,617	34
30–39	1,490,135	26	2,129,017	27	2,452,999	25
40–49	967,573	17	1,392,223	18	1,829,599	19
50–59	575,685	10	835,350	11	1,209,855	12
60 and over	479,962	8	679,194	9	985,721	10

NOTE: Additional data from *Historical Statistics of the United States.*

[a] A direct comparison between local and national figures is not possible, because the national figures are not based only on employed males. To avoid distorting the national figures as a result of including teenagers, I have ignored teenagers and calculated percentages among men over twenty.

TABLE 3
Relationships of Cabin-mates by Place of Origin, 1850–1870

Relationship and place of origin	Grass Valley			Nevada City		
	1850	1860	1870	1850	1860	1870
At least two:						
Relatives	16	10	6	4	7	4
From same state	35	17	1	37	12	6
From adjacent states	25	7	2	26	4	4
From same foreign country	—	10	29	—	16	16
All from different countries or sections of the United States	12	33	9	19	34	21

NOTE: Numbers are number of cabins from a random sample of 50; in Grass Valley in 1850, then, sixteen cabins of the sample contained at least one man related to another cabin resident.

TABLE 4
Regional Origins of American-born Residents, 1850–1870

Residence and region of origin	1850		1860		1870	
	N	Percent	N	Percent	N	Percent
Grass Valley						
North	179	47%	1,028	73%	505	64%
South	132	35	190	14	162	20
Frontier	68	18	190	14	128	16
TOTAL	379	100%	1,408	100%	795	100%
Nevada City						
North	433	48%	1,029	69%	553	73%
South	292	32	291	20	99	13
Frontier	180	20	172	12	101	13
TOTAL	905	100%	1,492	100%	753	100%

TABLE 5
Men's Occupations, 1850–1870

	Grass Valley			Nevada City		
Occupation	1850	1860	1870	1850[a]	1860	1870
Professional						
Attorney	3	10	12	10	23	14
Manufacturer	—	11	19	—	13	10
Mine officer	1	14	12	1	9	10
Newspaperman	—	4	6	4	10	13
Physician	5	13	19	9	12	11
Teacher or minister	1	6	10	3	5	12
Businessman						
Hotel keeper	—	20	12	2	21	5
Lumberman	—	7	16	1	8	14
Merchant	70	93	99	87	134	72
Multiple interests	—	4	4	5	13	7
Artisan or farmer						
Amalgamator	—	4	10	—	—	2
Blacksmith	3	21	53	2	26	22
Butcher	2	17	23	7	14	17
Carpenter	12	47	67	8	75	51
Clerk	—	47	67	2	62	31
Engineer	—	21	51	—	10	14
Saloon keeper	—	15	66	3	23	19
Other artisan	—	65	153	8	124	97
Farmer	5	20	89	2	26	66
Miner	228	2,357	1,693	765	1,665	978
Unskilled						
Laborer	2	196	107	1	151	72
Servant	—	2	6	1	6	10
Teamster	9	47	122	8	48	40
Unskilled mine worker	1	2	97	—	—	4
Woodchopper	—	1	102	—	—	35
Other unskilled	2	77	228	—	54	213
Professional	3%	2%	3%	3%	3%	4%
Businessman	17	4	4	10	7	5
Artisan or farmer	6	8	18	4	14	17
Miner	71	76	54	82	66	53
Unskilled	4	10	21	1	10	20
TOTAL	100%	100%	100%	100%	100%	100%

[a] Nevada City 1850 figures are a 25 percent sample.

TABLE 6

Continuity of Residence of Male Workers by Occupation, 1850–1860

Town	Professional or businessman		Artisan or farmer		Miner or unskilled		Total	
	N	Percent	N	Percent	N	Percent	N	Percent
Grass Valley								
Total in 1850	84	100%	26	100%	294	100%	404	100%
Still there in 1856[a]	7	8	2	8	10	3	19	5
Still there in 1860	4	5	2	8	9	3	15	4
Nevada City								
Total in 1850	123	100	33	100	773[b]	100	929	100
Still there in 1856	27	22	10	30	25	3	62	7
Still there in 1860	25	20	10	30	21	3	56	6

NOTE: Additional data from Brown and Dallison; Nevada City *Journal*; Nevada City *Democrat*; Byrne; Grass Valley *Telegraph*.
[a] Figures for artisans and farmers and for miners and unskilled are based on newspaper references, not on directory listings, and should be regarded as approximations.
[b] These figures are a 25 percent sample.

TABLE 7
Married Men by Occupation, 1850–1870

Occupation	Grass Valley					Nevada City				
	Total males in occupation	Percent of all males in occupation	Number married	Percent married	Percent of all married men	Total males in occupation	Percent of all males in occupation	Number married	Percent married	Percent of all married men
1850										
Professional or businessman	80	20%	6	8%	46%	122	13%	15	12%	71%
Artisan or farmer	22	6	1	5	8	32	4	2	6	10
Miner	288	71	6	2	46	765	82	4	1	19
Unskilled	14	4	—	—	—	10	1	—	—	—
TOTAL	404	100%	13	3%	100%	929[a]	100%	21	2%	100%
1860										
Professional or businessman	182	6%	51	28%	24%	248	10%	85	34%	26%
Artisan or farmer	257	8	54	21	25	360	14	87	24	27
Miner	2,357	76	91	4	42	1,665	66	128	8	40
Unskilled	325	10	19	6	9	259	10	21	8	7
TOTAL	3,121	100%	215	7%	100%	2,532	100%	321	13%	100%
1870										
Professional or businessman	209	7%	149	71%	15%	168	9%	105	63%	21%
Artisan or farmer	579	18	287	50	30	319	17	147	46	29
Miner	1,693	54	419	25	43	978	53	212	22	42
Unskilled	662	21	116	18	12	374	20	38	10	8
TOTAL	3,143	100%	971	31%	100%	1,839	100%	502	27%	100%

[a] Nevada City 1850 figures are a 25 percent sample.

TABLE 8
Countries of Origin of Male Workers, 1850–1870

Residence and country of origin	1850[a] N	1850[a] Percent	1860 N	1860 Percent	1870 N	1870 Percent
Grass Valley						
United States	379	95%	1,408	42%	795	25%
Great Britain	5	1	685	20	1,213	39
Ireland	4	1	749	22	463	15
Germany and Scandinavia	6	2	112	3	150	5
France and Italy	2	0+	91	3	97	3
Canada	5	1	9	0+	92	3
Latin America	—	—	1	0+	—	—
China	—	—	304	9	325	10
Nevada City						
United States	905	95	1,492	54	753	38
Great Britain	13	1	321	12	249	13
Ireland	13	1	197	7	101	5
Germany and Scandinavia	12	1	198	7	161	8
France and Italy	3	0+	59	2	53	3
Canada	3	0+	18	1	69	4
Latin America	3	0+	1	0+	—	—
China	—	—	459	17	573	29

[a] Nevada City figures in 1850 are a 25 percent sample.

TABLE 9
Occupations of Black Males, 1850–1870

Occupation	Grass Valley 1850	Grass Valley 1860	Grass Valley 1870	Nevada City 1850	Nevada City 1860	Nevada City 1870
Teacher or minister	—	—	1	—	—	—
Merchant	—	1	—	—	—	3
Blacksmith	—	—	—	—	—	1
Carpenter	—	1	—	—	1	—
Other artisan	1	3	2	—	1	2
Farmer	—	—	—	—	—	2
Miner	3	13	1	1	5	4
Laborer	—	4	11	—	6	9
Teamster	—	2	2	—	2	—
Servant	—	1	—	3	1	—
Other unskilled	2	10	8	2	9	8
TOTAL	6	35	25	6	25	29
Professional	—	—	4%	—	—	—
Businessman	—	3%	—	—	—	10%
Artisan or farmer	17%	11	8	—	8%	17
Miner	50	37	4	17%	20	14
Unskilled	33	49	84	83	72	59
TOTAL	100%	100%	100%	100%	100%	100%

TABLE 10

Property Holdings of Miners and Unskilled Workers, 1860 and 1870

Occupation and form of property	1860				1870			
	N	$0, percent	$100–1,000, percent	Over 1,000, percent	N	$0, percent	$100–1,000, percent	Over $1,000, percent
GRASS VALLEY								
MINERS[a]	494				334			
Real estate		96%	2%	2%		78%	18%	4%
Personal estate		92	6	2		75	22	4
UNSKILLED WORKERS								
Laborer	189				107			
Real estate		97	2	1		80	16	4
Personal estate		89	10	1		78	21	1
Mariner	—				1			
Real estate		—	—	—		100	—	—
Personal estate		—	—	—		100	—	—
Servant	2				6			
Real estate		100	—	—		100	—	—
Personal estate		100	—	—		100	—	—
Teamster	46				122			
Real estate		91	2	7		70	23	7
Personal estate		63	33	4		51	43	7
Woodchopper	1				102			
Real estate		100	—	—		94	4	2
Personal estate		100	—	—		92	8	—
Unskilled mine job	—				98			
Real estate		—	—	—		81	19	1
Personal estate		—	—	—		78	21	—
Other unskilled	71				227			
Real estate		99	1	—		96	1	3
Personal estate		92	8	—		94	6	—
TOTAL UNSKILLED	309				663			
Real estate		97	2	2		86	11	3

	N	%	%	%	N	%	%	%
MINERS[a]	325				201			
Real estate		94%	3%	3%		87%	8%	5%
Personal estate		91	7	2		82	11	7
UNSKILLED WORKERS								
Laborer	145				72			
Real estate		97	1	2		90	7	3
Personal estate		98	0+	1		82	18	—
Mariner	1				2			
Real estate		—	100	—		50	50	—
Personal estate		100	—	—		100	—	—
Servant	6				10			
Real estate		100	—	—		100	—	—
Personal estate		67	33	—		90	10	—
Teamster	43				40			
Real estate		79	4	16		73	15	13
Personal estate		63	21	16		53	33	15
Woodchopper	—				35			
Real estate		—	—	—		97	—	3
Personal estate		—	—	—		91	3	6
Unskilled mine job	—				4			
Real estate		—	—	—		75	25	—
Personal estate		—	—	—		75	—	25
Other unskilled	47				213			
Real estate		98	2	—		98	1	0+
Personal estate		94	6	—		96	4	—
TOTAL UNSKILLED	242				376			
Real estate		94	2	4		93	4	2
Personal estate		90%	6%	4%		88	10	2

[a] Miner figures are a 20 percent sample.

Table 11
Property Holdings of Artisans and Farmers, 1860 and 1870

Occupation and form of property	1860				1870			
	N	$0, percent	$100–1,000, percent	Over 1,000, percent	N	$0, percent	$100–1,000, percent	Over $1,000, percent
GRASS VALLEY								
ARTISANS								
Amalgamator	4				10			
Real estate		75%	25%	—		90%	10%	—
Personal estate		50	25	25%		80	20	—
Blacksmith	18				53			
Real estate		78	6	17		77	19	9%
Personal estate		83	11	6		60	38	2
Butcher	16				23			
Real estate		75	6	19		52	17	30
Personal estate		63	25	13		48	35	17
Carpenter	41				67			
Real estate		85	5	10		54	28	18
Personal estate		80	15	5		43	48	9
Clerk	46				67			
Real estate		93	6	—		78	10	12
Personal estate		67	15	17		60	28	12
Engineer	16				51			
Real estate		100	—	—		69	28	4
Personal estate		88	6	6		67	29	4
Saloon keeper	13				66			
Real estate		69	15	15		52	30	18
Personal estate		46	39	15		12	77	11
Other artisan	57				153			
Real estate		81	11	9		63	24	12
Personal estate		70	19	11		45	46	9
FARMERS	6				89			
Real estate		50	—	50		11	7	82

Real estate		83	7	9		56	20	24
Personal estate		70%	19%	11%		41%	42%	17%
NEVADA CITY								
ARTISANS								
Amalgamator	—				2			
Real estate		—	—	—		50%	—	50%
Personal estate		—	—	—		100	—	—
Blacksmith	22				22			
Real estate		73%	9%	18%		77	5%	18
Personal estate		73	14	14		64	27	9
Butcher	13				17			
Real estate		38	8	54		71	6	24
Personal estate		39	31	31		77	6	18
Carpenter	64				51			
Real estate		70	16	14		69	10	22
Personal estate		59	30	11		63	33	4
Clerk	61				31			
Real estate		85	3	12		81	7	13
Personal estate		57	23	20		65	13	23
Engineer	6				14			
Real estate		83	17	—		71	14	14
Personal estate		67	16	16		71	29	—
Saloon keeper	16				19			
Real estate		56	13	31		58	16	26
Personal estate		19	50	31		26	37	37
Other artisan	106				97			
Real estate		75	9	15		66	18	17
Personal estate		67	26	7		57	35	8
FARMERS	8				66			
Real estate		50	25	25		47	9	44
Personal estate		63	25	13		33	30	36
TOTAL ARTISANS AND FARMERS	296				319			
Real estate		73	10	17		65	12	24
Personal estate		60%	27%	14%		54%	29%	17%

TABLE 12
Property Holdings of Professionals and Businessmen, 1860 and 1870

Occupation and form of property	1860				1870			
	N	$0, percent	$100–1,000, percent	Over $1,000, percent	N	$0, percent	$100–1,000, percent	Over $1,000, percent
GRASS VALLEY								
Attorney	5				12			
Real estate		40%	—	60%		25%	33%	42%
Personal estate		—	20%	80		17	42	42
Hotel keeper	16				12			
Real estate		25	6	69		17	—	83
Personal estate		38	19	44		17	8	75
Lumberman	10				16			
Real estate		70	10	20		50	12	38
Personal estate		60	10	30		38	19	44
Manufacturer	4				19			
Real estate		25	—	75		47	—	53
Personal estate		75	—	25		26	37	37
Merchant	71				99			
Real estate		49	7	44		40	10	50
Personal estate		37	18	45		7	61	32
Mine officer	1				12			
Real estate		—	—	100		33	16	50
Personal estate		—	—	100		8	33	58
Newspaperman	2				6			
Real estate		50	—	50		50	50	—
Personal estate		100	—	—		50	17	33
Physician	10				19			
Real estate		50	—	50		53	5	42
Personal estate		30	30	40		21	42	37
Teacher or minister	3				10			
Real estate		100	—	—		70	30	—
Personal estate		67	33	—		40	50	10
Multiple interests	2				4			
Real estate				100		—	—	100

Personal estate 39%

NEVADA CITY

	N	39%	19%	43%	N	16%	45%	39%
Attorney	16				14			
Real estate		56%	13%	31%		36%	—	64%
Personal estate		31	13	56		21	36%	43
Hotel keeper	21				5			
Real estate		38	14	48		40	—	60
Personal estate		38	24	38		20	—	80
Lumberman	5				14			
Real estate		20	—	80		71	—	29
Personal estate		—	—	100		50	7	43
Manufacturer	10				10			
Real estate		40	10	50		50	10	40
Personal estate		40	20	40		50	20	30
Merchant	120				72			
Real estate		39	11	50		39	15	46
Personal estate		37	19	44		18	25	57
Mine officer	2				10			
Real estate		—	—	100		10	—	90
Personal estate		—	50	50		30	30	40
Newspaperman	3				13			
Real estate		67	—	33		46	15	39
Personal estate		—	—	100		39	39	23
Physician	10				11			
Real estate		70	—	30		55	27	18
Personal estate		30	20	50		27	36	36
Teacher or minister	5				12			
Real estate		80	—	20		92	—	8
Personal estate		80	20	—		67	33	—
Multiple interests	11				7			
Real estate		45	—	55		—	—	100
Personal estate		18	—	82		—	—	100
TOTAL	203				168			
Real estate		43	9	48		44	10	46
Personal estate		34%	18%	48%		29%	25%	46%

TABLE 13

Residents with Property Holdings of over $10,000, by Occupation, 1860 and 1870

Occupation and form of property	Grass Valley		Nevada City	
	1860	1870	1860	1870
Attorney				
Real estate	—	—	1	—
Personal estate	1	1	—	1
Clerk				
Real estate	—	—	—	—
Personal estate	—	—	—	1
Farmer				
Real estate	—	1	—	3
Personal estate	—	1	—	—
Hotel keeper				
Real estate	—	2	—	2
Personal estate	—	1	—	—
Lumberman				
Real estate	—	—	—	1
Personal estate	—	—	—	—
Manufacturer				
Real estate	—	2	1	1
Personal estate	—	2	—	—
Merchant				
Real estate	—	3	5	4
Personal estate	4	6	2	7
Mine officer				
Real estate	—	1	—	4
Personal estate	—	3	—	1
Miner				
Real estate	—	1	1	—
Personal estate	2	1	—	3
Multiple investments				
Real estate	—	2	4	5
Personal estate	—	2	1	4
Physician				
Real estate	—	1	—	1
Personal estate	—	1	—	1
TOTAL				
Real estate	—	13	12	21
Personal estate	7	18	3	18

TABLE 14
Ethnic Groups by Occupation, 1860 and 1870

Country of origin	Professional or businessman		Artisan or farmer		Miner[a]		Unskilled	
	N	Percent	N	Percent	N	Percent	N	Percent
Grass Valley, 1860								
United States	79	6%	148	11%	201	71%	178	13%
Great Britain	40	6	40	6	113	83	40	6
Ireland	21	3	31	4	128	85	57	8
Germany and Scandinavia	30	27	32	29	8	36	10	9
France and Italy	5	6	5	6	11	60	26	29
China	4	1	—	—	54	89	30	10
Nevada City, 1860								
United States	146	10	222	15	194	65	154	10
Great Britain	15	5	39	12	47	73	32	10
Ireland	4	2	25	13	26	66	38	19
Germany and Scandinavia	52	26	58	29	14	35	18	9
France and Italy	16	27	12	20	5	42	6	10
China	14	3	4	1	85	93	16	3
Grass Valley, 1870								
United States	101	13	262	33	39	25	237	30
Great Britain	42	4	136	12	197	80	50	5
Ireland	15	3	84	19	50	57	87	20
Germany and Scandinavia	32	21	60	40	4	13	38	25
France and Italy	4	4	18	19	6	31	45	46
Canada	6	7	26	28	2	11	50	54
China	12	4	4	1	33	51	144	44
Nevada City, 1870								
United States	107	15	199	27	60	41	127	17
Great Britain	14	6	39	16	37	74	11	4
Ireland	3	3	17	17	12	59	21	21
Germany and Scandinavia	34	21	51	32	9	28	31	19
France and Italy	8	15	13	25	3	28	17	32
Canada	4	4	13	17	6	38	22	41
China	3	3	4	1	82	72	156	27

[a] Miner figures are a 20 percent sample.

TABLE 15

Ethnic Groups as Percentage of Male Working Population, 1860 and 1870

Country of origin	Professional or businessman		Artisan or farmer		Miner [a]		Unskilled		Percent of male workers
	N	Percent	N	Percent	N	Percent	N	Percent	
Grass Valley, 1860									
United States	79	44%	148	58%	201	39%	178	52%	42%
Great Britain	40	22	40	16	113	22	40	12	20
Ireland	21	12	31	12	128	25	57	17	22
Germany and Scandinavia	30	17	32	13	8	2	10	3	3
France and Italy	5	3	5	2	11	2	26	8	3
China	4	2	—	—	54	11	30	9	9
TOTAL	179	100%	256	100%	515	100%	341	100%	100%
Nevada City, 1860									
United States	146	59%	222	62%	194	52%	154	58%	54%
Great Britain	15	6	39	11	47	13	32	12	12
Ireland	4	2	25	7	26	7	38	14	7
Germany and Scandinavia	52	21	58	16	14	4	18	7	7
France and Italy	16	6	12	3	5	1	6	2	2
China	14	6	4	1	85	23	16	6	17
TOTAL	247	100%	360	100%	371	100%	264	100%	100%
Grass Valley, 1870									
United States	101	48%	262	44%	39	12%	237	36%	25%
Great Britain	42	20	136	23	197	60	50	8	39
Ireland	15	7	84	14	50	15	87	13	15
Germany and Scandinavia	32	15	60	10	4	1	38	6	5
France and Italy	4	2	18	3	6	2	45	7	3
Canada	6	3	26	4	2	1	50	8	3
China	12	6	4	1	33	10	144	22	10
TOTAL	212	100%	590	100%	331	100%	651	100%	100%
Nevada City, 1870									
United States	107	62%	199	59%	60	29%	127	33%	38
Great Britain	14	8	39	12	37	18	11	3	13
Ireland	3	2	17	5	12	6	21	5	5
Germany and Scandinavia	34	20	51	15	9	4	31	8	8
France and Italy	8	5	13	4	3	1	17	4	3
Canada	4	2	13	4	6	3	22	6	4
China	3	2	4	1	82	39	156	41	29
TOTAL	173	100%	336	100%	209	100%	385	100%	100%

[a] Miner figures are a 20 percent sample.

TABLE 16

Household Heads by Property Holdings and Country of Origin, 1860 and 1870

Residence and country of origin	Real property				Personal property			
	N	$0	$100–1,000	Over $1,000	N	$0	$100–1,000	Over $1,000
Grass Valley, 1860								
United States	88	42%	15%	43%	88	53%	18%	28%
Great Britain	56	41	23	36	56	54	27	20
Ireland	59	61	22	17	59	73	19	8
Germany and Scandinavia	15	53	7	40	15	67	7	27
France and Italy	4	75	—	25	4	75	25	—
Canada	—	—	—	—	—	—	—	—
Nevada City, 1860								
United States	204	44	10	46	204	49	19	32
Great Britain	44	48	16	36	44	66	14	20
Ireland	36	47	17	36	36	67	19	14
Germany and Scandinavia	33	39	18	42	33	42	18	39
France and Italy	21	71	—	29	21	48	33	19
Canada	—	—	—	—	—	—	—	—
Grass Valley, 1870								
United States	324	31	32	37	324	17	50	33
Great Britain	322	27	55	18	322	22	67	11
Ireland	239	24	63	13	239	20	71	9
Germany and Scandinavia	59	32	34	34	59	10	44	46
France and Italy	17	41	29	29	17	35	47	18
Canada	17	24	47	29	17	18	65	18
Nevada City, 1870								
United States	274	31	23	46	274	48	28	24
Great Britain	84	49	31	20	84	68	25	7
Ireland	63	44	40	16	63	60	35	5
Germany and Scandinavia	51	16	29	55	51	26	43	31
France and Italy	22	36	9	55	22	50	23	27
Canada	19	47	11	42	19	47	32	21

TABLE 17
Married Men by Real Property Holdings and Occupation, 1860 and 1870

Real property	Professionals and businessmen		Artisans and farmers		Miners		Unskilled	
	Married	All	Married	All	Married	All	Married	All
Grass Valley, 1860								
$0	34%	46%	40%	83%	53%	96%	80%	97%
$100–1,000	6	6	17	7	26	2	7	2
Over $1,000	60	48	43	9	21	2	13	2
Nevada City, 1860								
$0	30	43	33	73	61	94	52	94
$100–1,000	5	9	17	10	13	3	14	2
Over $1,000	64	48	50	17	26	3	33	4
Grass Valley, 1870								
$0	28	41	27	56	27	78	33	86
$100–1,000	27	12	29	20	64	18	54	11
Over $1,000	46	47	44	24	9	4	14	3
Nevada City, 1870								
$0	21	44	23	65	47	87	47	93
$100–1,000	17	10	25	12	30	7	34	4
Over $1,000	62	46	52	24	24	5	18	2

TABLE 18
Miners' Living Arrangements, 1860 and 1870

Living arrangement	Grass Valley				Nevada City			
	1860		1870		1860		1870	
	N	Percent	N	Percent	N	Percent	N	Percent
Lives alone	16	1%	88	5%	30	2%	184	19%
Cabin with males	2,078	88	851	50	1,250	75	333	34
Boarding house	38	2	135	8	96	6	201	21
With family	105	5	416	25	131	8	221	23
With common-law wife	30	1	2	0+	41	3	2	0+
Boards with mining family	68	3	117	7	57	3	13	1
Boards with non-mining family	12	1	56	3	46	3	6	1
With parents	10	0+	28	2	14	1	18	2
TOTAL	2,357	100%	1,693	100%	1,665	100%	978	100%

TABLE 19
Occupations of White Female Heads of Household, 1860 and 1870

| | Grass Valley | | | | Nevada City | | | |
| | 1860 | | 1870 | | 1860 | | 1870 | |
Occupation	N	Percent	N	Percent	N	Percent	N	Percent
Keeps house	7	25%	17	29%	4	18%	28	49%
Takes in boarders	1	4	9	15	2	9	5	9
Prostitute	16	57	5	9	6	27	11	19
Merchant	—	—	3	5	1	5	1	2
Seamstress or milliner	—	—	4	7	1	32	3	5
Servant	3	11	2	3	—	—	5	9
Washwoman	—	—	9	15	—	—	2	4
Cook	1	4	—	—	—	—	—	—
Miner	—	—	—	—	1	5	—	—
Nun	—	—	2	3	—	—	—	—
Schoolteacher	—	—	6	10	—	—	—	—
Student	—	—	—	—	1	5	—	—
None listed	—	—	2	3	—	—	2	4
TOTAL	28	100%	59	100%	22	100%	57	100%

TABLE 20
Occupations of White Female Boarders, 1860 and 1870

| | Grass Valley | | | | Nevada City | | | |
| | 1860 | | 1870 | | 1860 | | 1870 | |
Occupation	N	Percent	N	Percent	N	Percent	N	Percent
Keeps house	—	—	8	9%	—	—	10	21%
Prostitute	5	21%	3	4	5	11%	4	9
Servant	10	42	40	46	25	54	18	38
Seamstress or milliner	—	—	9	10	3	7	1	2
Schoolteacher	—	—	3	4	4	9	1	2
Washwoman	1	4	1	1	2	4	—	—
Merchant	—	—	—	—	—	—	1	2
Cook	—	—	—	—	—	—	1	2
Nun	—	—	6	7	—	—	—	—
None listed	8	33	17	20	7	15	11	23
TOTAL	24	100%	87	100%	46	100%	47	100%

TABLE 21
Occupations of White Women, 1860 and 1870

Occupation	1860			1870		
	N	Percent of women	Percent of employed women	N	Percent of women	Percent of employed women
Grass Valley						
Keeps house	129	48%	—	715	64%	—
Takes in boarders	96	36	70%	294	26	72%
Prostitute	24	9	17	8	1	2
Merchant	1	0+	1	11	1	3
Miner	1	0+	1	—	—	—
Servant	13	5	9	42	4	10
Washwoman	1	0+	1	11	1	3
Cook	1	0+	1	—	—	—
Baker	1	0+	1	—	—	—
Schoolteacher	—	—	—	10	1	3
Seamstress or milliner	—	—	—	19	2	5
Nurse	—	—	—	2	0+	1
Waitress	—	—	—	2	0+	1
Nun	—	—	—	8	1	2
Nevada City						
Keeps house	202	50	—	456	76	—
Takes in boarders	135	33	66	87	15	60
Prostitute	19	5	9	17	3	12
Merchant	3	1	2	3	1	2
Miner	1	0+	1	—	—	—
Servant	26	6	13	23	4	16
Washwoman	2	1	1	2	0+	1
Cook	—	—	—	—	—	—
Baker	—	—	—	—	—	—
Schoolteacher	4	1	2	3	1	2
Seamstress or milliner	11	3	5	4	1	3
Nurse	—	—	—	5	1	3
Waitress	—	—	—	1	0+	1
Doctor	1	0+	1	—	—	—
Hostler	1	0+	1	—	—	—
Student	1	0+	1	—	—	—

TABLE 22
Occupations of White Women, by Husband's Occupation, 1860 and 1870

Occupation of husband and of wife	Grass Valley				Nevada City			
	1860		1870		1860		1870	
	N	Percent	N	Percent	N	Percent	N	Percent
Professional or businessman								
Wife keeps house	31	62%	102	65%	49	53%	70	71%
Wife takes in boarders	19	38	50	32	40	44	27	27
Wife has other work	—	—	4	3	3	3	2	2
Artisan or farmer								
Wife keeps house	30	64	158	60	45	55	119	82
Wife takes in boarders	16	34	105	40	32	39	23	16
Wife has other work	1	2	2	1	5	6	4	3
Miner								
Wife keeps house	41	43	322	77	82	59	186	87
Wife takes in boarders	53	55	94	23	51	36	27	13
Wife has other work	2	2	1	0+	7	5	—	—
Unskilled								
Wife keeps house	10	67	89	70	12	57	32	80
Wife takes in boarders	4	27	36	28	9	43	5	13
Wife has other work	1	7	2	2	—	—	3	8

TABLE 23

Occupations of White Women, by Real Property, 1860 and 1870

	1860				1870			
	N	$0	$100–1,000	Over $1,000	N	$0	$100–1,000	Over $1,000
Grass Valley								
Keeps house	121	100%	—	—	690	97%	2%	1%
Takes in boarders	96	100	—	—	296	98	1	1
Prostitute	19	100	—	—	5	100	—	—
Merchant	1	—	—	100%	11	55	36	9
Miner	1	100	—	—	—	—	—	—
Servant	3	100	—	—	6	83	17	—
Cook	1	100	—	—	—	—	—	—
Baker	1	—	—	100	—	—	—	—
Washwoman	—	—	—	—	10	70	30	—
Schoolteacher	—	—	—	—	7	100	—	—
Seamstress or milliner	—	—	—	—	10	90	10	—
Nun	—	—	—	—	2	100	—	—
TOTAL	243	99%	—	1%	1,036	97%	3%	1%
Nevada City								
Keeps house	195	97%	2%	2%	436	96%	3%	2%
Takes in boarders	136	99	0+	0+	87	98	—	2
Prostitute	14	86	—	14	13	85	8	8
Merchant	3	67	—	33	2	100	—	—
Miner	1	—	—	100	—	—	—	—
Seamstress or milliner	8	63	—	37	3	100	—	—
Servant	2	50	50	—	6	100	—	—
Physician	1	100	—	—	—	—	—	—
Washwoman	—	—	—	—	2	50	—	50
TOTAL	360	96%	1%	3%	549	96%	2%	2%

TABLE 24
Real Property Holdings of Boarding and Non-boarding
White Families, 1860 and 1870

Husband's occupation and real property	1860				1870			
	Wife keeps house		Wife takes in boarders		Wife keeps house		Wife takes in boarders	
	N	Percent	N	Percent	N	Percent	N	Percent
Grass Valley								
Professional or businessman								
$0	9	29%	8	42%	28	28%	12	24%
$100–1,000	—	—	3	16	30	29	10	20
Over $1,000	22	71	8	42	44	43	28	56
Artisan or farmer								
$0	11	37	7	44	46	29	23	22
$100–1,000	3	10	5	31	56	35	21	20
Over $1,000	16	53	4	25	56	35	61	58
Miner								
$0	23	56	27	51	86	27	29	31
$100–1,000	9	22	15	28	213	66	55	59
Over $1,000	9	22	11	21	24	7	10	11
Unskilled								
$0	7	70	4	100	30	34	11	31
$100–1,000	1	10	—	—	47	53	20	56
Over $1,000	2	20	—	—	11	13	5	14
Nevada City								
Professional or businessman								
$0	17	35	9	23	17	24	3	11
$100–1,000	1	2	4	10	14	20	3	11
Over $1,000	31	63	27	68	39	56	21	78
Artisan or farmer								
$0	15	33	7	22	29	24	2	9
$100–1,000	6	13	8	25	32	27	3	13
Over $1,000	24	53	17	53	58	49	18	78
Miner								
$0	46	56	33	65	87	47	13	48
$100–1,000	11	13	7	14	58	31	4	15
Over $1,000	25	31	11	22	41	22	10	37
Unskilled								
$0	7	58	4	44	12	40	3	60
$100–1,000	1	8	2	22	12	40	1	20
Over $1,000	4	33	3	33	6	20	1	20

TABLE 25

Relationships of Boarders to Hosts, by Host's Occupation, 1860 and 1870

Host's occupation and boarder's status	Grass Valley				Nevada City			
	1860		1870		1860		1870	
	N	Percent	N	Percent	N	Percent	N	Percent
Professional or businessman								
1. Same occupational level	4	31%	3	9%	4	13%	5	28%
2. Dependent	2	15	11	33	5	16	4	22
3. Occupation not related to host's	7	54	8	24	15	48	8	44
4. Employee	—	—	8	24	—	—	1	6
5. 1, 2, and 3	—	—	—	—	3	10	—	—
6. Both 2 and 3	—	—	3	9	4	13	—	—
TOTAL	13	100%	33	100%	31	100%	18	100%
Artisan or farmer								
1. Same occupational level	4	31%	21	22%	8	26%	7	39%
2. Superior status	—	—	2	2	1	3	—	—
3. Occupation not related to host's	8	62	30	31	15	48	3	17
4. Employee	—	—	29	30	2	7	7	39
5. Apprentice	—	—	2	2	—	—	1	6
6. Both 1 and 2	1	8	—	—	1	3	—	—
7. Both 1 and 3	—	—	4	4	2	7	—	—
8. Both 2 and 3	—	—	—	—	1	3	—	—
9. Both 3 and 4	—	—	9	9	1	3	—	—
TOTAL	13	100%	97	100%	31	100%	18	100%
Miner								
1. Employed in mining	34	76%	69	74%	20	61%	10	83%
2. Superior status	6	13	11	12	4	12	1	8
3. Unskilled	2	4	10	11	—	—	1	8
4. Both 1 and 2	1	2	2	2	4	12	—	—
5. 1, 2, and 3	—	—	—	—	1	3	—	—
6. Both 1 and 3	2	4	1	1	4	12	—	—
TOTAL	45	100%	93	100%	33	100%	12	100%
Unskilled								
1. Employed in mining	1	25%	6	23%	3	38%	1	100%
2. Same occupational level	1	25	11	42	3	38	—	—
3. Superior status	1	25	4	15	—	—	—	—
4. Both 1 and 2	—	—	2	8	2	25	—	—
5. Both 1 and 3	1	25	3	12	—	—	—	—
TOTAL	4	100%	26	100%	8	100%	1	100%

NOTE: Age has been used as a variable in determining status and dependency.

TABLE 26

*Households with Servants, by Married Male Occupation
and Real Property, 1860 and 1870*

Occupation and real property	1860				1870			
	N	No servants	One servant	Two or more	N	No servants	One servant	Two or more
Grass Valley								
Professional or businessman	50	94%	4%	2%	158	73%	22%	5%
Artisan or farmer	47	96	4	—	266	92	8	—
Miner	96	99	1	—	419	98	2	0+
Unskilled	15	100	—	—	126	96	3	1
TOTAL	208	97%	2%	1%	969	92%	7%	1%
No real estate	104	100%	—	—	272	96%	4%	0+%
$100–1,000	37	100	—	—	458	97	3	0+
More than $1,000	72	92	7	1	241	78	18	3
Nevada City								
Professional or businessman	92	85%	14%	1%	99	90%	7%	3%
Artisan or farmer	82	94	6	—	147	93	6	1
Miner	140	96	4	—	214	95	5	—
Unskilled	21	91	10	—	38	97	3	—
TOTAL	335	92%	8%	0+%	498	94%	5%	1%
No real estate	155	98%	2%	—	173	94%	6%	—
$100–1,000	40	95	5	—	129	100	—	—
More than $1,000	144	85	14	1	196	89	9	2

TABLE 27

Households with Servants, by White Female Occupation, 1860 and 1870

Woman's occupation	1860				1870			
	N	No servants	One servant	Two or more	N	No servants	One servant	Two or more
Grass Valley								
Keeps house	127	97%	3%	—	690	95%	5%	0+%
Takes in boarders	96	98	1	1%	295	88	10	2
All others	36	97	3	—	51	86	8	6
TOTAL	259	97%	2%	0+%	1,036	92%	7%	1%
Nevada City								
Keeps house	195	94%	6%	—	436	95%	4%	1%
Takes in boarders	135	89	10	1%	87	87	10	2
All others	30	100	—	—	26	96	4	—
TOTAL	360	93%	7%	0+%	549	94%	5%	1%

TABLE 28

Households with Children, by White Female Occupation, 1860 and 1870

Number of children	Keeps house		Takes in boarders		Prostitute		All others	
	N	Percent	N	Percent	N	Percent	N	Percent
Grass Valley, 1860								
None	—	—	2	4%	2	100%	—	—
One	24	25%	26	48	—	—	2	67%
Two	33	35	14	26	—	—	1	33
Three	18	19	6	11	—	—	—	—
Four	11	12	3	6	—	—	—	—
Five or more	9	10	3	6	—	—	—	—
Nevada City, 1860								
None	2	1	4	5	1	25	—	—
One	52	34	26	31	2	50	4	57
Two	44	29	25	30	1	25	1	14
Three	29	19	15	18	—	—	2	29
Four	16	11	7	8	—	—	—	—
Five or more	9	6	6	7	—	—	—	—
Grass Valley, 1870								
None	129	19	58	20	5	100	20	44
One	124	18	62	21	—	—	2	4
Two	123	18	57	19	—	—	8	18
Three	111	16	43	15	—	—	7	16
Four	83	12	31	11	—	—	6	13
Five or more	118	17	44	15	—	—	2	4
Nevada City, 1870								
None	90	21	10	12	11	85	11	73
One	76	18	20	23	—	—	—	—
Two	65	15	18	21	1	8	1	7
Three	69	16	15	17	1	8	2	13
Four	55	13	10	12	—	—	1	7
Five or more	80	18	14	16	—	—	—	—

NOTE: Women were married or living with an adult male.

TABLE 29
*Households with Children at School or at Work, by White
Female Occupation, 1860*

Number of children	Keeps house		Takes in boarders		All others		Total	
	N	Percent	N	Percent	N	Percent	N	Percent
Enrolled in school								
Grass Valley								
None	58	61%	39	74%	5	100%	102	67%
One	20	21	7	13	—	—	27	18
Two	10	11	4	8	—	—	14	9
Three	2	2	2	4	—	—	4	3
Four	3	3	—	—	—	—	3	2
Five or more	2	2	1	2	—	—	3	2
Nevada City								
None	96	63	47	57	7	58	150	61
One	31	20	18	22	4	33	53	22
Two	17	11	16	19	1	8	34	14
Three	3	2	2	2	—	—	5	2
Four	4	3	—	—	—	—	4	2
Five or more	1	1	—	—	—	—	1	0+
Listed with occupations								
Grass Valley								
None	85	90	52	96	5	100	142	92
One	7	7	2	4	—	—	9	6
Two	—	—	—	—	—	—	—	—
Three	3	3	—	—	—	—	3	2
Nevada City								
None	163	95	77	93	10	91	250	94
One	5	3	4	5	1	9	10	4
Two	3	2	1	1	—	—	4	2
Three	1	1	1	1	—	—	2	1

TABLE 30
Households with Children, by White Male Occupation, 1860 and 1870

Number of children	Professional or businessman		Artisan or farmer		Miner		Unskilled	
	N	Percent	N	Percent	N	Percent	N	Percent
Grass Valley, 1860								
None	19	38%	13	28%	32	33%	6	40%
One	13	26	13	28	16	17	4	27
Two	12	24	10	21	22	23	2	13
Three	2	4	6	13	12	13	2	13
Four	2	4	3	6	7	7	1	7
Five or more	2	4	2	4	7	7	—	—
Nevada City, 1860								
None	24	26	28	34	51	36	10	48
One	26	28	21	26	26	19	4	19
Two	22	24	16	20	26	19	3	14
Three	9	10	8	10	21	15	2	10
Four	7	8	5	6	9	6	2	10
Five or more	4	4	4	5	7	5	—	—
Grass Valley, 1870								
None	35	22	43	16	73	17	40	32
One	27	17	55	21	75	18	24	19
Two	27	17	59	22	75	18	16	13
Three	28	18	36	14	73	17	13	10
Four	18	12	28	11	48	12	15	12
Five or more	22	14	45	17	75	18	18	14
Nevada City, 1870								
None	18	18	31	21	37	17	14	37
One	23	24	27	18	40	19	4	11
Two	17	17	24	16	26	12	8	21
Three	16	16	24	16	36	17	4	11
Four	9	9	17	12	31	15	4	11
Five or more	15	15	24	16	44	21	4	11

Table 31
Households with Children at School or at Work, by
White Male Occupation, 1860 and 1870

Number of children	Professional or businessman		Artisan or farmer		Miner		Unskilled	
	N	Percent	N	Percent	N	Percent	N	Percent
Enrolled in school								
Grass Valley, 1860								
None	44	88%	32	68%	71	74%	13	87%
One	3	6	9	19	12	13	2	13
Two	—	—	5	11	8	8	—	—
Three	1	2	—	—	3	3	—	—
Four	1	2	1	2	—	—	—	—
Five or more	1	2	—	—	2	2	—	—
Nevada City, 1860								
None	66	72	60	73	101	72	18	86
One	18	20	10	12	20	14	1	5
Two	7	8	9	11	13	9	2	10
Three	—	—	3	4	2	1	—	—
Four	1	1	—	—	3	2	—	—
Five or more	—	—	—	—	1	1	—	—
Grass Valley, 1870								
None	78	49	137	52	229	55	71	56
One	30	19	54	20	78	19	26	21
Two	26	17	35	13	54	13	13	10
Three	18	11	29	11	37	9	11	9
Four	5	3	9	3	18	4	4	3
Five or more	1	1	1	0+	3	1	1	1
Nevada City, 1870								
None	46	47	81	55	94	44	26	68
One	24	24	20	14	26	12	4	11
Two	11	11	22	15	43	20	3	8
Three	12	12	10	7	28	13	3	8
Four	3	3	8	5	19	9	2	5
Five or more	3	3	6	4	4	2	—	—
Listed with occupations								
Grass Valley, 1860								
None	49	98	44	94	89	93	15	100
One	1	2	2	4	5	5	—	—
Two	—	—	—	—	—	—	—	—
Three	—	—	1	2	2	2	—	—
Nevada City, 1860								
None	90	98	78	95	132	94	21	100
One	1	1	2	2	6	4	—	—
Two	—	—	1	1	2	1	—	—
Three	1	1	1	1	—	—	—	—
Grass Valley, 1870								
None	145	92	233	88	394	94	119	94
One	10	6	23	9	19	5	4	3
Two	2	1	8	3	5	1	3	2
Three	—	—	1	0+	—	—	—	—
Four	—	—	1	0+	1	0+	—	—
Nevada City, 1870								
None	88	89	127	86	196	92	36	95
One	9	9	15	10	13	6	1	3
Two	2	2	5	3	2	1	1	3
Three	—	—	—	—	1	1	—	—
Four	—	—	—	—	2	1	—	—

TABLE 32

Households with Children at School or at Work, by White Male's Real Property, 1860 and 1870

Number of children	1860						1870					
	$0		$100–1,000		Over $1,000		$0		$100–1,000		Over $1,000	
	N	Percent	N	Percent	N	Percent	N	Percent	N	Percent	N	Percent
Grass Valley												
In household												
None	39	38%	14	38%	19	26%	71	26%	78	17%	42	18%
One	22	21	4	11	22	31	67	25	65	15	49	20
Two	27	26	4	11	15	21	48	18	88	20	41	17
Three	8	8	8	22	6	8	34	13	83	19	33	14
Four	5	5	3	8	5	7	32	12	56	13	23	10
Five or more	3	3	4	11	5	7	20	7	78	17	52	22
Enrolled in school												
None	83	80	26	70	55	76	159	59	241	53	116	48
One	12	12	5	14	9	13	56	21	81	18	51	21
Two	7	7	3	8	4	6	29	11	67	15	33	14
Three	—	—	2	5	2	3	24	9	47	10	24	10
Four	1	1	—	—	1	1	3	1	20	4	13	5
Five or more	1	1	1	3	1	1	1	0+	2	0+	3	1
Listed with occu-												
pations												
None	99	95	36	97	66	92	259	95	422	92	212	88
One	3	3	1	3	5	7	11	4	27	6	18	8
Two	—	—	—	—	—	—	2	1	9	2	7	3
Three	2	2	—	—	1	1	—	—	—	—	1	0+
Four	—	—	—	—	—	—	—	—	—	—	2	1

Nevada City

In household												
None	71	46%	10	25%	34	24%	43	25%	22	17%	35	18%
One	29	19	6	15	43	30	40	23	19	15	35	18
Two	27	17	9	23	32	22	23	13	24	19	28	14
Three	15	10	7	18	18	13	28	16	20	16	32	16
Four	9	6	3	8	11	8	14	8	17	13	30	15
Five or more	4	3	5	13	6	4	25	15	27	21	36	18
Enrolled in school												
None	125	81	21	53	103	72	98	57	59	46	90	46
One	18	12	11	28	20	14	25	15	15	12	34	17
Two	8	5	6	15	17	12	26	15	23	18	30	15
Three	3	2	1	3	1	1	11	6	19	15	23	12
Four	1	1	—	—	3	2	9	5	10	8	13	7
Five or more	—	—	1	3	—	—	4	2	3	2	6	3
Listed with occupations												
None	148	96	37	93	139	97	160	93	110	85	177	90
One	6	4	1	3	2	1	11	6	15	12	12	6
Two	1	1	1	3	2	1	1	1	4	3	5	3
Three	—	—	1	3	1	1	1	1	—	—	—	—
Four	—	—	—	—	1	—	—	—	—	—	2	1

TABLE 33
Chinese Population, 1860 and 1870

| | Grass Valley | | | | Nevada City | | | |
| | 1860 | | 1870 | | 1860 | | 1870 | |
Category	N	Percent	N	Percent	N	Percent	N	Percent
Men	305	95%	339	89%	439	91%	639	95%
Boys	—	—	4	1	2	0+	3	0+
Women	15	5	39	10	40	8	27	4
Girls	—	—	1	0+	1	0+	1	0+
TOTAL	320	100%	383	100%	482	100%	670	100%

TABLE 34
Black Married and Unmarried Men, 1860 and 1870

| | 1860 | | | | 1870 | | | |
| | Married | | Unmarried | | Married | | Unmarried | |
Town	N	Percent	N	Percent	N	Percent	N	Percent
Grass Valley	10	28%	26	72%	13	52%	12	48%
Nevada City	8	35	15	65	17	59	12	41

TABLE 35
Occupations of Black Women, 1860 and 1870

| | Grass Valley | | | | Nevada City | | | |
| | 1860 | | 1870 | | 1860 | | 1870 | |
Occupation	N	Percent	N	Percent	N	Percent	N	Percent
Keeps house	4	36%	11	73%	6	60%	12	63%
Takes in boarders	3	27	1	7	1	10	2	11
Washwoman	2	18	—	—	1	10	1	5
Servant	1	9	2	13	—	—	3	16
Seamstress	1	9	—	—	1	10	—	—
Prostitute	—	—	1	7	1	10	—	—
Merchant	—	—	—	—	—	—	1	5
TOTAL	11	100%	15	100%	10	100%	19	100%

TABLE 36

Married Men by Country of Origin, 1860 and 1870

Residence and country of origin	1860 Total males	Married N	Married Percent	1870 Total males	Married N	Married Percent
Grass Valley						
United States	1,408	90	6%	795	323	41%
Great Britain	685	57	8	1,213	327	27
Ireland	749	51	7	436	243	56
Germany and Scandinavia	112	17	15	150	57	38
France and Italy	91	2	2	97	15	16
Canada	9	—	—	92	17	19
China	305	2	1	339	5	2
TOTAL	3,359	219	7%	3,122	987	32%
Nevada City						
United States	1,492	191	13%	753	268	36%
Great Britain	321	43	13	249	81	33
Ireland	197	33	17	101	61	60
Germany and Scandinavia	198	35	18	161	47	29
France and Italy	59	19	32	53	24	45
Canada	18	—	—	69	18	26
China	437	3	1	639	2	0+
TOTAL	2,722	324	12%	2,025	501	25%

TABLE 37

White Women Who Keep House or Take In Boarders, by Country of Origin, 1860 and 1870

Residence and country of origin	1860 N	Keeps house	One boarder	Two or more	1870 N	Keeps house	One boarder	Two or more
Grass Valley								
United States	78	68%	23%	9%	330	65%	17%	19%
Great Britain	56	54	25	21	279	68	18	14
Ireland	57	32	42	26	267	80	14	6
Germany and Scandinavia	13	77	15	8	43	63	30	7
France and Italy	7	71	29	—	21	52	29	19
Canada	—	—	—	—	31	58	7	36
Latin America	—	—	—	—	4	75	25	—
Nevada City								
United States	166	69	18	13	235	81	16	3
Great Britain	55	62	26	13	71	87	11	1
Ireland	41	46	32	22	107	87	10	3
Germany and Scandinavia	32	53	28	19	44	75	18	7
France and Italy	20	75	10	15	17	71	18	12
Canada	—	—	—	—	17	77	12	12
Latin America	3	67	—	33	7	71	29	—

TABLE 38

Men's Occupations by Household Head's Country of Origin, 1860 and 1870

Residence and country of origin	Professional or businessman	Artisan or farmer	Miner	Unskilled	Total N
Grass Valley, 1860					
United States	26%	35%	32%	8%	78
Great Britain	29	18	47	6	55
Ireland	11	7	75	7	57
Germany and Scandinavia	57	21	14	7	14
France and Italy	—	75	—	25	4
Nevada City, 1860					
United States	29	26	38	6	197
Great Britain	9	27	57	7	44
Ireland	11	11	69	9	35
Germany and Scandinavia	49	30	15	6	33
France and Italy	45	15	35	5	20
Latin America	—	33	67	—	3
Grass Valley, 1870					
United States	24	42	15	19	315
Great Britain	11	18	68	3	321
Ireland	8	17	57	18	239
Germany and Scandinavia	39	41	17	3	59
France and Italy	19	25	19	38	16
Canada	12	41	18	29	17
Nevada City, 1870					
United States	27	32	33	9	259
Great Britain	6	18	75	1	84
Ireland	2	14	75	10	63
Germany and Scandinavia	31	57	—	12	51
France and Italy	18	27	50	5	22
Canada	21	32	42	5	19

TABLE 39
Households with Children, by Household Head's Country of Origin, 1860 and 1870

Number of children	United States		Great Britain		Ireland		Germany and Scandinavia		France and Italy	
	N	Percent	N	Percent	N	Percent	N	Percent	N	Percent
Grass Valley, 1860										
None	23	29%	17	30%	25	42%	4	27%	3	75%
One	25	32	9	16	10	17	4	27	—	—
Two	17	22	15	27	10	17	3	20	1	25
Three	4	5	5	9	10	17	3	20	—	—
Four	3	4	6	11	3	5	1	7	—	—
Five or more	7	9	4	7	1	2	—	—	—	—
Nevada City, 1860										
None	69	35	14	32	14	39	10	30	7	33
One	44	22	10	23	10	28	6	18	7	33
Two	44	22	5	11	6	17	10	30	3	14
Three	22	11	8	18	3	8	2	6	2	10
Four	13	7	4	9	1	3	2	6	2	10
Five or more	7	4	3	7	2	6	3	9	—	—
Grass Valley, 1870										
None	76	24	63	20	33	14	11	19	3	18
One	61	19	60	19	39	16	11	19	5	29
Two	66	21	56	17	31	13	16	27	4	24
Three	36	11	60	19	45	19	8	14	1	6
Four	40	13	26	8	38	16	3	5	2	12
Five or more	36	11	57	18	53	22	10	17	2	12
Nevada City, 1870										
None	49	19	19	23	13	21	9	18	5	23
One	57	22	14	17	9	14	7	14	2	9
Two	45	18	15	18	4	6	5	10	2	9
Three	44	17	9	11	11	18	9	18	3	14
Four	26	10	15	18	9	14	7	14	4	18
Five or more	36	14	12	14	17	27	14	28	6	27

TABLE 40

Households with Children, by Male Household Head's Real Property and Country of Origin, 1860 and 1870

Country of origin and number of children	Grass Valley, 1860					
	$0		$100–1,000		Over $1,000	
	N	Percent	N	Percent	N	Percent
United States						
None	10	29%	6	60%	7	20%
One	9	27	4	40	12	34
Two	9	27	—	—	8	23
Three	2	6	—	—	2	6
Four	1	3	—	—	2	6
Five or more	3	9	—	—	4	11
Great Britain						
None	8	35	2	15	7	35
One	5	22	—	—	4	20
Two	8	35	3	23	4	20
Three	2	9	2	15	1	5
Four	—	—	3	23	3	15
Five or more	—	—	3	23	1	5
Ireland						
None	17	47	6	46	2	20
One	5	14	—	—	5	50
Two	7	19	1	8	2	20
Three	4	11	5	39	1	10
Four	3	8	—	—	—	—
Five or more	—	—	1	8	—	—
Germany and Scandi- navia						
None	2	25	—	—	2	33
One	3	38	—	—	1	17
Two	2	25	—	—	1	17
Three	—	—	1	100	2	33
Four	1	13	—	—	—	—
Five or more	—	—	—	—	—	—
France and Italy						
None	2	67	—	—	1	100
One	—	—	—	—	—	—
Two	1	33	—	—	—	—
Three	—	—	—	—	—	—
Four	—	—	—	—	—	—
Five or more	—	—	—	—	—	—

TABLE 40—*continued*

Country of origin and number of children	Nevada City, 1860					
	$0		$100–1,000		Over $1,000	
	N	Percent	N	Percent	N	Percent
United States						
None	47	54%	4	20%	18	20%
One	15	17	4	20	25	27
Two	15	17	5	25	24	26
Three	5	6	2	10	15	16
Four	3	4	3	15	7	8
Five or more	2	2	2	10	3	3
Great Britain						
None	8	38	1	14	5	31
One	3	14	1	14	6	38
Two	1	5	2	29	2	13
Three	4	19	3	43	1	6
Four	3	14	—	—	1	6
Five or more	2	10	—	—	1	6
Ireland						
None	8	47	3	50	3	23
One	5	29	—	—	5	39
Two	2	12	1	17	3	23
Three	1	6	2	33	—	—
Four	1	6	—	—	—	—
Five or more	—	—	—	—	2	15
Germany and Scandinavia						
None	2	15	2	33	6	43
One	1	8	—	—	5	36
Two	7	54	1	17	2	14
Three	2	15	—	—	—	—
Four	1	8	—	—	1	7
Five or more	—	—	3	50	—	—
France and Italy						
None	6	40	—	—	1	17
One	5	33	—	—	2	33
Two	2	13	—	—	1	17
Three	1	7	—	—	1	17
Four	1	7	—	—	1	17
Five or more	—	—	—	—	—	—

Continued

TABLE 40—*continued*
Households with Children, by Male Household Head's Real Property
and Country of Origin, 1860 and 1870

Country of origin and number of children	Grass Valley, 1870					
	$0		$100–1,000		Over $1,000	
	N	Percent	N	Percent	N	Percent
United States						
None	21	21%	29	30%	26	22%
One	30	31	8	8	23	19
Two	17	17	24	25	25	21
Three	9	9	13	13	14	12
Four	14	14	12	12	14	12
Five or more	7	7	12	12	17	14
Great Britain						
None	25	29	31	18	7	12
One	16	19	33	19	11	19
Two	15	17	35	20	6	10
Three	16	19	32	18	12	20
Four	7	8	15	9	4	7
Five or more	7	8	31	18	19	32
Ireland						
None	15	26	13	9	5	16
One	12	21	19	13	8	25
Two	9	16	20	13	2	6
Three	6	11	34	23	5	16
Four	10	18	26	17	2	6
Five or more	5	9	38	25	10	31
Germany and Scandinavia						
None	6	32	3	15	2	10
One	4	21	2	10	5	25
Two	5	26	7	35	4	20
Three	3	16	3	15	2	10
Four	—	—	1	5	2	10
Five or more	1	5	4	20	5	25
France and Italy						
None	2	29	—	—	1	20
One	4	57	1	20	—	—
Two	1	14	1	20	2	40
Three	—	—	1	20	—	—
Four	—	—	1	20	1	20
Five or more	—	—	1	20	1	20

TABLE 40—*continued*

Country of origin and number of children	Nevada City, 1870					
	$0		$100–1,000		Over $1,000	
	N	Percent	N	Percent	N	Percent
United States						
None	14	18%	12	20%	23	19%
One	21	27	8	14	28	23
Two	11	14	14	24	20	17
Three	15	19	12	20	17	14
Four	7	9	4	7	15	13
Five or more	10	13	9	15	17	14
Great Britain						
None	10	24	6	23	3	18
One	11	27	1	4	2	12
Two	7	17	5	19	3	18
Three	3	7	3	12	3	18
Four	5	12	6	23	4	24
Five or more	5	12	5	19	2	12
Ireland						
None	11	39	1	4	1	10
One	2	7	7	28	—	—
Two	2	7	1	4	1	10
Three	4	14	4	16	3	30
Four	1	4	4	16	4	40
Five or more	8	29	8	32	1	10
Germany and Scandinavia						
None	3	38	3	20	3	11
One	1	13	2	13	4	14
Two	1	13	2	13	2	7
Three	1	13	1	7	7	25
Four	1	13	2	13	4	14
Five or more	1	13	5	33	8	29
France and Italy						
None	3	38	—	—	2	17
One	—	—	1	50	1	8
Two	1	13	—	—	1	8
Three	3	38	—	—	—	—
Four	—	—	1	50	3	25
Five or more	1	13	—	—	5	42

TABLE 41
Continuity of Residence of Male Workers by Occupation, 1860–1870

Town	Professional or businessman		Artisan or farmer		Miner[a]		Unskilled		Total, percent
	N	Percent	N	Percent	N	Percent	N	Percent	
Grass Valley									
Total in 1860	123	100%	238	100%	511	100%	319	100%	100%
Still there in 1865	58	47	93	39	74	15	43	14	23
Still there in 1867	55	45	86	36	62	12	36	11	20
Still there in 1870	41	33	63	27	29	6	23	7	13
Nevada City[b]									
Total in 1860	126	100	294	100	335	100	249	100	100
Still there in 1867	41	33	79	27	32	10	23	9	17
Still there in 1870	30	24	59	20	16	5	18	7	12

NOTE: Additional data drawn from *Bean's History* and Byrne.
[a] Miner figures are a 20 percent sample.
[b] No data are available for Nevada City in 1865.

TABLE 42
White Children's Occupations, by Father's Occupation, 1870

Child's occupation	Miner	Professional or businessman	Artisan or farmer	Unskilled
Grass Valley				
Professional	—	—	1	—
Merchant	—	1	—	—
Artisan	4	1	5	—
Clerk	—	8	3	1
Apprentice	4	—	6	2
Miner	13	—	10	2
Unskilled	9	3	9	2
Farm laborer	2	—	12	—
Helps parent	—	1	1	1
Seamstress or milliner	—	1	—	—
Percentage of working children	31%	15%	46%	8%
Nevada City				
Professional	2	—	5	—
Merchant	—	—	2	—
Artisan	6	3	8	—
Clerk	1	7	—	—
Apprentice	1	—	2	—
Miner	16	1	1	—
Unskilled	2	—	1	3
Farm laborer	—	—	5	—
Helps parent	—	2	2	—
Percentage of working children	40%	19%	37%	4%

TABLE 43

Women's Occupations, by Husband's Occupation and Country of Origin, 1870

Husband's country of origin and wife's work	Professional or businessman		Artisan or farmer		Miner		Unskilled	
	N	Percent	N	Percent	N	Percent	N	Percent
Grass Valley								
United States								
Keeps house	46	61%	77	58%	37	77%	41	70%
Takes in boarders	27	36	55	41	11	23	18	31
All others	2	3	1	1	—	—	—	—
Great Britain								
Keeps house	26	72	33	59	161	74	5	50
Takes in boarders	9	25	23	41	57	26	4	40
All others	1	3	—	—	—	—	1	10
Ireland								
Keeps house	13	72	31	76	111	82	33	77
Takes in boarders	4	22	9	22	24	18	10	23
All others	1	6	1	2	1	1	—	—
Germany and Scandinavia								
Keeps house	15	65	12	50	9	90	2	100
Takes in boarders	7	30	12	50	1	10	—	—
All others	1	4	—	—	—	—	—	—
France and Italy								
Keeps house	2	67	3	75	2	67	5	83
Takes in boarders	1	33	1	25	1	33	1	17
All others	—	—	—	—	—	—	—	—
Nevada City								
United States								
Keeps house	50	73	70	86	73	87	18	78
Takes in boarders	18	26	10	12	11	13	3	13
All others	1	1	1	1	—	—	2	9
Great Britain								
Keeps house	5	100	11	79	53	86	1	100
Takes in boarders	—	—	3	21	9	15	—	—
All others	—	—	—	—	—	—	—	—
Ireland								
Keeps house	1	100	5	56	41	87	4	67
Takes in boarders	—	—	3	33	6	13	2	33
All others	—	—	1	11	—	—	—	—
Germany and Scandinavia								
Keeps house	9	56	22	76	—	—	6	100
Takes in boarders	7	44	6	21	—	—	—	—
All others	—	—	1	3	—	—	—	—
France and Italy								
Keeps house	2	50	5	83	11	100	—	—
Takes in boarders	1	25	1	17	—	—	—	—
All others	1	25	—	—	—	—	1	100

TABLE 44
Married Men in Western and Frontier Areas, 1850–1880

Place or region	1850	1860	1870	1880
San Francisco	15%[a]	—	—	—
Jacksonville, Illinois	60	—	—	—
Clarence, Iowa	—	82%	—	58%
Crawford Township, Iowa	63	61	62%	—
Roseburg, Oregon	—	46	54	49
North Central Texas	70	—	—	—
Kanab, Utah	—	—	90[b]	—
Trempealeau County, Wisconsin	33	69	66	—
Grass Valley	3	7	31	—
Nevada City	2	13	27	—

SOURCES: P. R. Decker, p. 210; Doyle, p. 156; R. O. Davis, p. 133; Bowers, pp. 12–13; Robbins, "Social and Economic Change," p. 87; Williams, p. 56; May, p. 185; Curti, p. 57.
[a] 1852.   [b] 1874.

TABLE 45
Sex Ratios in Western and Frontier Areas, 1850–1870

Place or region	1850	1860	1870
United States	104	105	102
Mountain and Pacific states	279	—	147
Selected agricultural frontier counties	125[a]	125[a]	—
Arizona Territory	—	—	400
California	—	—	200
Butte County, California	3,329	—	—
San Francisco	650[b]	250	—
California mines	2,300	—	—
Colorado Territory	—	3,400	—
Montana and Idaho Territories	—	—	800
Nebraska frontier	—	150	—
Nevada	—	—	500
Virginia City, Nevada	—	—	203
Oregon	—	—	200
North Central Texas	320	—	—
Trempealeau County, Wisconsin	120	—	—
Wyoming Territory	—	—	600
Grass Valley	1,716	712	180
Nevada City	4,447	373	208

SOURCES: D. Bogue, p. 164; Eblen, pp. 411–12; Jensen and Miller, p. 189; Larson, pp. 3, 5; Ricards, p. 474; P. R. Decker, p. 211; Wishart, p. 109; Blackburn and Ricards, "Virginia City," p. 246; "Nueces County," p. 9; "Manistee County," p. 603; Williams, p. 54.
NOTE: Sex ratios are the number of men per 100 women.
[a] Figures are for 1840 to 1860.
[b] 1852.

TABLE 46

Continuity of Residence in Frontier Areas, 1850–1880

Place or region	1850	1855	1860	1865	1870	1875	1880
San Francisco	100%[a]	—	25%	—	—	—	—
Jacksonville, Illinois	100	—	25	—	—	—	—
			100	—	21%	—	—
Wapello County, Iowa	100	—	30	—	—	—	—
Central Kansas	—	—	100	58%	42	—	—
			100		43	—	—
Eastern Kansas	—	—	100	36	26	—	—
			100		43	36%	—
					100	52	41%
East Central Kansas	—	—	100	35	31	—	—
			100		67	64	—
					100	66	59
Holland, Michigan	100	—	61	—	—	—	—
			100	—	61	—	—
					100	—	55
Roseburg, Oregon	—	—	—	—	100	—	34
Trempealeau County, Wisconsin	—	—	100	—	25	—	—
					100	—	29
Grass Valley	100	5%[b]	4	—	—	—	—
			100	23	13	—	—
Nevada City	100	7[b]	6	—	—	—	—
			100	17[c]	12	—	—

SOURCES: P. R. Decker, pp. 74–75; Doyle, p. 95; Throne, p. 310; Malin, "Turnover," pp. 365–69; Kirk, p. 51; Robbins, "Opportunity and Persistence," pp. 286–88; Curti, p. 67.

NOTE: Where two or more figures are given for the same town in the same year, two or more separate populations were used to calculate persistence.

[a] 1852.   [b] 1856.   [c] 1867.

Notes

Complete authors' names, titles, and publication data are given in the References Cited, pp. 287–95. I use the abbreviation CHS for the California Historical Society, San Francisco, and CSL for the California State Library, Sacramento.

The titles of these newspapers vary from year to year, and I use the following standard forms.

California Mining Journal (Grass Valley), 1856–58
Democrat (Nevada City), 1853–63
Gazette (Nevada City), 1864–67
Journal (Nevada City), 1851–61
National (Grass Valley), 1861–70
National Gazette (Nevada City), 1870
Telegraph (Grass Valley), 1853–58
Transcript (Nevada City), 1861–70
Union (Grass Valley), 1864–70
Young America (Nevada City), 1853

Introduction

1. The classic statement of the theme of continuity is Pomeroy, "Toward a Reorientation of Western History." For the unique quality of Grass Valley, see Paul, *California Gold*, p. 324.

2. For popular images of women, children, and home, see Welter, pp. 4, 21, 31, and *passim*; Wishy, esp. Chapter 3; Tyack, pp. 72–75; K. Jeffrey, p. 22. On churches, see Hanchett, esp. p. 158; on schools, see Tyack, *passim*.

3. For nineteenth-century stereotypes, see Fredrickson, esp. Chapter 5; Berkhofer, esp. Part 3; Gibson, pp. 4–22. On defensiveness, cf. Welter, pp. 26, 91–92; Lotchin, pp. 304–5; 310–11; Wright, pp. 128–31; Starr, pp. 69–73, 85–86; Doyle, *Jacksonville*, pp. 25, 29, 120; Wallace, p. 65.

4. Cf. Griffen and Griffen, p. 236; Yans-McLaughlin, p. 206.

5. On moral reform in Gold Rush California, see Margo, *passim;* Ostrander, pp. 1–22; Hanchett, *passim.* On politics and the Chinese, see Saxton, pp. 80–81, 99–103.

Chapter 1

1. Bean, p. 185; Brown and Dallison, pp. 35–37; Morse, p. 224; Wells, p. 64; Delano, *Pen Knife Sketches,* p. 95.

2. Bean, pp. 11–13, 74–76; Brown and Dallison, p. 19; Sheldon, pp. 61–62; Wilson, pp. 24–25.

3. Brown and Dallison, p. 19; Bean, pp. 76–78; Ferguson, p. 148.

4. Brown and Dallison, pp. 21–22; Bean, pp. 65, 77, 79; Fairchild, p. 27; Ferguson, p. 159; Steele, pp. 23–25. On coyoteing, see Kelley, p. 25.

5. Sawyer, pp. 118–20; Bean, pp. 65, 69, 80; Brown and Dallison, pp. 11–13; Ferguson, p. 173; Hill, p. 57; Litton, Nov. 30, 1850; Peter Decker, pp. 246, 256; Wells, p. 80.

6. Bean, pp. 48, 184; Wells, p. 64; Morse, p. 222; Elder, Jan. 8, 1851; *Delano's California Correspondence,* pp. 112–13; Schaeffer, pp. 120–24; Brown and Dallison, pp. 22, 38.

7. U.S. Census Bureau, *Population Schedules,* 1850, pp. 547–610, 619–30; Wells, p. 80; Ferguson, p. 148.

8. Morse, p. 336; Borthwick, p. 182; Payne, Apr. 27, 1851; McKeeby, pp. 129, 131; *Journal,* Nov. 27, 1851, p. 2.

9. Delano, *Pen Knife Sketches,* pp. 52, 72; Borthwick, p. 182; Morse, pp. 224–25; Sawyer, pp. 118, 121; Wilson, p. 36.

10. Morse, pp. 222, 340; Hill, pp. 58, 61–63; Elder, Jan. 8, 1851; Ferguson, pp. 134, 141, 155–56; Crandall, p. 97; *Journal,* Dec. 25, 1851, p. 1, Sept. 13, 1851, p. 1; Wells, p. 107.

11. Peter Decker, p. 236; Bean, pp. 33, 75; Delano, *Pen Knife Sketches,* pp. 100–105; Wells, p. 121; Stewart, pp. 88, 90; *Young America,* Sept. 28, 1853, p. 2. Cf. Lotchin, pp. 126–29.

12. Low, pp. 160–65, 177; Schaeffer, pp. 190, 210; Ferguson, pp. 160, 182; Gill, pp. 22–24; Fletcher, pp. 32, 34–36, 56, 80; Borthwick, p. 186.

13. Scamehorn, pp. 157, 160–61; Schaeffer, p. 143; Stewart, p. 72; Morse, pp. 225, 232; Crandall, p. 132; Hill, p. 50; Delano, *Pen Knife Sketches,* p. 23.

14. *Journal,* Apr. 22, 1852, p. 2; Fletcher, pp. 61, 72; Stewart, pp. 74–76, 88; Peter Decker, pp. 238–42.

15. Mann, "National Party Fortunes," pp. 273–74; Stewart, pp. 90–93; Wells, p. 121; Bean, p. 33.

16. *Journal,* Apr. 19, 1851, p. 3, Nov. 1, 1851, p. 1; Wells, p. 81; Bean, pp. 83–84; Crandall, p. 89.

17. Bean, p. 83; *Delano's California Correspondence,* pp. 112–13, 115, 122–23; Delano, *Pen Knife Sketches,* pp. 95–96; Winchester Papers, May 1, 1851, CHS; Brown and Dallison, p. 37.

18. Bean, p. 187. For examples of the fortunes of quartz operations, see *Journal,* Jan. 7, 1852, p. 2, Feb. 26, 1852, p. 2, Feb. 5, 1852, p. 3.

19. Wells, pp. 83–84; Bean, pp. 82–84; Hill, pp. 68, 79; Wilson, p. 35; *Journal*, Sept. 13, 1851, p. 1, Oct. 23, 1851, p. 2, Dec. 20, 1851, p. 2.

20. Bean, p. 83; Browne, p. 128; Wells, pp. 100, 108; Scamehorn, pp. 158–59; *Journal*, Oct. 30, 1851, p. 2, Jan. 29, 1852, p. 2, Mar. 6, 1852, p. 2, Jan. 22, 1852, p. 2.

21. Bean, pp. 49, 190; Browne, p. 128; Schaeffer, p. 156; Scamehorn, pp. 155, 157, 160; Morse, pp. 229–30; Borthwick, pp. 259–60; Dornin, p. 56; *Journal*, Feb. 18, 1853, p. 2; Delano, *Pen Knife Sketches*, pp. 40–41.

22. Brown and Dallison, p. 33; Wells, p. 82; Bean, pp. 14, 86; *Journal*, Jan. 27, 1853, p. 2; *Young America*, Nov. 9, 1853, p. 2, Nov. 30, 1853, p. 2; *Telegraph*, Sept. 29, 1853, p. 2.

23. *Journal*, Feb. 19, 1853, p. 1, Apr. 29, 1853, p. 2, June 24, 1853, p. 2; *Telegraph*, Sept. 22, 1853, p. 2; Winchester Papers, Mar. 3, 1853, Sept. 28, 1853, Feb. 11, 1853, Jan. 25, 1853, Oct. 15, 1853, CHS.

24. Bean, pp. 61–68, 79, 84; Stewart, p. 98; Scamehorn, pp. 156–57; Stafford, p. 80; Browne, p. 119; Crandall, pp. 98, 127; *Journal*, Nov. 23, 1855, p. 2, Mar. 13, 1853, p. 2, July 1, 1853, p. 2, Feb. 4, 1853, p. 2, Apr. 10, 1856, p. 2. For an account of the roles played by the two towns in mining innovation, see Paul, *California Gold*, pp. 64–65, 151–53, 156–57.

25. Crandall, pp. 120–21, 133; Morse, p. 332; Hill, p. 81; Fletcher, pp. 30, 51, 56–57; Borthwick, p. 183; Winchester Papers, Feb. 25, 1854, Nov. 19, 1853, CSL; Winchester Papers, July 14, 1852, CHS.

26. See the *Journal* and the *Democrat* for discussions of departures during 1854 and 1855. Crandall, Introduction; Stafford, p. 78.

27. *Democrat*, Feb. 22, 1854, p. 2, Mar. 15, 1854, p. 2, Aug. 20, 1856, p. 1; *Telegraph*, Mar. 9, 1854, p. 2, Oct. 31, 1854, p. 2, Oct. 9, 1855, p. 2; *Journal*, Sept. 21, 1855, p. 2, Nov. 3, 1854, p. 2, Jan. 26, 1856, p. 2, June 22, 1855, p. 1, Aug. 8, 1856, p. 1, Aug. 9, 1856, p. 2; *California Mining Journal*, Aug. 1, 1856, p. 33; Stafford, p. 89; Dornin, p. 58; Wells, pp. 66, 82, 85, 98.

28. *Journal*, Apr. 21, 1854, p. 2, Apr. 18, 1856, p. 2, Mar. 16, 1855, p. 2; *Telegraph*, Apr. 13, 1854, p. 2, May 18, 1854, p. 2; Wells, pp. 65, 82.

29. Mann, "National Party Fortunes," p. 274; Stewart, p. 86; *Journal*, May 9, 1856, p. 2, June 30, 1854, p. 2; *Democrat*, Aug. 23, 1854, p. 2, May 7, 1856, p. 2.

30. Morse, p. 336. For examples of editorials on the theme of permanency, see *Telegraph*, Oct. 31, 1854, p. 1; *Democrat*, Nov. 26, 1856, p. 2; *Journal*, Oct. 9, 1851, p. 2, Dec. 17, 1852, p. 2; cf. Lotchin, pp. 100–101.

Chapter 2

1. Peter Decker, p. 235; Ferguson, pp. 9–11; Low, p. 174; Morse, pp. 226–27; Sheldon, p. 65; Bean, pp. 77, 81; Brown and Dallison, pp. 23–25, 30; Wilson, p. 29; *Journal*, Dec. 11, 1851, p. 2, Oct. 23, 1851, p. 2; Hill, pp. 68–69; Winchester Papers, Aug. 14, 1853, CSL. On reasons for coming to California, see Holliday, p. 31.

2. McKeeby, pp. 131–33; Wells, pp. 150–52; Peter Decker, pp. 234,

236; Low, p. 171; Wilson, p. 30; *Journal*, Dec. 20, 1851, p. 2, Mar. 14, 1852, p. 3, Dec. 24, 1852, pp. 1–2; Steele, p. 100.

3. *Journal*, Apr. 15, 1853, p. 2, Jan. 20, 1853, p. 2, Mar. 10, 1854, p. 2, Sept. 2, 1853, p. 2; *Democrat*, June 7, 1854, p. 2; Wells, p. 150.

4. Schaeffer, pp. 70–71, 127, 142; Wilson, p. 31; *Telegraph*, Oct. 23, 1853, p. 2, Apr. 27, 1854, p. 1, May 18, 1854, p. 2, Feb. 23, 1854, p. 2, Nov. 23, 1853, p. 2; Delano, *Pen Knife Sketches*, pp. 32–34, 37–39; *Journal*, Nov. 1, 1852, p. 2, Oct. 2, 1851, p. 2. On the two views of society, see Royce, pp. 272–73.

5. *Journal*, Apr. 19, 1851, p. 2, Oct. 9, 1851, p. 2, Apr. 8, 1853, p. 2; *California Mining Journal*, May 1, 1856, p. 10. The values and social place of Ewer, Sargent, and Delano exactly parallel those of the Eastern urban reformers described by Boyer; likewise, their moral writings follow the format and examples of the tract literature of the reform societies. See Boyer, pp. 2, 5–6, 29–31.

6. *Telegraph*, Oct. 9, 1855, p. 2, Apr. 6, 1854, p. 2, Oct. 31, 1854, p. 1; *Journal*, Nov. 22, 1851, p. 2.

7. *Journal*, Oct. 2, 1851, p. 2, Sept. 13, 1851, p. 1; Delano, *Pen Knife Sketches*, pp. 69–71; Brown and Dallison, p. 19. Cf. Bender, *Toward*, pp. 110–11.

8. *Journal*, Apr. 19, 1851, p. 1; Delano, *Pen Knife Sketches*, pp. 14–15, 28, 35; Stafford, pp. 81–82; Schaeffer, pp. 140, 183.

9. *Journal*, Oct. 9, 1851, p. 2, Apr. 19, 1851, p. 2, Oct. 16, 1851, p. 2; *Young America*, Dec. 14, 1853, p. 2; *Telegraph*, Nov. 24, 1853, p. 3, Feb. 16, 1854, p. 2, Mar. 2, 1854, p. 2; Ferguson, pp. 153–54; Stafford, p. 77; Schaeffer, pp. 77–78.

10. *Telegraph*, Oct. 15, 1853, p. 2; *Journal*, Nov. 1, 1851, p. 2, Dec. 6, 1851, p. 2; Foley and Morley, p. 52; Crandall, pp. 129–30; Delano, *Pen Knife Sketches*, pp. 34, 37; Delano, *Woman*, pp. 18–19, 21.

11. Bean, p. 74; Ferguson, pp. 148–49; Wilson, pp. 27–28, 31; *Journal*, Apr. 22, 1852, p. 4; Crandall, p. 86.

12. Women in households figures drawn from U.S. Census Bureau, *Population Schedules*, 1850, pp. 547–610, 619–30.

13. Ferguson, pp. 177, 150–151; Wilson, pp. 32–34; Stewart, pp. 64–66; Elder, Mar. 20, 1851, Apr. 6, 1851; Delano, *Pen Knife Sketches*, p. 4; *Delano's California Correspondence*, p. 133. Cf. Lotchin, pp. 255–57.

14. *Journal*, Dec. 21, 1855, p. 2, Apr. 11, 1852, p. 2, Feb. 25, 1853, p. 2, Nov. 29, 1851, p. 2; *Telegraph*, Oct. 6, 1853, p. 2, Mar. 2, 1854, p. 3; Schaeffer, p. 195.

15. Brown and Dallison, pp. 22–23; Bean, pp. 80, 105; Crandall, p. 109; Stewart, p. 95; Fletcher, pp. 62–63; *Journal*, Sept. 20, 1851, p. 2, June 25, 1858, p. 1; Low, p. 163; *Telegraph*, Nov. 27, 1855, p. 2, Mar. 2, 1854, p. 5; Hanchett, p. 92.

16. Bean, p. 187; Wells, pp. 65, 123; *Journal*, Apr. 15, 1852, p. 2, Oct. 13, 1854, p. 2, Apr. 29, 1853, p. 2.

17. *Journal*, Aug. 26, 1853, p. 1, Nov. 9, 1855, p. 2.

18. *Journal*, Sept. 18, 1851, p. 1; Sawyer, p. 124; Peter Decker, p. 254.

19. Morse, p. 226; *Journal,* Nov. 15, 1851, p. 2, Oct. 23, 1851, p. 2, Nov. 20, 1851, p. 2, Feb. 25, 1853, p. 2; *Democrat,* Feb. 21, 1855, p. 2, Mar. 28, 1855, p. 2. Cf. Pitt, pp. 53–55, 69–71.

20. Levinson, pp. 45–46, 66; *Journal,* Sept. 1, 1854, p. 2, June 17, 1853, p. 2, Mar. 28, 1856, p. 2; Dornin, pp. 55, 57; Morse, p. 226; Peter Decker, p. 254.

21. Peter Decker, pp. 252–54; Elder, Mar. 20, 1851; Brown and Dallison, pp. 35–37; Wells, p. 53; Lopes, pp. 62–64; Morse, p. 234; Schaeffer, pp. 118–19; *Journal,* Mar. 3, 1854, p. 2, Nov. 27, 1851, p. 2; *Telegraph,* May 25, 1854, p. 2, Feb. 14, 1854, p. 2, Oct. 30, 1855, p. 2; *Democrat,* Oct. 31, 1855, p. 2, Oct. 24, 1855, p. 2; *Young America,* Dec. 23, 1853, p. 2.

22. Black occupations and living arrangements are taken from the U.S. Census Bureau, *Population Schedules,* 1850. Morse, p. 223; Kinyon, pp. 60–62; *Journal,* Nov. 13, 1851, p. 2, Mar. 13, 1852, p. 2, Apr. 21, 1854, p. 2, Apr. 6, 1855, p. 2, Dec. 4, 1855, p. 2; Lapp, pp. 75, 179, 91, 64–65; *Telegraph,* Dec. 4, 1855, p. 2.

23. Sawyer, pp. 124–25; *Journal,* Dec. 9, 1853, p. 2, Feb. 25, 1853, p. 2, Oct. 9, 1851, p. 2, May 8, 1852, p. 1, June 30, 1854, p. 1, Mar. 24, 1854, p. 2; *Democrat,* Mar. 22, 1854, p. 2; *Telegraph,* May 4, 1854, p. 2.

24. Winchester Papers, Nov. 19, 1853, CHS; Tinloy, pp. 1–4; Lyman, pp. 41–45, 72A, 97, 277–80; *National,* Nov. 5, 1861, p. 3; *Journal,* Dec. 16, 1853, p. 2. Cf. Siu, pp. 34–36, 42.

25. Wells, p. 65; Scamehorn, p. 161; *Journal,* Nov. 20, 1851, p. 2, May 1, 1852, p. 2, June 12, 1852, p. 2, May 8, 1852, p. 2, Feb. 18, 1853, p. 1; cf. Pitt, p. 61.

26. *Journal,* Aug. 28, 1852, p. 2, Dec. 3, 1852, p. 2, June 30, 1854, p. 2, July 14, 1854, p. 2, Feb. 11, 1853, p. 2, Dec. 14, 1855, p. 2, Sept. 14, 1855, p. 2; *Democrat,* July 5, 1854, p. 3, July 12, 1854, p. 2; *Telegraph,* Dec. 22, 1852, p. 2, Oct. 31, 1854, p. 2; Wells, p. 162; Ostrander, pp. 8, 14–19, 20–21.

27. *Journal,* Oct. 2, 1851, p. 2, Jan. 21, 1853, p. 4, July 22, 1853, p. 1, July 6, 1855, p. 2; *Telegraph,* Oct. 27, 1853, p. 2, Dec. 4, 1855, p. 2; *Democrat,* Oct. 24, 1855, p. 2.

28. *Journal,* Sept. 23, 1853, p. 2, Dec. 12, 1856, p. 2, Mar. 10, 1854, p. 2; *Democrat,* Mar. 22, 1854, p. 3; Margo, pp. 226–27.

29. *Journal,* Sept. 2, 1853, p. 2, Nov. 9, 1855, p. 2; *Democrat,* Mar. 1, 1854, p. 2, Oct. 31, 1855, p. 2. Cf. Lotchin, p. 12; Goldman, p. 38.

30. *Telegraph,* Sept. 4, 1855, p. 2; *Journal,* Aug. 4, 1854, p. 2, Apr. 6, 1855, p. 1, Oct. 3, 1856, p. 2. Cf. Lotchin, pp. 255–66; Hurt, pp. 18, 28.

31. *Journal,* May 23, 1856, p. 2, June 15, 1855, p. 2, Feb. 8, 1856, p. 2; *Democrat,* Feb. 21, 1855, p. 2, Sept. 19, 1855, p. 2. On anti-Semitism, see "Anti-Jewish Sentiment in California," pp. 15, 19, 21. On the Whigs and reform, cf. Johnson, pp. 129–30, 132–33; Feldburg, pp. 11–15.

32. *Journal,* Feb. 22, 1856, p. 2, Dec. 16, 1853, p. 2, Feb. 8, 1856, p. 1, Mar. 22, 1854, p. 2, Oct. 27, 1854, p. 2, Aug. 8, 1856, p. 2, Apr. 28, 1854, p. 2; *Telegraph,* Aug. 3, 1854, p. 2, Jan. 19, 1854, p. 2.

33. *Journal*, Aug. 25, 1854, p. 2, Oct. 20, 1854, p. 2, Mar. 9, 1855, p. 1, Mar. 23, 1855, p. 2; *Democrat*, Aug. 23, 1854, p. 2.

34. Coolidge, p. 59; Sandmeyer, pp. 41–43; *Journal*, Nov. 23, 1855, p. 2, Feb. 9, 1855, p. 2, Oct. 26, 1855, p. 2; *Democrat*, Feb. 21, 1855, p. 2, Oct. 17, 1855, p. 2. Cf. Feldburg, pp. 91, 98.

35. *Journal*, May 19, 1854, p. 2, Nov. 17, 1854, p. 2, Aug. 4, 1854, p. 2, Feb. 3, 1854, p. 2, Dec. 16, 1853, p. 2, June 24, 1853, p. 2, Mar. 10, 1854, p. 2, July 6, 1855, p. 2, Dec. 12, 1856, p. 2, Nov. 9, 1855, p. 2, Oct. 20, 1854, p. 2, Feb. 22, 1856, p. 2, July 6, 1855, p. 2; *Democrat*, Oct. 4, 1854, p. 2, June 7, 1854, p. 2; *Telegraph*, Oct. 31, 1854, p. 2, June 22, 1854, p. 2, Dec. 4, 1855, p. 2, Sept. 4, 1855, p. 2; Brown and Dallison, p. 23. Cf. Hanchett, pp. 23–24; Lotchin, p. 206.

36. The beginnings of middle-class concentrations can be shown by correlating occupations and street addresses in Brown and Dallison. Crandall, p. 200; *Young America*, Sept. 28, 1853, p. 2; *Journal*, July 28, 1854, p. 2, Apr. 28, 1854, p. 2; Stafford, p. 80.

37. Morse, p. 337; Searls, pp. 83–84; *Telegraph*, Aug. 24, 1854, p. 2, Mar. 2, 1854, p. 3, Nov. 6, 1855, p. 2, May 13, 1856, p. 2, July 4, 1854, p. 2; *Journal*, Jan. 28, 1853, p. 1, Jan. 6, 1854, p. 2, Apr. 8, 1853, p. 2, May 13, 1853, p. 2, Dec. 19, 1856, p. 3; Bean, pp. 99–104, 195–97; Rolfe, pp. 2–3; *Democrat*, Jan. 30, 1856, p. 2, June 14, 1854, p. 2; Winchester Papers, Dec. 25, 1853, CHS.

38. *Journal*, July 6, 1855, p. 2; *Democrat*, July 11, 1855, p. 2.

Chapter 3

1. *Journal*, June 5, 1857, p. 2, Jan. 2, 1857, p. 2, Aug. 14, 1857, p. 3, Feb. 27, 1857, p. 2, Jan. 23, 1857, p. 2, Feb. 18, 1857, p. 2, Feb. 20, 1857, p. 2, May 17, 1857, p. 2; Wells, pp. 82–83.

2. Bean, pp. 49–50, 207; *Democrat*, Apr. 1, 1857, p. 2; Morse, p. 335; Byrne, pp. 71, 80, 82.

3. *Democrat*, June 30, 1858, p. 3, May 9, 1863, pp. 2–3; *Telegraph*, June 12, 1858, p. 2; *Journal*, Oct. 28, 1859, p. 3, Mar. 11, 1861, p. 2; Coad, Jan. 16, 1858, May 9, 1859, Dec. 6, 1860, Apr. n.d., 1860; Bean, pp. 14, 50; Morse, p. 341.

4. *Journal*, Apr. 6, 1860, p. 2, Mar. 16, 1860, p. 3; *Democrat*, Mar. 14, 1860, p. 2; Hittell, *Resources*, p. 295; Byrne, pp. 82–83.

5. Bean, pp. 50, 91; *National*, Sept. 12, 1861, p. 2; *Democrat*, Jan. 11, 1862, p. 3, Jan. 23, 1862, p. 3; *Transcript*, Feb. 15, 1862, p. 3, Jan. 30, 1863, p. 3, Feb. 6, 1863, p. 3, June 4, 1863, p. 3, Oct. 9, 1863, p. 3; Wells, p. 83.

6. Wells, p. 117; *Journal*, Apr. 5, 1861, p. 3; *Democrat*, Mar. 10, 1858, p. 3, Feb. 8, 1860, p. 3, Feb. 15, 1860, p. 3, Jan. 25, 1860, p. 2, Feb. 4, 1862, p. 3, Jan. 30, 1862, p. 3; Bean, pp. 135, 197; *National*, Aug. 27, 1863, p. 3; *Transcript*, May 11, 1862, p. 3, Feb. 20, 1863, p. 3; Byrne, pp. 14–15.

7. *Democrat*, Feb. 11, 1857, p. 2, Oct. 31, 1861, p. 3, July 2, 1861, p. 2; *Journal*, Jan. 8, 1858, p. 2, Feb. 27, 1857, p. 2; *Transcript*, Mar. 31, 1865, p. 3; Wells, pp. 65–66. Cf. Dykstra, *Cattle Towns*, pp. 116, 131–32.

8. *National,* Dec. 21, 1861, p. 3; *Democrat,* May 15, 1862, p. 3, Jan. 8, 1861, p. 3; *Transcript,* Apr. 30, 1864, p. 3; *Gazette,* May 4, 1866, p. 3.

9. Wells, p. 164; *Journal,* May 18, 1860, p. 2; *Democrat,* Feb. 17, 1858, p. 2.

10. Bean, pp. 92–95, 189, 196; Wells, pp. 66–67, 85–86; *Journal,* Jan. 30, 1857, p. 2, Sept. 18, 1857, p. 2, May 1, 1857, p. 2, Aug. 28, 1857, p. 2, May 28, 1858, p. 2, July 8, 1858, pp. 1–2, June 1, 1860, pp. 1–2, Nov. 23, 1860, p. 3; *Democrat,* June 13, 1860, p. 3, July 7, 1858, p. 3, July 25, 1860, p. 2, May 30, 1860, p. 2, May 26, 1858, p. 2, Aug. 16, 1862, p. 2; *National,* Aug. 16, 1862, p. 2; English, Nov. 8, 1863, Nov. 13, 1863; McConahy, p. 66; *Transcript,* Nov. 10, 1863, p. 3, Nov. 28, 1863, p. 3.

11. *Journal,* Oct. 21, 1859, p. 2, Oct. 5, 1860, p. 2, Jan. 6, 1860, p. 2, Feb. 5, 1858, p. 2, Dec. 9, 1859, p. 2, Oct. 19, 1860, p. 2, Oct. 14, 1859, p. 2; *Transcript,* Oct. 6, 1860, p. 2, Apr. 22, 1862, p. 3, May 26, 1863, p. 3, Mar. 14, 1863, p. 3; Wells, pp. 132, 165, 167, 170; Hittell, *Resources,* p. 406.

12. *National,* May 26, 1860, p. 2, Oct. 13, 1863, p. 3; Hittell, *Resources,* p. 295; Wells, p. 198; Browne, p. 8; Brewer, pp. 453–54; Byrne, pp. 70, 72, 80, 82; Bean, pp. 127–28. I have depended on Paul, *California Gold,* for information on the chlorination process, pp. 142–43, 292–93.

13. *Journal,* Feb. 13, 1857, p. 2, Mar. 20, 1857, p. 2; Hittell, *Mining,* pp. 80, 119; Wells, p. 198; *National,* Nov. 19, 1861, p. 1; Bean, pp. 50, 108, 114, 117; Byrne, pp. 71, 80, 82.

14. *Democrat,* Mar. 25, 1857, p. 2; *Journal,* Mar. 20, 1857, p. 2; Coad, Jan. 16, 1858, May 2, 1859; Abbott, p. 150.

15. Advertisements in the *Journal,* Jan. 1860.

16. *California Mining Journal,* Feb. 1, 1857, p. 58; *National,* Oct. 8, 1863, p. 3. Cf. Wyman, pp. 35–36, 63, 68.

17. Soltow, pp. 17, 22–23, 33; Gitelman, pp. 80, 84–85, 12.

18. *National,* Nov. 19, 1861, p. 1, Nov. 5, 1861, p. 2; Coad, Jan. 16, 1858, Dec. 6, 1860; Rowse, pp. 21, 179; Rowe, pp. 113, 115.

19. *Telegraph,* June 12, 1858, p. 2; *California Mining Journal,* June 1, 1858, p. 90; *Journal,* June 18, 1858, p. 2.

20. Mann, "National Party Fortunes," pp. 275–76; *Journal,* Aug. 13, 1858, p. 2, Nov. 9, 1860, p. 2, Sept. 6, 1861, p. 2; *Democrat,* Sept. 4, 1862, p. 3; *Transcript,* Aug. 29, 1863, p. 3, Sept. 4, 1863, p. 2.

21. *Transcript,* May 5, 1863, p. 3, Nov. 9, 1864, p. 2; *Gazette,* July 9, 1864, p. 3, Oct. 14, 1864, p. 3, Nov. 7, 1864, p. 2, Dec. 1, 1864, p. 2.

22. *Transcript,* Nov. 10, 1864, p. 3; *Gazette,* Nov. 10, 1864, p. 2, Jan. 14, 1865, p. 2, Jan. 17, 1865, p. 3, Jan. 19, 1865, pp. 2–3, Jan. 21, 1865, p. 3; *National,* Jan. 19, 1865, p. 3, Jan. 20, 1865, pp. 2–3.

Chapter 4

1. Brown and Dallison and Thompson list residents by streets; I have correlated them with occupations taken from the manuscript census of 1860. *Journal,* Oct. 12, 1860, p. 3, May 4, 1864, p. 3, Feb. 15, 1861, p. 2; Putnam, pp. 197, 231; *Democrat,* Aug. 20, 1861, p. 3, May 13, 1862, p. 3, Feb. 15, 1860, p. 3, Apr. 15, 1857, p. 3; *Transcript,* Jan. 22, 1863, p. 3,

Sept. 6, 1860, p. 3; *National,* Sept. 19, 1861, p. 3, Aug. 10, 1861, p. 3. Cf. Blumin, pp. 105–110.

2. *Transcript,* Feb. 7, 1862, p. 3, May 4, 1862, p. 3; *Journal,* Oct. 28, 1859, p. 2, Feb. 25, 1859, p. 2, Nov. 23, 1860, p. 2; *National,* Jan. 15, 1859, p. 2.

3. *Democrat,* July 21, 1858, p. 3; *Journal,* Mar. 4, 1859, p. 3, Apr. 10, 1857, p. 2; Brewer, p. 454; Byrne, p. 90.

4. *Democrat,* Oct. 24, 1860, p. 3, Feb. 3, 1863, p. 3, Nov. 8, 1862, p. 3, May 4, 1861, p. 3; *Transcript,* Jan. 21, 1863, p. 3, Jan. 24, 1863, p. 3, Jan. 11, 1862, p. 3; *Journal,* Oct. 21, 1859, p. 3, Dec. 4, 1858, p. 2, Dec. 30, 1859, p. 3. Cf. Bode, pp. 19–26, 177–82.

5. *Democrat,* Aug. 21, 1862, p. 3; *Journal,* Jan. 9, 1857, p. 2, Feb. 20, 1857, p. 2.

6. Putnam, pp. 239–41; English, Nov. 1–5, 1863; *Democrat,* Jan. 5, 1859, p. 2; *Transcript,* Oct. 2, 1863, p. 3; *Union,* Oct. 20, 1870, p. 3.

7. *Journal,* Nov. 20, 1857, p. 2, Oct. 30, 1857, p. 2; *Democrat,* Nov. 5, 1861, p. 3, Mar. 17, 1858, p. 3, Oct. 27, 1858, p. 3; *National,* Jan. 4, 1862, p. 3; *Transcript,* Nov. 24, 1863, p. 3, Mar. 7, 1863, p. 3.

8. *Transcript,* Sept. 15, 1860, p. 3; *National,* Jan. 8, 1859, p. 2, Apr. 7, 1860, p. 2, Jan. 18, 1862, p. 3; *Journal,* July 15, 1859, p. 3; *Democrat,* Aug. 21, 1862, p. 3, Jan. 4, 1862, p. 3.

9. *Journal,* Jan. 8, 1858, p. 2; *National,* Dec. 22, 1863, p. 3; *Transcript,* May 2, 1863, p. 3, Dec. 23, 1862, p. 3, Dec. 23, 1863, p. 2, Apr. 1, 1862, p. 3; *Democrat,* May 29, 1862, p. 3, May 24, 1862, p. 3, May 6, 1857, p. 2, Apr. 25, 1863, p. 3, May 2, 1863, p. 3.

10. *Democrat,* Feb. 18, 1857, p. 2, Feb. 25, 1857, p. 2, June 10, 1862, p. 3, Oct. 6, 1858, p. 3; Putnam, pp. 193, 209–10.

11. *Journal,* June 11, 1858, p. 2, Feb. 19, 1858, p. 3, Oct. 4, 1861, p. 3, Feb. 10, 1860, p. 2; *National,* Aug. 10, 1861, p. 2, Aug. 13, 1861, p. 3, Oct. 29, 1861, p. 3, Dec. 5, 1861, p. 3; *Democrat,* Oct. 8, 1861, p. 3, Apr. 29, 1857, p. 2.

12. *Democrat,* Apr. 26, 1862, p. 3, Apr. 13, 1859, p. 3; *Journal,* Feb. 25, 1859, p. 2, Sept. 28, 1860, p. 3, June 29, 1860, p. 3, June 17, 1859, p. 2, Aug. 3, 1860, p. 3; *National,* Feb. 8, 1862, p. 3; *Transcript,* Oct. 6, 1860, p. 2, May 11, 1862, p. 3; Wells, p. 83.

13. *Journal,* Jan. 2, 1857, p. 2, May 1, 1857, p. 2, Oct. 9, 1857, p. 2; *Democrat,* Sept. 29, 1858, p. 3, May 6, 1857, p. 3, Oct. 6, 1858, p. 2, Mar. 16, 1859, p. 3, Aug. 17, 1859, p. 3; *Transcript,* Feb. 15, 1863, p. 3; McConahy, p. 50.

14. *Democrat,* Oct. 4, 1862, p. 3, Sept. 8, 1858, p. 3.

15. *Democrat,* July 10, 1862, p. 3, July 24, 1862, p. 3; *Transcript,* July 8, 1862, p. 3, July 9, 1862, p. 3, July 25, 1862, p. 3; *National,* Oct. 3, 1861, p. 3.

16. *Journal,* Apr. 3, 1857, p. 2; *National,* Nov. 21, 1863, p. 3; *Transcript,* Sept. 15, 1860, p. 3.

17. Putnam, p. 231; Rowe, pp. 151, 165n. Cf. Modell and Hareven, pp. 165–67; and Griffen and Griffen, p. 251.

18. Morse, p. 337; Caswell household as shown in U.S. Census Bureau, *Population Schedules*, 1860.

19. *Democrat*, Jan. 27, 1858, p. 2, Aug. 11, 1858, p. 3, May 27, 1862, p. 3, May 24, 1862, p. 3; *Gazette*, Sept. 14, 1867, p. 3; *National Gazette*, Sept. 14, 1870, p. 3.

20. *Journal*, Feb. 22, 1861, p. 3, Feb. 3, 1860, p. 2.

21. *Journal*, Aug. 19, 1860, p. 2, Feb. 11, 1859, p. 2, Jan. 18, 1861, p. 3, Sept. 7, 1860, p. 3; *National*, Aug. 30, 1860, p. 3; *Democrat*, Feb. 7, 1861, p. 3; *Union*, Jan. 27, 1865, p. 3.

22. *Journal*, Apr. 26, 1861, p. 3, Aug. 24, 1860, p. 3, Jan. 4, 1861, p. 3, Oct. 14, 1859, p. 3; *Democrat*, Jan. 18, 1860, p. 3, Jan. 10, 1863, p. 3; *Transcript*, Oct. 30, 1860, p. 3, Jan. 23, 1862, p. 3, May 20, 1862, p. 3, Feb. 11, 1863, p. 3; Searls, pp. 89–90.

23. *Journal*, Aug. 24, 1860, p. 3; *Democrat*, Aug. 22, 1860, p. 3; *Transcript*, Dec. 28, 1860, p. 3.

24. Putnam, pp. 242–45; *Journal*, Oct. 4, 1861, p. 3; *Transcript*, Feb. 18, 1863, p. 3, Feb. 6, 1862, p. 2; *Union*, Jan. 4, 1865, p. 3.

25. *Democrat*, Jan. 19, 1859, p. 2, Nov. 3, 1858, p. 3, May 18, 1859, p. 3, Aug. 8, 1860, p. 3; *Journal*, Nov. 5, 1858, p. 2, May 4, 1860, p. 3, Nov. 4, 1863, p. 3, Oct. 18, 1861, p. 3, Jan. 14, 1863, p. 3; *Transcript*, Jan. 14, 1863, p. 3, July 31, 1862, p. 3, Aug. 2, 1862, p. 3.

26. *Journal*, Feb. 27, 1857, p. 2, Jan. 28, 1859, p. 2, Nov. 18, 1859, p. 3, Apr. 16, 1858, p. 2, July 9, 1858, p. 1, Oct. 14, 1859, p. 2; *Democrat*, Jan. 19, 1859, p. 2, Apr. 15, 1862, p. 3, Nov. 12, 1861, p. 3, Oct. 12, 1859, p. 2; *Telegraph*, July 3, 1858, p. 2; *National*, Nov. 26, 1859, p. 2, Aug. 17, 1861, p. 2, Mar. 20, 1862, p. 3, Sept. 28, 1861, p. 3; *Transcript*, Mar. 19, 1863, p. 3, July 6, 1862, p. 3; Byrne, pp. 14–15; Benjamin, vol. 2, p. 47; Levinson, pp. 132–34, 180, 115; Bramall, pp. 31–32.

27. This becomes clear when Thompson is correlated with occupations and ethnicity taken from the manuscript census of 1860.

28. *Journal*, Apr. 8, 1859, p. 2, Apr. 22, 1859, p. 2, Apr. 29, 1859, p. 3, June 3, 1859, p. 3; *Democrat*, Apr. 20, 1859, p. 3, May 4, 1859, p. 2. See Feldburg, pp. 9–23, for the results of a controversy over Bibles in schools during a time of ethnic tension.

Chapter 5

1. Paul, *California Gold*, pp. 289–92, 255–56, 260; Browne, pp. 129–32; Bean, pp. 50–51, 53, 232–33, 238, 133, 247; Wells, p. 187; *Gazette*, Apr. 27, 1864, p. 3; *Transcript*, Aug. 18, 1864, p. 2.

2. Bean, pp. 204–10, 212–13; Wells, pp. 189–93; Byrne, pp. 69, 71, 79–85; *National Gazette*, Oct. 3, 1870, p. 2.

3. *Transcript*, May 24, 1866, p. 2, Apr. 18, 1866, p. 3, Sept. 29, 1864, p. 3; *Union*, Mar. 7, 1865, p. 2, June 21, 1865, p. 3, Sept. 12, 1865, p. 3, June 20, 1868, p. 3, Nov. 10, 1868, p. 2, Aug. 13, 1869, p. 3; *National*, Dec. 26, 1868, p. 3; Bean, p. 19; Hittell, *Resources*, p. 449; Hittell quoted in the *Union*, Dec. 27, 1866, p. 2; Browne, p. 132; *Gazette*, Jan. 24, 1865, p. 3.

4. Morse, p. 353; *National*, Jan. 24, 1865, pp. 2–3; Byrne, pp. 10, 15;

Union, Sept. 13, 1865, p. 3, Nov. 9, 1865, p. 2; *Gazette,* Feb. 8, 1865, p. 3, Mar. 1, 1865, p. 2; Browne, p. 103; Paul, *California Gold,* p. 260; Hittell, *Resources,* p. 295; Bean, p. 204.

5. *Transcript,* Apr. 5, 1864, p. 3, May 4, 1866, p. 3, Jan. 17, 1865, p. 3, Apr. 22, 1864, p. 2, Feb. 3, 1865, p. 3; *Gazette,* Jan. 7, 1865, p. 3, July 7, 1864, p. 3, Jan. 3, 1865, p. 3, Dec. 1, 1866, p. 2, Mar. 26, 1865, p. 2; *National,* Jan. 10, 1865, p. 3; Bean, pp. 54–55, 108–109, 114; Kelley, p. 35.

6. *Union,* Nov. 1, 1867, p. 3, Aug. 18, 1866, p. 3; *Gazette,* Feb. 1, 1865, p. 2; *Transcript,* July 11, 1865, p. 3; Browne, pp. 132, 137; Byrne, p. 83; Bean, pp. 50–54, 247.

7. Browne, p. 135, 120; Bean, pp. 120–21, 123–24, 108–109; *Transcript,* Sept. 13, 1866, p. 3, Apr. 13, 1866, p. 3, June 16, 1866, p. 3; *Gazette,* June 14, 1866, p. 3, Jan. 22, 1866, p. 2.

8. *National,* July 14, 1867, p. 3; Bean, pp. 204–207, 213, 215; *National Gazette,* Apr. 16, 1870, p. 3, Oct. 3, 1870, p. 2; *Transcript,* Oct. 2, 1867, p. 2; *Union,* Feb. 14, 1868, p. 3, Oct. 20, 1870, p. 3.

9. Bean, p. 65; Wells, p. 171; *Gazette,* Apr. 23, 1866, p. 3, Dec. 11, 1868, p. 1, Dec. 17, 1868, p. 1; *Union,* Feb. 14, 1868, p. 3.

10. *Union,* Nov. 10, 1867, p. 3, Mar. 23, 1869, p. 3, Sept. 8, 1869, p. 3, Dec. 10, 1868, p. 2; *Transcript,* Jan. 12, 1869, p. 3, Jan. 31, 1869, p. 3, Mar. 3, 1868, p. 3; *Gazette,* Jan. 26, 1869, p. 1, Oct. 19, 1869, p. 3; *National Gazette,* May 28, 1870, p. 3, Sept. 28, 1870, p. 3; Wells, pp. 55, 176; Browne, pp. 129–32, 37.

11. *Union,* Dec. 27, 1866, p. 3, Feb. 24, 1866, p. 3; *National,* Dec. 6, 1864, p. 3; *Gazette,* Mar. 11, 1870, p. 3, June 1, 1867, p. 3, Feb. 6, 1866, p. 3; *Transcript,* Jan. 23, 1866, p. 3.

12. Soltow, p. 22; U.S. Census Bureau, *Compendium of the Ninth Census,* vol. 1, pp. 91–93.

13. Increased residential segregation is shown by correlating names and occupations taken from Bean with ethnicity taken from the manuscript census of 1870. Rowe, pp. 113, 155; Todd, pp. 64, 67; Bramall, p. 75; *Gazette,* Mar. 27, 1867, p. 3, Aug. 1, 1864, p. 3; *Transcript,* Nov. 21, 1867, p. 3.

14. *Gazette,* July 20, 1865, p. 3, Dec. 28, 1865, p. 3; *Union,* Apr. 6, 1867, p. 3.

15. Mann, "National Party Fortunes," pp. 281–82.

16. *National Gazette,* May 17, 1870, p. 3; *National,* May 29, 1869, p. 2; *Transcript,* Oct. 2, 1867, p. 2; *Gazette,* Apr. 9, 1869, p. 2, Feb. 1, 1865, p. 2.

17. *Union,* Feb. 26, 1866, p. 3; *Gazette,* Apr. 9, 1869, p. 3, Apr. 15, 1869, p. 3, Nov. 3, 1869, p. 3; *National Gazette,* Apr. 27, 1870, p. 3; Bean, pp. 43, 47; Wells, p. 171. For attitudes toward town merchants and township miners, see Bean, pp. 73–96, and Waite in Bean, pp. 9–47, esp. p. 19.

18. *Union,* Jan. 3, 1868, p. 2. Cf. *Gazette,* Mar. 19, 1869, p. 3; *National,* Mar. 26, 1869, p. 3.

Chapter 6

1. *National*, Apr. 7, 1869, p. 3, May 26, 1868, p. 3, Mar. 19, 1868, p. 3; Putnam, pp. 253–55; *Gazette*, Jan. 21, 1868, p. 3, Jan. 31, 1868, p. 2, Aug. 18, 1869, p. 3, Jan. 24, 1870, p. 3, July 19, 1864, p. 3, Jan. 30, 1866, p. 3, Dec. 11, 1868, p. 1, Feb. 8, 1869, p. 3, Sept. 2, 1869, p. 3; *National Gazette*, May 2, 1870, p. 3; *Transcript*, June 15, 1867, p. 3, July 1, 1866, p. 2, Jan. 1, 1868, p. 2, Aug. 22, 1868, p. 3; *Union*, June 3, 1865, p. 3; Rowe, pp. 24, 57; Todd, pp. 24–25.

2. *Gazette*, July 14, 1864, p. 2, Aug. 13, 1868, p. 1, July 1, 1869, p. 3; *Transcript*, July 30, 1864, p. 3, Aug. 1, 1864, p. 3, June 30, 1870, p. 2; *National*, July 1, 1868, p. 3; *Union*, July 1, 1868, p. 3.

3. Bean, pp. 107, 198–99; *Union*, Jan. 10, 1865, p. 3, Oct. 25, 1867, p. 3, Nov. 10, 1870, p. 2, Sept. 7, 1870, p. 3; *Gazette*, Jan. 4, 1867, p. 3, Jan. 6, 1868, p. 2, Feb. 22, 1869, p. 3, Mar. 26, 1870, p. 3; *Transcript*, Jan. 3, 1864, p. 3, Oct. 28, 1870, p. 2; *National Gazette*, Oct. 17, 1870, p. 3, Nov. 1, 1870, p. 3.

4. *Transcript*, Nov. 10, 1866, p. 3, Nov. 28, 1868, p. 3, Sept. 23, 1869, p. 3, Oct. 1, 1870, p. 3, Nov. 9, 1865, p. 3, Nov. 3, 1869, p. 3, Apr. 20, 1870, p. 3, May 6, 1869, p. 3; *Gazette*, Oct. 27, 1869, p. 3, Nov. 28, 1869, p. 3; *Union*, Nov. 16, 1869, p. 3, Nov. 24, 1869, p. 3.

5. *National Gazette*, Nov. 7, 1870, p. 3; *Transcript*, Mar. 23, 1870, p. 2, Mar. 18, 1869, p. 3, Apr. 9, 1870, p. 3; *National*, June 28, 1868, p. 3.

6. *National*, May 2, 1865, p. 3, Jan. 3, 1870, p. 2; *Union*, Dec. 9, 1865, p. 3; *Gazette*, Feb. 14, 1865, p. 3, May 28, 1868, p. 1, Oct. 28, 1865, p. 3, Feb. 11, 1865, p. 3.

7. *Gazette*, Oct. 9, 1867, p. 3, Feb. 10, 1870, p. 3, Feb. 22, 1866, p. 3, Feb. 21, 1867, p. 3; *Transcript*, Jan. 29, 1867, p. 3; *Union*, May 12, 1869, p. 3.

8. *Gazette*, Jan. 25, 1867, p. 3, Jan. 16, 1867, p. 3, Dec. 28, 1866, p. 3, Jan. 21, 1868, p. 3, June 5, 1869, p. 3; *Transcript*, Jan. 24, 1867, p. 2, Mar. 11, 1870, p. 3, Mar. 1, 1868, p. 2, June 5, 1869, p. 3, Mar. 5, 1868, p. 3; *National*, June 9, 1868, p. 3, May 11, 1869, p. 3, Jan. 6, 1869, p. 3, Apr. 2, 1869, p. 3; *Union*, Apr. 23, 1870, p. 3. Cf. Hirsch, p. 102.

9. *Gazette*, Oct. 16, 1869, p. 3, Oct. 22, 1869, p. 2, Oct. 23, 1869, p. 3, Nov. 1, 1869, p. 2, Jan. 13, 1870, p. 3; *Transcript*, Mar. 26, 1870, p. 3, Aug. 23, 1870, p. 3; *National*, Aug. 19, 1869, p. 2; *National Gazette*, June 17, 1870, p. 3, May 25, 1870, p. 3; *Nevada Women's Suffrage Association Constitution, passim; Minutes*, May 5, 1870, Mar. 24, 1870, Mar. 17, 1870.

10. *Union*, Apr. 23, 1865, p. 3, May 23, 1865, p. 3, Aug. 3, 1865, p. 3; *Transcript*, Apr. 28, 1869, p. 3, June 26, 1869, p. 3; *Gazette*, Nov. 25, 1869, p. 3, June 26, 1865, p. 2, Feb. 3, 1865, p. 3; *National*, Oct. 21, 1864, p. 3.

11. *Union*, Mar. 1, 1870, p. 2; *Gazette*, Jan. 28, 1867, p. 2, Sept. 14, 1865, p. 3, Dec. 4, 1868, p. 1; *National Gazette*, Sept. 14, 1870, p. 3.

12. *Transcript*, Jan. 1, 1864, p. 3, Jan. 3, 1864, p. 2, Dec. 31, 1869, p. 3,

Apr. 13, 1870, p. 3; *Gazette,* Jan. 3, 1867, p. 3, Jan. 1, 1868, p. 3, Feb. 7, 1870, p. 3; *Union,* Jan. 1, 1865, p. 3, Apr. 8, 1870, p. 3, Jan. 3, 1865, p. 3; *National Gazette,* Apr. 8, 1870, p. 3, Apr. 12, 1870, p. 3, May 2, 1870, p. 3.

13. Wells, p. 153; *Union,* Nov. 3, 1865, p. 3; *Gazette,* Aug. 3, 1864, p. 3, Feb. 1, 1865, p. 3, May 31, 1865, p. 3, Nov. 27, 1866, p. 3; *Transcript,* Sept. 16, 1864, p. 3, Jan. 18, 1865, p. 3, Mar. 22, 1865, p. 2, Apr. 5, 1867, p. 3; *National,* Mar. 1, 1865, p. 3, Feb. 10, 1868, p. 3, July 2, 1868, p. 3, Dec. 11, 1869, p. 3. Cf. Lapp, p. 167.

14. *Gazette,* Apr. 21, 1865, p. 2, Apr. 22, 1865, p. 2, Nov. 25, 1867, p. 3, Oct. 28, 1868, p. 1; *National,* Apr. 18, 1865, p. 3; *Transcript,* Feb. 9, 1865, p. 3, Feb. 10, 1865, p. 3, Aug. 3, 1866, p. 3, Feb. 20, 1867, p. 2, Oct. 1, 1867, p. 3, Aug. 17, 1870, p. 2; *National Gazette,* Aug. 9, 1870, p. 3, Aug. 27, 1870, p. 3, Sept. 2, 1870, p. 3, Nov. 25, 1870, p. 3; *Union,* Sept. 20, 1865, p. 3; Sept. 23, 1865, p. 3, Aug. 16, 1870, p. 3, Oct. 10, 1868, p. 3; Levinson, pp. 190–91, 195–6, 214.

15. *Gazette,* Mar. 11, 1864, p. 3, Apr. 3, 1868, p. 1; *National,* Mar. 17, 1864, p. 3, Mar. 18, 1869, p. 3; *Union,* Mar. 3, 1865, p. 3, Mar. 18, 1867, p. 3, Dec. 21, 1865, p. 3, July 14, 1866, p. 3, Sept. 26, 1868, p. 3, Mar. 18, 1870, p. 3.

16. *National,* May 19, 1865, p. 3, May 24, 1865, p. 3, Mar. 16, 1868, p. 3, Mar. 19, 1868, p. 3; *Transcript,* June 10, 1866, p. 3; *Gazette,* June 22, 1865, p. 3, June 29, 1865, p. 3, July 12, 1865, p. 3, Oct. 6, 1865, p. 3, Dec. 30, 1865, p. 3, Mar. 7, 1866, p. 3, Mar. 17, 1866, p. 3, June 12, 1866, p. 3, June 11, 1866, p. 3, Feb. 12, 1868, p. 1, July 8, 1868, p. 3; *Union,* June 21, 1865, p. 2, Apr. 22, 1866, p. 3.

17. *Transcript,* May 14, 1869, p. 3, Jan. 12, 1870, p. 3; *Gazette,* Feb. 14, 1870, p. 3; *Union,* Sept. 6, 1868, p. 2, Jan. 29, 1868, p. 3; *National,* Mar. 22, 1864, p. 3. For evidence of Chinese community institutions, see U.S. Census Bureau, *Population Schedules,* 1870, esp. pp. 144–45, 206, 296, 311.

18. *Gazette,* Nov. 28, 1867, p. 3; *Transcript,* Aug. 28, 1868, p. 3, July 9, 1869, p. 3, Nov. 18, 1870, p. 3; *National Gazette,* Nov. 18, 1870, p. 3.

19. *Gazette,* Aug. 23, 1866, p. 3, Aug. 19, 1865, p. 3; *Union,* Aug. 24, 1866, p. 3, May 9, 1867, p. 3, June 17, 1869, p. 3; *Transcript,* Oct. 2, 1870, p. 3, Oct. 11, 1870, p. 3, June 8, 1870, p. 3; *National Gazette,* Aug. 6, 1870, p. 3, Oct. 12, 1870, p. 3, Nov. 26, 1870, p. 3.

20. *Union,* June 6, 1869, p. 3, Jan. 10, 1867, p. 3, Apr. 29, 1870, p. 3, Aug. 14, 1870, p. 3, Dec. 16, 1866, p. 2, June 30, 1868, p. 3, July 2, 1868, p. 3, Feb. 20, 1869, p. 2, Feb. 27, 1869, p. 3, Mar. 15, 1869, p. 3, Apr. 19, 1869, p. 3; *Transcript,* Dec. 23, 1865, p. 3, Feb. 28, 1869, p. 3, June 8, 1869, p. 2; *National,* Jan. 28, 1865, p. 3; Seager, p. 51.

21. *Gazette,* Apr. 20, 1870, p. 2, Apr. 4, 1870, p. 2; *National,* Aug. 28, 1869, p. 2, June 28, 1869, p. 3.

22. Bramall, pp. 25–26, 30, 34–35; Rowe, pp. 82–83; *Gazette,* Feb. 13, 1865, p. 3, July 8, 1869, p. 3, Jan. 10, 1868, p. 2, June 13, 1866, p. 3; *National,* Feb. 13, 1865, p. 3; *Union,* June 22, 1865, p. 3, Dec. 28, 1869, p. 3.

23. *Union,* June 27, 1865, p. 3, Jan. 30, 1866, p. 3; *National,* Oct. 3, 1864, p. 3; *Gazette,* Dec. 11, 1865, p. 3.

24. *Union,* Nov. 17, 1865, p. 3, Sept. 28, 1865, p. 3; *Gazette,* Sept. 28, 1865, p. 3, Oct. 15, 1866, p. 3, Apr. 25, 1868, p. 1, Jan. 3, 1868, p. 3, Mar. 25, 1869, p. 3; *Transcript,* May 4, 1870, p. 3, Oct. 23, 1870, p. 3; *National Gazette,* Dec. 20, 1870, p. 3; *National,* Dec. 21, 1869, p. 2. Cf. Lingenfelter, pp. 10–11.

25. *Gazette,* Apr. 16, 1869, p. 3; *National,* Jan. 28, 1864, p. 2; Morse, pp. 344, 347, 350, 354–56.

26. *Gazette,* July 17, 1867, p. 3, Nov. 10, 1868, p. 1, May 18, 1869, p. 3, July 7, 1868, p. 1; *National,* Aug. 10, 1868, p. 3; *Transcript,* June 22, 1870, p. 2; Jenkin, p. 265; Lingenfelter, pp. 8, 19, 23; Wyman, p. 179.

27. *Union,* Apr. 18, 1867, p. 3, Mar. 26, 1869, p. 3, May 6, 1869, p. 3; *National,* Feb. 12, 1868, p. 3, Apr. 28, 1869, p. 2, Jan. 11, 1869, p. 3; Morse, p. 353.

28. *National,* Apr. 22, 1869, p. 3, Apr. 28, 1869, p. 3, May 1, 1869, p. 3, May 5, 1869, p. 3, May 6, 1869, p. 3, May 10, 1869, p. 2; *Gazette,* Apr. 27, 1869, p. 3, Apr. 30, 1869, p. 3, May 11, 1869, p. 3; *Union,* Apr. 22, 1869, p. 3, May 8, 1869, p. 3, May 11, 1869, p. 2; *Transcript,* Apr. 22, 1869, p. 3, May 4, 1869, p. 3; Lingenfelter, p. 84.

29. *Union,* May 12, 1869, p. 3, May 19, 1869, p. 3, May 9, 1869, p. 2; *Gazette,* May 11, 1869, p. 3, May 12, 1869, pp. 2–3; *National,* May 12, 1869, p. 3, May 18, 1869, p. 3.

30. *Gazette,* May 14, 1869, p. 2, May 17, 1869, p. 2, May 24, 1869, p. 3, May 25, 1869, pp. 2–3, May 26, 1869, p. 3; *Union,* May 14, 1869, pp. 2–3; *Transcript,* May 19, 1869, p. 2, May 25, 1869, p. 3, May 26, 1869, p. 3; *National,* May 17, 1869, p. 3, May 23, 1869, p. 3, May 24, 1869, pp. 2–3, May 25, 1869, p. 3.

31. *Union,* May 26, 1869, p. 3, May 27, 1869, p. 3, May 28, 1869, p. 3; *Transcript,* May 26, 1869, p. 2, May 27, 1869, p. 2, May 29, 1869, p. 2; *Gazette,* May 27, 1869, pp. 2–3, May 28, 1869, p. 3.

32. *Union,* May 29, 1869, p. 3, June 11, 1869, p. 3, June 18, 1869, p. 2, July 3, 1869, p. 2, July 28, 1869, p. 3, Aug. 11, 1869, p. 3; *Transcript,* June 2, 1869, p. 2; *Gazette,* June 12, 1869, p. 3, June 14, 1869, pp. 2–3, July 17, 1869, p. 3; *National,* July 15, 1869, p. 2; Lingenfelter, pp. 85–86, 88.

33. *Gazette,* Apr. 30, 1869, p. 3, May 7, 1869, p. 2, May 12, 1869, p. 2, May 18, 1869, p. 2, May 19, 1869, p. 3, May 22, 1869, p. 3; *National,* May 18, 1869, p. 2; *Transcript,* May 18, 1869, pp. 2–3, May 14, 1869, p. 2, May 26, 1869, p. 3; *Union,* May 16, 1869, p. 3.

34. *Union,* May 21, 1869, p. 2, May 25, 1869, p. 3, June 2, 1869, p. 2; *Gazette,* May 12, 1869, p. 2, May 25, 1869, p. 2, Aug. 14, 1869, p. 2, July 7, 1869, p. 2; Saxton, pp. 88, 98.

35. *National,* May 24, 1869, p. 2, May 25, 1869, p. 2, May 27, 1869, p. 2, May 29, 1869, p. 2, May 31, 1869, p. 2, July 15, 1869, p. 2. But see Lingenfelter, pp. 86–87.

36. *Transcript,* May 14, 1869, p. 2; *National,* June 22, 1869, p. 3, May 24, 1869, p. 3.

37. *Gazette*, Sept. 18, 1869, p. 3; *National*, Sept. 1, 1869, p. 3, Oct. 1, 1869, p. 3, Nov. 13, 1869, p. 2, Dec. 21, 1869, p. 2; *National Gazette*, Dec. 22, 1870, p. 3.

38. *National*, June 15, 1869, p. 2, Sept. 15, 1869, p. 3, Sept. 22, 1869, p. 2, Oct. 2, 1869, p. 2; *Gazette*, Aug. 13, 1869, p. 2, Jan. 27, 1867, p. 2, July 7, 1869, p. 2, June 21, 1869, p. 3, Aug. 12, 1869, p. 3; *Transcript*, Sept. 1, 1869, p. 2, Aug. 1, 1869, p. 2, Aug. 14, 1869, p. 2; *Union*, Sept. 2, 1869, pp. 2–3.

39. *Gazette*, Feb. 18, 1870, p. 2, Mar. 23, 1870, p. 2, Oct. 13, 1869, p. 3, Dec. 2, 1869, p. 3, Mar. 18, 1870, p. 3, Sept. 3, 1869, p. 2; *National Gazette*, Sept. 16, 1870, p. 3; *Transcript*, Apr. 7, 1870, p. 3, Sept. 2, 1869, p. 2.

40. *Union*, Dec. 5, 1869, p. 3; *National*, Sept. 6, 1869, p. 3, Oct. 4, 1869, p. 3, Oct. 18, 1869, p. 3, Nov. 13, 1869, p. 3, Dec. 18, 1869, p. 3, Oct. 17, 1870, p. 3; *Gazette*, Sept. 30, 1869, p. 2, Nov. 12, 1869, p. 3.

41. Wells, pp. 163–65; Todd, pp. 72–73; Kelley, p. 55; Paul, *California Gold*, p. 331.

Conclusion

1. See the discussion in Gitelman, p. xiv.

2. Pomeroy, "Toward," pp. 581–82, 585, 593, 597; Pomeroy, "Urban," *passim;* Merriam, p. 52. Cf. Billington, pp. 28, 94; Larsen, pp. xi, 19.

3. Paul, *Mining Frontiers*, pp. 9, 15, 57, 93, 193–94, 22; Jackson, pp. 48–49, 33, 216, 220; Lingenfelter, pp. 4, 10–11; Paul, *California Gold*, p. 257.

4. Paul, *Mining Frontiers*, p. 26; Jackson, p. 12; Ricards, pp. 473–74, 478, 480, 482, 488; D. Smith, "San Juaner," pp. 140–43.

5. Goldman, p. 38; Lingenfelter, p. 8; R. Brown, pp. 22, 31; D. Smith, *Rocky Mountain*, pp. 29, 60, 228, 232–33; Jackson, pp. 86, 94, 225; Faulk, p. 104; Landis, pp. 32–34, 62; Blackburn and Ricards, "Virginia City," pp. 248–50, 254.

6. Paul, *Mining Frontiers*, pp. 68–69, 122, 56; D. Smith, *Rocky Mountain*, pp. 26, 28, 160, 182; Paul, "Mining History," pp. 27–28; D. Smith, "San Juaner," pp. 142, 146–47, 150–51; Lingenfelter, pp. 6–7, 9, 19, 28, 31, 109, 119; Jackson, pp. 27, 135–37; R. Brown, pp. 8, 102, 201.

7. Billington, pp. 25, 27, 60, 168.

8. Curti, pp. 1–2, 17, 20, 184, 447–48.

9. Curti, pp. 140, 78, 108–9, 100, 126–27.

10. Curti, pp. 84, 184–88, 196, 198–99, 202, 205, 207.

11. D. Bogue, p. 114; Eblen, pp. 411–13; Hudson, pp. 44–45; Faragher, pp. 34–36; May, p. 185; Blackburn and Ricards, "Manistee," pp. 603–4; Blackburn and Ricards, "Nueces," p. 9; R. Davis, p. 133; Robbins, "Social and Economic Change," p. 87.

12. A. Bogue, *Prairie*, pp. 22–25; D. Bogue, p. 114; Bowers, p. 26; Wishart, p. 111; Throne, pp. 313–14. Cf. Blackburn and Ricards, "Nueces," p. 11; J. Davis, p. 117.

13. J. Jeffrey, pp. 79, 94, 106, 125–26, 12, 53, 60; Doyle, *Jacksonville,* p. 119; D. Smith, *Rocky Mountain,* p. 22; Lotchin, pp. 255–57.

14. Modell and Hareven, pp. 165–67, 175; de Graaf, p. 311; Goldman, pp. 32–33; Riley, pp. 240, 262–64; Faragher, pp. 62, 83, 87, 187; J. Jeffrey, pp. 86, 95, 128; Larson, pp. 5–7; Griswold, pp. 267–68, 273–74.

15. Steffen, pp. xv, 89, 23, 95; R. Brown, pp. 166, 36; D. Smith, *Rocky Mountain,* 57, 10, 243–44, 134; Dykstra, "Great Plains," p. 216.

16. Atherton, *Main Street,* pp. 163–65; Doyle, *Jacksonville,* pp. 156–93; P. Smith, pp. 157–82; Hine, pp. 80–81; Dykstra, "Great Plains," pp. 220–21; Dykstra, *Cattle Towns,* pp. 3, 74, 149; Lingeman, p. 60; Esslinger, pp. 23–24; Blumin, pp. 22–23.

17. Wallace, pp. 48–49; Throne, pp. 326–29; Peter R. Decker, pp. 106–7, 233; Atherton, *Merchant,* pp. 38–39, 32; Billington, pp. 122–24.

18. Dykstra, *Cattle Towns,* pp. 3–6, 365–66; A. Bogue, "Social History," pp. 33, 31.

19. Dykstra, *Cattle Towns,* pp. 112, 116, 122, 131–32, 239–41, 252.

20. Dykstra, *Cattle Towns,* pp. 87, 100, 128, 254, 260, 263, 294.

21. Dykstra, *Cattle Towns,* pp. 178–79, 183–84, 188, 206.

22. Dykstra, *Cattle Towns,* pp. 212, 237, 365–66.

23. Doyle, *Jacksonville,* pp. 2, 4–5, 9, 12–13, 15.

24. Doyle, *Jacksonville,* pp. 18–19, 25, 29–30; Hine, pp. 139–40; Starr, pp. 93–94; Peter R. Decker, pp. 107–8, 125–29; Merriam, p. 41; Blumenthal, pp. 264–66; Lotchin, p. 248.

25. P. Smith, pp. 17–36; cf. Russo, pp. 26–28.

26. Doyle, *Jacksonville,* pp. 92, 111, 186–87, 194, 217.

27. Doherty, pp. 35, 41, 43; Yans-McLaughlin, pp. 82–87, 260–64; Golab, p. 247; Griffen and Griffen, p. 21; Robbins, "Opportunity and Persistence," p. 285.

28. Thernstrom, pp. 222–24, 227; Doyle, *Jacksonville,* pp. 96, 98; Peter R. Decker, pp. 74–75; Doyle, "Social Theory," p. 155; Alcorn and Knights, p. 100.

29. Griffen and Griffen, p. 17; Doyle, *Jacksonville,* pp. 107, 98–99, 101; Malin, *Grassland,* pp. 281–83; Bowers, pp. 22–24; Chudacoff, pp. 86, 90, 92, 59; Doherty, pp. 36, 40; Gitelman, pp. 43–44; Alcorn, p. 72; Golab, pp. 113, 142.

30. Thernstrom, pp. 226–27; A. Bogue, *Prairie,* p. 25; Throne, pp. 310, 321, 324; Bowers, p. 25; R. Davis, p. 137. On wealth, see Soltow, pp. 22–24.

31. Peter R. Decker, pp. 81–84; cf. Rowe, pp. vi, 119.

32. Seward, pp. 92–94, 101–103; Furstenberg *et al.,* pp. 215–17; Soltow, pp. 22–23; Modell and Hareven, pp. 165, 169, 182; Bodnar, pp. 34–35; Katz, pp. 222, 277; Yans-McLaughlin, p. 172.

33. On industrialization and workers, see Dawley, p. 223 and *passim;* Hirsch, pp. xv, 15, 22, 37, and *passim.* On the concentration of immigrants into specific occupations, see Esslinger, pp. 99, 77–78; Bodnar, p. 6; Golab, pp. 200–202, 213. On residential separation see Esslinger, pp. 21–

22, 67; Bodnar, pp. 20, 153; Gitelman, pp. 6, 132–33, 136–37; Conzen, pp. 5, 126–27, 131. On ethnic elite residential patterns, see Esslinger, p. 104, and Conzen, p. 137.

34. Peter R. Decker, p. 172; Conzen, pp. 65–68, 72, 120–21; Esslinger, pp. 84–88; cf. Doyle, *Jacksonville*, pp. 131, 137.

35. Walkowitz, "Statistics," 259–60, 220, 284–85; Hirsch, pp. 77–78; cf. Lieberson, pp. 171–81.

36. Thernstrom, p. 227; Malin, *Grassland*, p. 281. Cf. Gitelman, p. 18; Conzen, p. 42; Esslinger, pp. 42–44, 80; Katz, pp. 20–21, 119. On wealth, see Soltow, pp. 22–24, 33, 64. On sex ratios, see U.S. Census Bureau, *Historical Statistics*, p. 9. On Cornish migration see Rowse, pp. 268–69.

37. Doyle, "Social Theory," p. 155; Doyle, *Jacksonville*, p. 95; Lantz, pp. 117–18; Peter R. Decker, pp. 193–95. Cf. Kirk, p. 51; Esslinger, pp. 42–44. For criticism of Thernstrom, see Alcorn and Knights, p. 100.

38. For a more theoretical discussion of the point of view advanced here, and by Yans-McLaughlin, see Bender, *Community and Social Change*, pp. 31, 57, 72, and *passim*.

39. Walkowitz, *Worker City*, pp. 4, 13.

References Cited

·✥ REFERENCES CITED ✥·

Abbott, Carlisle S. *Recollections of a California Pioneer*. New York, 1917.
Alcorn, Richard S. "Leadership and Stability in Mid-Nineteenth Century America," *Journal of American History* 61 (1974), 685–702.
Alcorn, Richard S., and Peter R. Knights. "Most Uncommon Bostonians: A Critique of Stephan Thernstrom's *The Other Bostonians*," *Historical Methods Newsletter* 8 (1975), 98–114.
"Anti-Jewish Sentiment in California—1855," *American Jewish Archives* 12 (1960), 15–33.
Atherton, Lewis. *The Frontier Merchant in Mid-America*. Columbia, Mo., 1971.
————. *Main Street on the Middle Border*. Bloomington, Ind., 1954.
Bates, Mrs. D. B. *Incidents on Land and Water; or, Four Years on the Pacific Coast*. Boston, 1858.
Beals, Ralph L. "Ethnology of the Nisenan," *University of California Publications in American Archaeology and Ethnology* 31 (1931–33), 335–414.
Bean, Edwin. *Bean's History and Directory of Nevada County, California*. Nevada City, 1867.
Bender, Thomas. *Community and Social Change in America*. New Brunswick, N.J., 1978.
————. *Toward an Urban Vision: Ideas and Institutions in Nineteenth Century America*. Lexington, Ky., 1975.
Benjamin, I. J. *Three Years in America, 1859–1862*. 3 vols. Philadelphia, 1956.
Berkhofer, Robert F., Jr. *The White Man's Indian*. New York, 1978.
Billington, Ray A. *America's Frontier Heritage*. New York, 1966.
Blackburn, George, and Sherman L. Ricards, Jr. "A Demographic History of the West: Manistee County, Michigan, 1860," *Journal of American History* 57 (1970), 600–618.

————. "A Demographic History of the West: Nueces County, Texas, 1850," *Prologue: The Journal of the National Archives* 4 (1972), 3–20.

————. "The Prostitutes and Gamblers of Virginia City, Nevada: 1870," *Pacific Historical Review* 48 (1979), 235–59.

Blumenthal, Albert. *A Sociological Study of a Small Town.* Chicago, 1933.

Blumin, Stuart M. *The Urban Threshold: Growth and Change in a Nineteenth Century American Community.* Chicago, 1976.

Bode, Carl. *The American Lyceum.* New York, 1956.

Bodnar, John. *Immigration and Industrialization: Ethnicity in an American Mill Town.* Pittsburgh, 1977.

Bogue, Allan G. *From Prairie to Corn Belt: Farming on the Illinois and Iowa Prairies in the Nineteenth Century.* Chicago, 1963.

————. "Social History and the Pioneer," *Agricultural History* 34 (1960), 21–34.

Bogue, Donald J. *The Population of the United States.* Glencoe, Ill., 1959.

Borthwick, J. D. *The Gold Hunters.* New York, (1857) 1917.

Bowers, William L. "Crawford Township, 1850–1870: A Population Study of a Pioneer Community," *Iowa Journal of History* 58 (1960), 1–30.

Boyer, Paul. *Urban Masses and Moral Order in America, 1820–1920.* Cambridge, Mass., 1978.

Bramall, Kathleen L. "Cornish Miners of Grass Valley and Nevada City." M.A. diss., California State University, Chico, 1972.

Brewer, William H. *Up and Down California in 1860–1864: The Journal of William H. Brewer.* Francis P. Farquhar, ed. Berkeley, 1966.

Brown, Nat P., and John K. Dallison. *Brown and Dallison's Nevada, Grass Valley and Rough and Ready Directory.* San Francisco, 1856.

Brown, Ronald C. *Hard Rock Miners: The Intermountain West, 1860–1920.* College Station, Tex., 1979.

Browne, J. Ross. *Resources of the Pacific Slope.* San Francisco, 1869.

Byington, Margaret. "The Family in a Typical Mill Town," *American Journal of Sociology* 14 (1909), 648–59.

Byrne, William S. *Directory of Grass Valley Township for 1865.* San Francisco, 1865.

Chudacoff, Howard P. *Mobile Americans: Residential and Social Mobility in Omaha, 1880–1920.* New York, 1972.

Coad, John. Personal correspondence, 1858–60. In possession of Jepson Garland, Menlo Park, Calif.

Conzen, Kathleen N. *Immigrant Milwaukee, 1836–1860.* Cambridge, Mass., 1976.

Coolidge, Mary. *Chinese Immigration.* New York, 1909.

Crandall, Henry S. *Love and Nuggets.* Roland D. Crandall, ed. Old Greenwich, Conn., 1967.

Curti, Merle. *The Making of an American Community: A Case Study of Democracy in a Frontier County.* Stanford, Calif., 1959.

Davis, James E. *Frontier America, 1800–1840: A Comparative Demographic Analysis of the Frontier Process.* Glendale, Calif., 1977.

Davis, Rodney O. "Prairie Emporium: Clarence, Iowa, 1860–1880, a Study of Population Trends," *Mid-America* 51 (1969), 130–39.

Dawley, Alan. *Class and Community: The Industrial Revolution in Lynn.* Cambridge, Mass., 1976.

Decker, Peter. *The Diaries of Peter Decker.* Helen S. Giffen, ed. Georgetown, Calif., 1966.

Decker, Peter R. *Fortunes and Failures: White Collar Mobility in Nineteenth Century San Francisco.* Cambridge, Mass., 1978.

de Graaf, Lawrence B. "Race, Sex, and Region: Black Women in the American West, 1850–1920," *Pacific Historical Review* 49 (1980), 284–313.

Delano, Alonzo. *Alonzo Delano's California Correspondence.* Irving McKee, ed. Sacramento, 1952.

————. *A Live Woman in the Mines.* New York, n.d.

————. *Old Block's Sketch Book.* Santa Ana, Calif., (1856) 1947.

————. *Pen Knife Sketches; or, Chips of the Old Block.* San Francisco, (1853) 1934.

Dexter, A. Henry. *Early Days in California.* Denver, 1886.

Doherty, Robert. *Society and Power: Five New England Towns, 1800–1860.* Amherst, Mass., 1977.

Dornin, George D. *Thirty Years Ago, 1849–1879.* Berkeley, 1879.

Doyle, Don H. *The Social Order of a Frontier Community: Jacksonville, Illinois, 1825–1870.* Urbana, 1978.

————. "Social Theory and New Communities in Nineteenth Century America," *Western Historical Quarterly* 8 (1977), 151–65.

Dykstra, Robert R. *The Cattle Towns: A Social History of the Kansas Cattle Trading Centers; Abilene, Ellsworth, Wichita, Dodge City, and Caldwell, 1867 to 1885.* New York, 1968.

————. "Cities in the Sagebrush: Great Plains Urbanization, 1865–90," in James E. Wright and Sarah Z. Rosenberg, eds., *The Great Plains Experience.* Lincoln, Nebr., 1978, pp. 209–21.

Eblen, Jack. "An Analysis of Nineteenth Century Frontier Populations," *Demography* 2 (1965), 399–413.

Elder, William. William Elder Correspondence, 1851. Searls Memorial Library, Nevada City.

English, Joseph R. The Memory Book of Joseph R. English, Nevada City, Calif., 1863–1869, Vallejo, Calif., 1870–1916. Wells Fargo History Room, San Francisco.

Esslinger, Dean. *Immigrants and the City: Ethnicity and Mobility in a Nineteenth Century City.* Port Washington, N.Y., 1975.

Fairchild, Mahlon D. "Reminiscences of a Forty-Niner," *California Historical Society Quarterly* 13 (1934), 3–33.

Faler, Paul. "Cultural Aspects of the Industrial Revolution: Lynn, Massachusetts, Shoemakers and Industrial Morality, 1826–1860," in Milton

290   *References Cited*

Cantor, ed., *American Workingclass Culture*. Westport, Conn., 1979, pp. 121–48.

Faragher, John M. *Women and Men on the Overland Trail*. New Haven, 1979.

Faulk, Odie B. *Tombstone: Myth and Reality*. New York, 1972.

Feldburg, Michael. *The Turbulent Era: Riot and Disorder in Jacksonian America*. New York, 1980.

Ferguson, Charles D. *The Experiences of a Forty-Niner*. Cleveland, 1888.

Fletcher, Daniel C. *Reminiscences of California and the Civil War*. Ayer, Mass., 1894.

Foley, Doris, and Jim Morley. *Gold Cities: Grass Valley and Nevada City*. Berkeley, 1965.

Fredrickson, George M. *The Black Image in the White Mind*. New York, 1971.

Frisch, Michael H. *Town into City: Springfield, Massachusetts and the Meaning of Community, 1840–1880*. Cambridge, Mass., 1972.

Furstenberg, Frank, Theodore Herschberg, and John Modell. "The Origins of the Female-Headed Black Family: The Impact of the Urban Experience," *Journal of Interdisciplinary History* 6 (1975), 211–33.

Gibson, Charles, ed. *The Black Legend: Anti-Spanish Attitudes in the Old World and New*. New York, 1971.

Gill, William. *The California Letters of William Gill*. Eva T. Clark, ed. New York, n.d.

Gitelman, Howard M. *Workingmen of Waltham: Mobility in American Urban Industrial Development, 1850–1890*. Baltimore, 1974.

Golab, Caroline. *Immigrant Destinations*. Philadelphia, 1977.

Goldman, Marion. "Prostitution and Virtue in Nevada," *Society* 10 (1972), 32–38.

Griffen, Clyde, and Sally Griffen. *Natives and Newcomers: The Ordering of Opportunity in Mid-Nineteenth Century Poughkeepsie*. Cambridge, Mass., 1978.

Griswold, Robert C. "Apart but Not Adrift: Wives, Divorce, and Independence in California, 1850–1890." *Pacific Historical Review* 49 (1980), 265–83.

Hanchett, William F., Jr. "Religion and the Gold Rush, 1849–1854: The Christian Churches in the California Mines." Ph.D. diss., Univ. of California, Berkeley, 1952.

Hill, Jasper D. *The Letters of a Young Miner: Covering the Adventures of Jasper S. Hill during the California Gold Rush, 1849–1852*. Doyce B. Nunis, Jr., ed. San Francisco, 1964.

Hine, Robert V. *Community on the American Frontier: Separate But Not Alone*. Norman, Okla., 1980.

Hirsch, Susan E. *Roots of the American Working Class: The Industrialization of the Crafts in Newark, 1800–1860*. Philadelphia, 1978.

Hittell, John S. *Mining in the Pacific States of North America*. San Francisco, 1861.

——— . *The Resources of California*. San Francisco, 1863.

Holliday, Jaquelin S. "The Gold Rush in Myth and Reality." Ph.D. diss. Univ. of California, Berkeley, 1959.

Hudson, John N. "The Study of Western Frontier Populations," in Jerome O. Steffen, ed., *The American West*. Norman, Okla., 1979, pp. 35–60.

Hurt, Peyton. "The Rise and Fall of the 'Know Nothings' in California," *California Historical Society Quarterly* 9 (1930), 16–49, 99–128.

Jackson, W. Turrentine. *Treasure Hill: Portrait of a Silver Mining Camp*. Tucson, 1963.

Jeffrey, Julie R. *Frontier Women: The Trans-Mississippi West, 1840–1880*. New York, 1979.

Jeffrey, Kirk. "The Family as Utopian Retreat from the City: The Nineteenth Century Contribution," *Soundings* 55 (1972), 21–41.

Jenkin, A. K. H. *The Cornish Miner: An Account of His Life Above and Underground from Early Times*. London, 1962.

Jensen, Joan A., and Darlis Miller. "The Gentle Tamers Revisited," *Pacific Historical Review* 49 (1980), 173–214.

Johnson, Paul. *A Shopkeeper's Millennium: Society and Revivals in Rochester, New York, 1815–1837*. New York, 1978.

Katz, Michael B. *The People of Hamilton, Canada West: Family and Class in a Mid-Nineteenth Century City*. Cambridge, Mass., 1975.

Kelley, Robert C. *Gold versus Grain: The Hydraulic Mining Controversy in California's Sacramento Valley*. Glendale, Calif., 1959.

Kinyon, Edmund. *The Northern Mines*. Grass Valley, 1949.

Kirk, Gordon W., Jr. *The Promise of American Life: Social Mobility in a Nineteenth-Century Immigrant Community, Holland, Michigan, 1874–1894*. Philadelphia, 1978.

Landis, Paul H. *Three Iron Mining Towns*. New York, (1938) 1970.

Lantz, Herman R. *A Community in Search of Itself: A Case History of Cairo, Illinois*. Carbondale, Ill., 1972.

Lapp, Rudolph M. *Blacks in Gold Rush California*. New Haven, 1977.

Larsen, Lawrence H. *The Urban West at the End of the Frontier*. Lawrence, Kans., 1978.

Larson, T. A. "Women's Role in the American West," *Montana: The Magazine of Western History* 24 (1974), 2–11.

Levinson, Robert E. "The Jews in the California Gold Rush." Ph.D. diss., Univ. of Oregon, 1968.

Lieberson, Stanley. "Stratification and Ethnic Groups," in Edward O. Laumann, ed., *Social Stratification: Research and Theory for the 1970's*. Indianapolis, 1970, pp. 172–81.

Lingeman, Richard. *Small Town America: A Narrative History, 1620–the Present*. New York, 1980.

Lingenfelter, Richard E. *The Hardrock Miners: A History of the Mining Labor Movement in the American West*. Berkeley, 1974.

Litton, Solomon. Letter to His Wife, Nov. 30, 1850. Wells Fargo History Room, San Francisco.

Lopes, Frank A., Jr. "A History of Grass Valley, California, 1849–1855." M.A. diss., Sacramento State College, 1956.

Lotchin, Roger W. *San Francisco, 1846–1856: From Hamlet to City.* New York, 1974.

Low, Garrett W. *Gold Rush by Sea: From the Journal of Garrett W. Low.* Kenneth Haney, ed. Philadelphia, 1941.

Lyman, Stanford. "The Structure of Chinese Society in 19th Century America." Ph.D. diss., Univ. of California, Berkeley, 1961.

McConahy, A. P. *Incidents as I Remember Them, Closing 1865.* Van Wert, Ohio, 1927.

McKeeby, Lemuel C. "The Memoirs of Lemuel Clark McKeeby," *California Historical Society Quarterly* 3 (1924), 45–72, 126–70.

Malin, James C. *The Grassland of North America: Prolegomena to Its History with Addenda.* Lawrence, Kans., 1956.

—————. "The Turnover of Farm Population in Kansas," *Kansas Historical Quarterly* 4 (1935), 339–72.

Mann, Ralph. "National Party Fortunes and Local Political Structure: The Case of Two California Mining Towns, 1850–1870," *Southern California Quarterly* 57 (1975), 271–96.

—————. "The Social and Political Structure of Two California Mining Towns, 1850–1870." Ph.D. diss., Stanford Univ., 1970.

Margo, Elisabeth. *Taming the Forty-Niner.* New York, 1955.

May, Dean. "People on the Mormon Frontier: Kanab's Families of 1874," *Journal of Family History* 1 (1976), 169–92.

Merriam, Paul G. "Urban Elite in the Far West: Portland, Oregon, 1870–1890," *Arizona and the West* 18 (1976), 41–52.

Modell, John, and Tamara Hareven. "Urbanization and the Malleable Household: An Examination of Boarding and Lodging in American Families," in Tamara Hareven, ed., *Family and Kin in Urban Communities, 1700–1930.* New York, 1977, pp. 164–83.

Morse, Edwin F. "The Story of a Gold Miner," *California Historical Society Quarterly* 6 (1927), 205–37, 332–59.

Nevada Women's Suffrage Association. Minutes and Constitution, 1869–1872. California Historical Society, San Francisco.

Ostrander, Gilman. "The Prohibition Movement in California, 1848–1933," *University of California Publications in History,* vol. 57. Berkeley, 1957.

Paul, Rodman. *California Gold: The Beginnings of Mining in the Far West.* Cambridge, Mass., 1947.

—————. "Mining Frontiers as a Measure of Western Historical Writing," *Pacific Historical Review* 33 (1964), 25–34.

—————. *Mining Frontiers of the Far West: 1848–1880.* New York, 1963.

Payne, E. E. Personal Correspondence, 1851. California Historical Society, San Francisco.

Pitt, Leonard. *The Decline of the Californios.* Berkeley, 1966.

Pomeroy, Earl. *The Pacific Slope: A History of California, Oregon, Washington, Idaho, Utah and Nevada.* New York, 1966.

_____. "Toward a Reorientation of Western History: Continuity and Environment," *Mississippi Valley Historical Review* 41 (1955), 579–600.

_____. "The Urban Frontier of the Far West," in John Clark, ed., *The Frontier Challenge*. Lawrence, Kans., 1971, pp. 7–29.

Putnam, R. F. Diary of Rev. R. F. Putnam, Emmanuel Episcopal Church, Grass Valley, 1862–1863. California Historical Society, San Francisco.

Ricards, Sherman L., Jr. "A Demographic History of the West: Butte County, California, 1850," *Michigan Academy of Science, Arts and Letters* 46 (1961), 469–91.

Riley, Glenda. "Not Gainfully Employed: Women on the Iowa Frontier, 1833–1870," *Pacific Historical Review* 49 (1980), 237–64.

Robbins, William G. "Opportunity and Persistence in the Pacific Northwest: A Quantitative Study of Early Roseburg, Oregon," *Pacific Historical Review* 39 (1970), 279–96.

_____. "Social and Economic Change in Roseburg, Oregon, 1850–1885," *Pacific Northwest Quarterly* 64 (1973), 80–87.

Rolfe, Emily L. "The Reminiscences of Emily Lindsey Rolfe," Nevada County Historical Society *Bulletin* 20 (1966), 2–4.

Rowe, John. *The Hard Rock Men: Cornish Immigrants and the North American Mining Frontier*. New York, 1974.

Rowse, A. L. *The Cousin Jacks: The Cornish in America*. New York, 1969.

Royce, Josiah. *California*. Santa Barbara, (1886) 1970.

Russo, David J. *Families and Communities: A New View of American History*. Nashville, Tenn., 1974.

Sandmeyer, Elmer C. *The Anti-Chinese Movement in California*. Urbana, (1939) 1973.

Sawyer, Lorenzo. *Way Sketches: Across the Plains in 1850*. New York, 1926.

Saxton, Alexander. *The Indispensable Enemy: Labor and the Anti-Chinese Movement in California*. Berkeley, 1971.

Scamehorn, H. Lee, ed. *The Buckeye Rovers in the Gold Rush*. Athens, Ohio, 1965.

Schaeffer, Luther M. *Sketches of Travel in South America, Mexico and California*. New York, 1860.

Seager, Robert, II. "Some Denominational Reactions to Chinese Immigration to California, 1856–1892," *Pacific Historical Review* 28 (1959), 49–66.

Searls, Niles. *The Diary of a Pioneer and Other Papers*. San Francisco, 1940.

Seward, Rudy R. *The American Family: A Demographic Profile*. Beverly Hills, Calif., 1978.

Sheldon, Stewart. *Gleanings by the Way from '36 to '89*. Topeka, Kans., 1890.

Siu, Paul C. P. "The Sojourner," *American Journal of Sociology* 58 (1952), 34–44.

294   *References Cited*

Smith, Duane A. *Rocky Mountain Mining Camps: The Urban Frontier.* Bloomington, Ind., 1967.

————. "The San Juaner: A Computerized Portrait," *The Colorado Magazine* 52 (1975), 137–52.

Smith, Page. *As a City on a Hill: The Town in American History.* Cambridge, Mass., 1973.

Soltow, Lee. *Men and Wealth in the United States, 1850–1870.* New Haven, 1975.

Stafford, Mallie. *The March of History through Three Decades: Embracing Sketches of California History.* San Francisco, 1884.

Starr, Kevin. *Americans and the California Dream, 1850–1915.* New York, 1973.

Steele, John. *In Camp and Cabin: Mining Life and Adventure, in California during 1850 and Later.* New York, (1901) 1962.

Steffen, Jerome O. *Comparative Frontiers: A Proposal for Studying the American West.* Norman, Okla., 1980.

Stewart, William M. *Reminiscences of Senator William M. Stewart of Nevada.* New York, 1908.

Thernstrom, Stephan. *The Other Bostonians: Poverty and Progress in the American Metropolis, 1880–1970.* Cambridge, Mass., 1973.

Thompson, Hugh B. *Directory of the City of Nevada and Grass Valley.* San Francisco, 1861.

Throne, Mildred. "A Population Study of an Iowa County in 1850," *Iowa Journal of History* 57 (1959), 305–30.

Tinloy, Patrick. "Nevada County's Chinese," Nevada County Historical Society *Bulletin* 25 (1971), 1–4.

Todd, Arthur C. *The Cornish Miner in America.* Glendale, Calif., 1967.

Tyack, David. *The One Best System: A History of Urban Education.* Cambridge, Mass., 1974.

United States Bureau of the Census. *A Compendium of the Ninth Census* (1870). Washington, D.C., 1872.

————. *Historical Statistics of the United States: Colonial Times to 1957.* Washington, D.C., 1961.

————. *Population of the United States in 1860.* Washington, D.C., 1864.

————. *Population Schedules of the Seventh Census of the United States, 1850.* California, Yuba County. Washington, D.C., 1850.

————. *Population Schedules of the Eighth Census of the United States, 1860.* California, Nevada County. Washington, D.C., 1860.

————. *Population Schedules of the Ninth Census of the United States, 1870.* California, Nevada County. Washington, D.C., 1870.

————. *Statistical View of the United States . . . Being a Compendium of the Seventh Census.* Washington, D.C., 1854.

Walkowitz, Daniel. "Statistics and the Writing of Workingclass Culture: A Statistical Portrait of Iron Workers in Troy, New York, 1860–1880," in Milton Cantor, ed., *American Workingclass Culture.* Westport, Conn., 1979, pp. 241–85.

————. *Worker City, Company Town: Iron and Cottonworker Protest in Troy and Cohoes, New York, 1855–84.* Urbana, 1978.

Wallace, Anthony F. C. *Rockdale: The Growth of an American Village in the Early Industrial Revolution.* New York, 1978.

Wells, Harry L., compiler. *Thompson and West's History of Nevada County, California.* Oakland, Calif., 1880.

Welter, Barbara. *Dimity Convictions: The American Woman in the 19th Century.* Athens, Ohio, 1976.

Williams, Blaine T. "The Frontier Family," in Harold M. Hollingsworth and Sandra L. Myres, eds., *Essays on the American West.* Austin, 1969, pp. 40–65.

Wilson, Luzena S. *Luzena Stanley Wilson: '49er.* Oakland, Calif., 1937.

Winchester, Jonas. Jonas Winchester Papers. California Historical Society, San Francisco.

————. Jonas Winchester Papers. California State Library, Sacramento.

Wishart, David J. "The Age and Sex Composition of the Population on the Nebraska Frontier, 1860–1880," *Nebraska History* 54 (1973), 106–19.

Wishy, Bernard. *The Child and the Republic: The Dawn of American Child Nurture.* Philadelphia, 1968.

Wright, Louis B. *Culture on the Moving Frontier.* Bloomington, Ind., 1955.

Wyman, Marc. *Hard Rock Epic: Western Miners and the Industrial Revolution, 1860–1910.* Berkeley, 1979.

Yans-McLaughlin, Virginia. *Family and Community: Italian Immigrants in Buffalo, 1880–1930.* Ithaca, N.Y., 1977.

Occupational structure, 19–21, 81–83, 89–92, 109–15, 212; women and children in, 44–46, 107–15, 162–68; quartz boom's effect on, 138–40, 146, 151, 215
O'Connor, Miles P., 130
Oliver, J. W., 27, 37–38, 43, 57
Oregon, 201
Osborne Hill mine, 72
Out-migration, 31, 86, 144, 210–18 *passim*

Painter, Philip, 185, 191f
Paul, Rodman, 197
Penn, Madame, 44
Philips, Mrs., 44
Piety Hill, 96, 98, 124
Placer camps, 198
Placerville, 78
Political parties, 22f, 32–33, 58–63 *passim*, 87, 92–93, 147–48, 188–92, 210f, 220
Pomeroy, Earl, 196
Population: male preponderance in, 17, 36f, 154, 201–2; out-migration of, 31, 86, 144, 210–17 *passim;* foreign-born in, 48–56, 86–88, 142–51; changes in composition of (1856–63), 81–88; quartz boom and, 132–33, 138–39, 142–51
Poverty, 85, 96, 111–15 *passim*, 123
Pralus, A., 131
Professionals: (1849–56), 21f, 31; (1856–63), 83, 85, 89–90; (1863–70), 138–45 *passim*, 159f, 165–67
Property ownership, 83–85, 91, 98, 100–101, 153–54, 156, 167n, 217; by women, 109, 163–64; quartz boom's effect on, 139–41, 146
Prospect Hill, 96
Prostitution, 35ff, 38, 42f, 50, 108, 163, 220; reform movements against, 56f, 58–59, 60, 64; Chinese, 61–63, 116f, 181; segregation of, 57, 64–67 *passim*, 95–96, 104–5
Putnam, R. F., 101, 102–3, 109
Pyramid Lake Indian fight, 77

Quartz mining: (1849–56), 14, 20, 27–28, 40–41, 42; (1856–63), 72–73, 79–82 *passim*, 101; process of, 24–28 *passim;* (1863–70), 129–51; Cornish expertise

in, 129, 137, 142–47 *passim*, 151–55 *passim*, 169ff, 178–79, 183, 187, 214f

Racial discrimination, 48–56, 60, 117–20, 219. *See also* Chinese
Recreo Flor de Maria, 37
Reform movements, 34–35, 56–57, 103–5, 205f. *See also* Benevolent Societies; Morality
Religion, *see* Churches
Republican Party, 92–93, 188ff, 191, 211, 220
Residential areas, *see* Housing patterns and structures
Ricards, Sherman L., 197
Ridge, John Rollin, 93, 132
Riley, Glenda, 203
Ripert, S., 131
Roberts, E. W., 115, 185, 189
Robinson, Abbie, 182
Rocky Bar Company, 72
Rogers (spurious doctor), 25
Rolfe, Emily, 16, 66
Rolfe, Ianthus J., 125
Rolfe, T. H., 73, 106
Rosenthal, Jacob, 146
Rosiere, Jules, 10

Sabbatarianism, 58ff, 64, 103–4
Sacramento, 78, 207
St. Patrick's Day, 174–75, 218
Saloons, 57–58, 85, 103–6 *passim*
San Francisco, 214, 217; vigilance committees in, 59–60, 209; mine ownership in, 129, 135–36, 141, 185, 188f, 197; outmigration from, 212, 217–18
Sanitary Fund, 172
San Juan Mountains (Colorado), 197
Sargent, Aaron A., 26, 28, 38, 48f, 125, 149, 211
Saunders, Jacob, 172
Sawmills, 13–14, 16, 79
Sawyer, Lorenzo, 49, 53
Scadden mine, 73
Scandinavians, 87
Schaeffer, Luther Melanchthon, 37, 41
Schools: (1849–56), 46, 48, 52–53; (1856–63), 101–2, 123, 124–25; (1863–70), 154–56, 171
Searls, Niles, 59
Sears, W. H., 147